Cognitive Technologies

T0202736

Managing Editors: D. M. Gabbay   J. Siekmann

Editorial Board: A. Bundy   J. G. Carbonell
M. Pinkal   H. Uszkoreit   M. Veloso   W. Wahlster
M. J. Wooldridge

Artur S. d'Avila Garcez · Luís C. Lamb
Dov M. Gabbay

Neural-Symbolic Cognitive Reasoning

With 53 Figures and 6 Tables

 Springer

Authors:

Dr. Artur S. d'Avila Garcez
Reader in Computing
Department of Computing
School of Informatics
City University London
London EC1V 0HB, UK
aag@soi.city.ac.uk

Dr. Luís C. Lamb
Associate Professor
Institute of Informatics
Federal University of
Rio Grande do Sul
Porto Alegre, RS, 91501-970, Brazil
lamb@inf.ufrgs.br, luislamb@acm.org

Prof. Dov M. Gabbay
Augustus De Morgan Professor of Logic
Department of Computer Science
King's College London
Strand, London WC2R 2LS, UK
dov.gabbay@kcl.ac.uk

Managing Editors:

Prof. Dov M. Gabbay
Augustus De Morgan Professor of Logic
Department of Computer Science
King's College London
Strand, London WC2R 2LS, UK

Prof. Dr. Jörg Siekmann
Forschungsbereich Deduktions- und
Multiagentensysteme, DFKI
Stuhlsatzenweg 3, Geb. 43
66123 Saarbrücken, Germany

ISBN: 978-3-642-09229-9   e-ISBN: 978-3-540-73246-4
DOI: 10.1007/978-3-540-73246-4

Cognitive Technologies ISSN: 1611-2482

ACM Computing Classification (1998): F.1.1, F.4.1, I.2.3, I.2.4, I.2.6

© 2009 Springer-Verlag Berlin Heidelberg
Softcover reprint of the hardcover 1st edition 2009

Cover design: KünkelLopka, Heidelberg

Printed on acid-free paper

9 8 7 6 5 4 3 2 1

springer.com

To Simone, for giving me our little Max (AAG).
To Desirée (LCL).
To Lydia (DMG).

Preface

This book is about neural computation and applied reasoning, and about how they are related and can be integrated within a machine-learning framework. Logic has a long and solid tradition of principled research, and has been influential in virtually all fields of scientifically-based human knowledge. Neural computation has now achieved maturity. Practitioners have been able to use artificial connectionist models in a number of real-world problems, including machine learning, pattern recognition, vision, cognitive modelling, and artificial agents. However, the area still lacks sound computational foundations, as several features of neural-computation models are still under investigation.

The book presents a number of principled, sound neural-computation models. It makes use of a number of applied (nonclassical) logical systems in order to do so. Logics lie at the foundation of computer science and artificial intelligence. For instance, logic research has provided the foundations of the theories of computability, recursion, and complexity. In artificial intelligence, the construction of automated reasoning systems, knowledge representation languages and formalisms, and theorem proving have been pursued since at least the 1950s. All these are based on logics.

More recently, applications in planning, multiagent systems, expert systems, the Semantic Web, learning theory, cognitive modelling and robotics, constraint satisfaction, searching, and the traditional fields of knowledge representation and reasoning have benefited from research on nonclassical logics. In particular, research on temporal, modal, description, intuitionistic, fuzzy, and nonmonotonic logics has been influential in artificial intelligence, both in relation to theory and principled languages for building models and systems.

Recently, nonclassical logics[1] have been found relevant in relation to the formalisation of integrated learning and reasoning [66, 72, 77, 148, 222]. They have contributed to the construction of sound models of cognitive reasoning. As is well known, human cognition successfully integrates the connectionist (brain-inspired)

---

[1] Nonclassical logics depart from the Aristotelian tradition in the sense that these logics lack some properties of classical logic, such as the law of the excluded middle, or extend them with additional features. For instance, the development of nonmonotonic logics, which has contributed to

and symbolic (mind-inspired) paradigms of artificial intelligence, language being a compelling case in point. Yet the modelling of cognition develops these separately in the fields of neural computation (and statistical artificial intelligence) and symbolic logic/artificial intelligence. There is now a movement towards a fruitful middle way in between these extremes, in which the study of logic is combined with connectionism. It is essential that these be integrated, thereby enabling not only a technology for building better intelligent systems, but also the understanding of fully fledged computational cognitive models.

The aim of neural-symbolic computation is to explore the advantages that each paradigm presents. Among the advantages of artificial neural networks are massive parallelism, fault tolerance (robust learning), efficient inductive learning, and effective generalisation capabilities. On the other hand, symbolic systems provide descriptions (as opposed to only discriminations); can explain their inference process, for example through automatic theorem proving; and use powerful declarative languages for knowledge representation and reasoning.

In this book, we explore the synergies of neural-symbolic integration from the following perspective. We use a neural network to simulate a given task. The network is obtained by being programmed (set up) or by adapting to and generalising over well-known situations (learning). The network is the mechanism to execute the task, while symbolic logic enables the necessary interaction between the network and the outside world. Differently from and complementing [66], which set the scence for neural-symbolic integration with the use of standard networks and logic programming, we are concerned here with applied (and nonclassical) logical systems. With this consideration at the forefront, *the book presents a rich cognitive model for reasoning and learning based on neural-network ensembles*. The book also illustrates the effectiveness of the model by experimentation, and shows that the connectionist model can compute a number of combined nonclassical logical systems [42], including modal, temporal, epistemic, and intuitionist logics. Finally, the book investigates the issue of relational learning and the representation of first-order logic, the combination (fibring) of models/networks, qualitative reasoning under uncertainty, and how neural networks can offer an effective approach to learning in argumentation frameworks [39,212]. We conclude by summarising our case for a logic-based, cognitive connectionist model which we call *fibred network ensembles*. Overall, it offers a rich model from a symbolic computation/reasoning viewpoint, yet it is relatively simple and efficient as a learning model. We believe it strikes the right balance between expressiveness and computational feasibility. And, as a matter of principle, we believe that this is no coincidence, but a direct result of

---

the formalisation of practical or commonsense reasoning, led to the discovery of several new logical systems in which the principle of monotonicity may not hold. Further, several authors have defended a position that intuitionistic logics are more appropriate as a foundational basis of computation than classical logic [258]. Classical logic does not capture all of the nature of human practical reasoning. For instance, in order to formalise and automate computational (human) reasoning about time, knowledge, beliefs, or uncertainty several nonclassical logics have been found more appropriate than classical logic; see [42,87,100,102]. Our point will be made clearer as the reader proceeds to the coming chapters.

our methodology, which seeks to unify systematically the most advanced concepts of symbolic computation with the physical constraints of a realistic connectionist machine.

Our aim here is to offer a principled way in which robust learning and effective reasoning can be realised. In line with one of the recent grand challenges in computer science, according to the British Computer Society – nonclassical computation – we seek to unify the classical and nonclassical (natural) computational paradigms, with the nonclassical computational models presented here showing how alternative formulations can deal with cognitive dimensions usually studied under separate formalisms.

London, UK, and Porto Alegre, Brazil, February 2005 to June 2008.

Acknowledgements Over the last five years, we have had stimulating (brief and long) conversations about this book with several researchers in personal meetings, conferences, and workshops. We would like to acknowledge the feedback from Samson Abramsky, Sebastian Bader, Howard Barringer, Rodrigo de Salvo Braz, Krysia Broda, Jehoshua (Shuki) Bruck, Matthew Cook, Cicero Garcez, Robert Givan, Joe Halpern, Pascal Hitzler, Wilfrid Hodges, Ian Hodkinson, Steffen Hölldobler, Bob Kowalski, David Makinson, Ryszard Michalski, Sanjay Modgil, Stephen Muggleton, Vasile Palade, Günther Palm, Luc de Raedt, Oliver Ray, Odinaldo Rodrigues, Dan Roth, Stefan Rüger, Alessandra Russo, Jude Shavlik, Jörg Siekmann, Ron Sun, Guglielmo Tamburrini, John G. Taylor, Francesca Toni, Johan van Benthem, Moshe Vardi, John Woods, and Gerson Zaverucha. We thank them all for their challenging arguments and questioning on the subject, and we apologise for any omissions. We also would like to thank the participants of the International Workshops on Neural-Symbolic Learning and Reasoning (NeSy), organised yearly since 2005 either at IJCAI or ECAI, for the enjoyable research atmosphere and useful debates during our workshop meetings. We particularly would like to thank the NeSy keynote speakers Luc de Raedt, Marco Gori, Steffen Hölldobler, Lokendra Shastri, Ron Sun, Stefan Wermter, and Kai-Uwe Kuehnberger.

We also acknowledge our publisher, Ronan Nugent of Springer, for his support throughout the writing of the book.

Artur d'Avila Garcez has been partly supported by grants from the Nuffield Foundation and the Royal Society; Luís Lamb has been partly supported by grants from the Brazilian Research Council (CNPq) and the CAPES foundation; and Dov Gabbay has been partly supported by EPSRC and by the Leverhulme Trust. This manuscript was written using LaTeX.

Contents

1 Introduction 1
  1.1 Motivation 1
  1.2 Methodology and Related Work 3
  1.3 Structure of the Book 7

2 Logic and Knowledge Representation 9
  2.1 Preliminaries 10
  2.2 Classical Logic 11
    2.2.1 Propositional Logic 11
    2.2.2 First-Order Logic 12
  2.3 Nonclassical Logics 14
  2.4 Nonmonotonic Reasoning 16
  2.5 Logic Programming 17
    2.5.1 Stable-Model and Answer Set Semantics 19
  2.6 Discussion 20

3 Artificial Neural Networks 23
  3.1 Architectures of Neural Networks 23
  3.2 Learning Strategy 26
  3.3 Recurrent Networks 29
  3.4 Evaluation of Learning Models 31
  3.5 Discussion 33

4 Neural-Symbolic Learning Systems 35
  4.1 The CILP System 35
  4.2 Massively Parallel Deduction in CILP 43
  4.3 Inductive Learning in CILP 44
  4.4 Adding Classical Negation 45
  4.5 Adding Metalevel Priorities 49
  4.6 Applications of CILP 52
  4.7 Discussion 53

5   Connectionist Modal Logic 55
     5.1   Modal Logic and Extended Modal Programs 56
             5.1.1   Semantics for Extended Modal Logic Programs 58
     5.2   Connectionist Modal Logic 60
             5.2.1   Computing Modalities in Neural Networks 61
             5.2.2   Soundness of Modal Computation 66
             5.2.3   Termination of Modal Computation 67
     5.3   Case Study: The Muddy Children Puzzle 68
             5.3.1   Distributed Knowledge Representation in CML 69
             5.3.2   Learning in CML 71
     5.4   Discussion 73

6   Connectionist Temporal Reasoning 75
     6.1   Connectionist Temporal Logic of Knowledge 76
             6.1.1   The Language of CTLK 77
             6.1.2   The CTLK Algorithm 79
     6.2   The Muddy Children Puzzle (Full Solution) 81
             6.2.1   Temporal Knowledge Representation 81
             6.2.2   Learning in CTLK 83
     6.3   Discussion 84

7   Connectionist Intuitionistic Reasoning 87
     7.1   Intuitionistic Logic and Programs 88
     7.2   Connectionist Intuitionistic Reasoning 90
             7.2.1   Creating the Networks 92
             7.2.2   Connecting the Networks 93
     7.3   Connectionist Intuitionistic Modal Reasoning 95
     7.4   Discussion 100

8   Applications of Connectionist Nonclassical Reasoning 101
     8.1   A Simple Card Game 101
     8.2   The Wise Men Puzzle 102
             8.2.1   A Formalisation of the Wise Men Puzzle 103
             8.2.2   Representing the Wise Men Puzzle Using CML 104
     8.3   Applications of Connectionist Intuitionism 108
             8.3.1   Representing the Wise Men Puzzle Using CIL 109
     8.4   Discussion 112

9   Fibring Neural Networks 115
     9.1   The Idea of Fibring 115
     9.2   Fibring Neural Networks 117
     9.3   Examples of the Fibring of Networks 119
     9.4   Definition of Fibred Networks 121
     9.5   Dynamics of Fibred Networks 123
     9.6   Expressiveness of Fibred Networks 124
     9.7   Discussion 125

10 Relational Learning in Neural Networks 127
  10.1 An Example 128
  10.2 Variable Representation 130
  10.3 Relation Representation 131
  10.4 Relational Learning... 132
  10.5 Relational Reasoning 134
  10.6 Experimental Results 135
  10.7 Discussion 140

11 Argumentation Frameworks as Neural Networks 143
  11.1 Value-Based Argumentation Frameworks 144
  11.2 Argumentation Neural Networks.............................. 145
  11.3 Argument Computation and Learning.......................... 149
        11.3.1 Circular Argumentation 150
        11.3.2 Argument Learning 154
        11.3.3 Cumulative (Accrual) Argumentation 155
  11.4 Fibring Applied to Argumentation 157
  11.5 Discussion 159

12 Reasoning about Probabilities in Neural Networks 161
  12.1 Representing Uncertainty 161
  12.2 An Algorithm for Reasoning about Uncertainty 164
  12.3 The Monty Hall Puzzle...................................... 166
  12.4 Discussion 167

13 Conclusions 169
  13.1 Neural-Symbolic Learning Systems 170
  13.2 Connectionist Nonclassical Reasoning 172
        13.2.1 Connectionist Modal Reasoning 173
        13.2.2 Connectionist Temporal Reasoning 175
  13.3 Fibring Neural Networks 176
  13.4 Concluding Remarks.. 178

References 181

Index 193

Chapter 1
Introduction

1.1 Motivation

The construction of robust computational models integrating reasoning and learning is a key research challenge for artificial intelligence. Recently, this challenge was also put forward as a fundamental problem in computer science [255]. Such a challenge intersects with another long-standing entry in the research agenda of artificial intelligence: the integration of its symbolic and connectionist paradigms. Such integration has long been a standing enterprise, with implications for and applications in cognitive science and neuroscience [51,66,130,178,179,238,240,247,248,250]. Further, the importance of efforts to bridge the gap between the connectionist and symbolic paradigms of artificial intelligence has also been widely recognised (see e.g. [51,66,229,242,243]).

Valiant [255] has pointed out that the construction of rich computational cognitive models is one of the challenges computer science faces over the next few decades. A positive answer to this challenge would provide a characterisation of a semantics for cognitive computation,[1] as follows:

> The aim here is to identify a way of looking at and manipulating commonsense knowledge that is consistent with and can support what we consider to be the two most fundamental aspects of intelligent cognitive behaviour: the ability to learn from experience, and the ability to reason from what has been learned. We are therefore seeking a semantics of knowledge that can computationally support the basic phenomena of intelligent behaviour [255].

Valiant also described the characteristics of the semantic formalisation needed for supporting learning and reasoning:

> One set of requirements [for a semantics to be adequate for commonsense reasoning] is that it should support integrated algorithms for learning and reasoning that are computationally

---

[1] The article [255] was published in 2003 in the Journal of the ACM, in a special issue celebrating its 50th anniversary. In that issue, the editor-in-chief at the time (J.Y. Halpern) invited winners of the Turing Award and Nevanlinna Prize to discuss up to three problems that these prominent researchers thought would be major challenges for computer science in the next 50 years.

A.S. d'Avila Garcez et al., *Neural-Symbolic Cognitive Reasoning*, Cognitive Technologies,
© Springer-Verlag Berlin Heidelberg 2009

tractable and have some nontrivial scope. Another requirement is that it has a principled way of ensuring that the knowledge-base from which reasoning is done is robust, in the sense that errors in the deductions are at least controllable [255].

Aiming at building integrated reasoning and learning methods, our approach provides a unified computational foundation for neural networks and nonclassical reasoning. Knowledge is expressed by a symbolic language, whereas deduction and learning are carried out by a robust connectionist engine. This book also seeks to contribute to the long-term aim of representing expressive symbolic formalisms in learning systems [253], by means of neural-symbolic integration [66]. Ultimately, the goal is to produce biologically motivated models with integrated reasoning and learning capabilities, in which neural networks provide the inspiration and the machinery necessary for cognitive computation and learning, while several nonclassical logics provide practical reasoning and explanation capabilities to the models, facilitating the interaction between the models and the outside world. This book contributes to the integration of both research programmes into a unified foundation; both of these programmes are now widely but separately used in many areas of computer science and artificial intelligence [42, 66, 87, 125].

A historical criticism of neural networks was raised by McCarthy back in 1988 [176]. McCarthy referred to neural networks as having a "propositional fixation", in the sense that they were not able to represent first-order logic. This, per se, has remained a challenge for a decade, but several approaches have now dealt with first-order reasoning in neural networks (see e.g. [43] and Chap. 10). Perhaps in an attempt to address McCarthy's criticism, many researchers in the area have focused attention only on first-order logic. This has suppressed developments in other important fronts, mainly in nonclassical, practical reasoning, which also should be at the centre of neural-symbolic integration research owing to the practical nature of neural-network research. We have shown recently that nonclassical reasoning can be used in a number of applications in neural-symbolic systems [33, 68–72, 74, 76–79, 157]. This has been possible through the integration of nonclassical logics and neural networks.

Notwithstanding this evidence, little attention has been given to nonclassical reasoning and its integration with neural networks. We believe that for neural computation to achieve its promise, connectionist models must be able to cater for nonclassical reasoning. Research on nonclassical logics, including new results on modal, temporal, intuitionistic, and nonmonotonic logics and their combinations, has been relevant not only to computer science and artificial intelligence, but also to economics and the physical sciences. We believe that neural-symbolic systems can benefit from the results and achievements that nonclassical logics have had in all these areas.

In summary, we shall argue in this book that nonclassical reasoning is fundamental in the construction of computational connectionist models. If one assumes that neural networks can represent rich models of human reasoning and learning, and can offer an alternative solution to the challenges confronted by intelligent computation, it is undeniable that nonclassical logics should play a fundamental role at the centre of this enterprise.

1.2 Methodology and Related Work

Several approaches have been proposed for integrating the connectionist and symbolic paradigms of artificial intelligence. Most provide a solution to the learning of classical propositional logic or fragments of first-order logic by means of neural networks or related methods (see e.g. [12, 43, 148, 228, 229, 250, 254]). Our book [66] surveys the work on neural-symbolic integration done until 2002, and proposes a methodology for dealing with nonmonotonicity in artificial neural networks, including knowledge extraction. In [12], a survey of recent developments in classical-logic learning in neural networks is presented. Further, [66] showed that neural-symbolic systems are also appropriate for tackling learning in real-world problems. In particular, the analysis presented in [66] shows that neural-symbolic systems can be used effectively in a number of applications, ranging from the detection of large-scale power system failures to DNA sequence analysis.

Despite the significant contributions of the developments in first-order logic to knowledge representation, learning, and reasoning in artificial intelligence, a truly intelligent agent or multiagent system, in the sense defined in [271], has several dimensions that cannot be appropriately managed solely by the use of first-order classical logic.

There are several extensions and alternatives to classical logic. Nonclassical logics have become useful in computer science and artificial intelligence over the last few decades. Such logics have been shown to be adequate for expressing several features of reasoning, allowing for the representation of temporal, epistemic, and probabilistic abstractions in computer science and artificial intelligence, as shown for example, in [42, 87, 106, 121].

For instance, temporal, modal, and intuitionistic logics are now amongst the most successful logical languages used in computing. Born in philosophy and mathematics, they have benefited from research efforts in applications of computing. Several semantic models and (automated) proof systems have been designed for nonclassical logics [42, 88, 104]. Temporal logic has had a successful history in computer science and artificial intelligence since the pioneering work of Pnueli, back in 1977 [207], as it allows an accurate and elegant formalism for reasoning about the dynamics of computing systems. Temporal logic has had a large impact in both academia and industry [89, 103]. Modal logic, in turn, has also become a lingua franca in the areas of formalisation, specification, verification, theorem proving, and model checking in multiagent and distributed computing systems [42, 50, 87, 106, 143, 154]. Nonmonotonic reasoning dominated research in artificial intelligence in the 1980s and 1990s, and intuitionistic logic is considered by many to be an adequate logical foundation in several core areas of theoretical computer science, including type theory and functional programming [258]. Other applications of nonclassical logics include the characterisation of timing analysis in combinatorial circuits [180] and in spatial reasoning [23], with possible use in geographical information systems. For instance, Bennett's propositional intuitionistic approach provided for tractable yet expressive reasoning about topological and spatial relations. In [106], several applications of many-dimensional modal logic are illustrated.

Automated reasoning and learning theory have been the subject of intensive investigation since the early developments in computer science and artificial intelligence [81, 174, 251]. However, while machine learning has been developed mainly by the use of statistical and connectionist approaches (see e.g. [125, 173, 184, 262]), the reasoning component of intelligent systems has been developed using classical and nonclassical logics (see e.g. [42, 87, 100, 104]). The acceptance of the need for systems that integrate reasoning and learning into the same foundation, and the evolution of the fields of cognitive and neural computation, has led to a number of proposals integrating logic and machine learning [43, 51, 66, 77, 79, 118, 148, 164, 229, 250, 254, 255].

An effective model of integrated reasoning and learning has been shown to be attainable by means of neural-symbolic learning systems [66, 69–72, 74, 79]. This book advocates the use of nonclassical logics as a foundation for knowledge representation and learning in neural-symbolic systems. We propose a new approach for representing, reasoning with, and learning nonclassical logics in a connectionist framework, which leads, in a principled way, to a powerful but computationally light cognitive model combining expressive nonclassical reasoning and robust learning; we call it *fibred network ensembles*.

In contrast to symbolic learning systems, neural networks' learning implicitly encodes patterns and their generalisations in the networks' weights, so reflecting the statistical properties of the trained data [35]. The merging of theory (background knowledge) and data learning (learning from examples) into neural networks has been shown to provide a learning system that is more effective than purely symbolic or purely connectionist systems, especially when the data are noisy [246, 250]. This result has contributed to the growing interest in developing neural-symbolic learning systems. By integrating logic and neural networks, neural-symbolic systems may provide (i) a logical characterisation of a connectionist system, (ii) a connectionist (parallel) implementation of a logic, or (iii) a hybrid learning system that brings together features from connectionism and symbolic artificial intelligence.

Until recently, neural-symbolic systems were not able to fully represent, compute, and learn expressive languages other than propositional logic and fragments of first-order, classical logic [12, 43, 51, 238]. To the best of our knowledge, research efforts towards representing nonclassical logical formalisms in connectionist systems were scant until the early 2000s. However, in [67, 70, 73, 74, 76–78], a new approach to knowledge representation and reasoning in neural-symbolic systems based on neural-network ensembles was proposed, namely *connectionist nonclassical logics*. In [75], connectionist modal logic (CML) was introduced, showing that modalities can be represented effectively in neural networks. In [70, 72, 73], the language of the Connectionist Temporal Logic of Knowledge (CTLK) was introduced, and in [76–78] the computation of intuitionistic reasoning was shown to be learnable within neural networks. This new approach shows that a variety of nonclassical logics can be effectively represented in artificial neural networks. To the best of our knowledge, this was the first approach to combining nonclassical logics and neural networks.

Recently, it has also been shown that value-based argumentation frameworks can be integrated with neural networks, offering a unified model for learning and reasoning about arguments, including the computation of circular and accrual argumentation [68, 69]. The study of formal models of argumentation has also been a subject of intensive investigation in several areas, notably in logic, philosophy, decision theory, artificial intelligence, and law [25, 31, 39, 48, 83, 210, 212]. In artificial intelligence, models of argumentation have been one of the approaches used in the representation of commonsense, nonmonotonic reasoning. They have been particularly successful when modelling chains of *defeasible arguments* so as to reach a conclusion [194, 209]. Although logic-based models have been the standard for the representation of argumentative reasoning [31, 108], such models are intrinsically related to artificial neural networks, as we shall show in Chap. 11. This relationship between neural networks and argumentation networks provides a model in which the learning of arguments can be combined with argument computation.

This book also presents a new neural-network architecture based on the idea of fibring logical systems introduced by Gabbay [101]. Fibring allows one to combine different systems (here, neural networks) in a principled way. Fibred neural networks may be composed not only of interconnected neurons but also of other networks in a recursive architecture. A fibring function then defines how this recursive architecture must behave, by defining how the networks should relate to each other (typically by allowing the activation of one network to influence the changes of the weights of another). We show that, in addition to being universal approximators, fibred networks can approximate any polynomial function to any desired degree of accuracy, and are thus more expressive than standard feedforward neural networks.

Neural-symbolic systems that use simple neural networks, such as single-hidden-layer feedforward or recurrent networks [125], typically only manage to represent and reason about propositional symbolic knowledge or *if then else* rules [36, 66, 95, 205, 250]. On the other hand, neural-symbolic systems that are capable of representing and reasoning about (fragments of) first-order logic are normally less capable of learning new concepts efficiently [136, 149, 229, 243]. There is clearly a need to strike a balance between the reasoning and learning capabilities of such systems, and between expressiveness and computational complexity.

As argued in [43], if connectionism is an alternative paradigm to artificial intelligence, neural networks must be able to compute symbolic reasoning in an efficient and effective way. It is also argued that connectionist systems are usually fault-tolerant, whereas symbolic systems may be 'brittle and rigid'. We seek to tackle these problems by offering a principled way of computing, representing, and learning nonclassical logics within connectionist models.

The combination of nonclassical reasoning and connectionism is achieved by means of algorithms that translate logical clauses into neural-network ensembles. Such algorithms can be proved correct in the sense that the ensembles compute a semantics of the original theory. An immediate consequence of our approach is the ability to perform learning from examples efficiently, by applying, for example, the backpropagation learning algorithm [224] to each network of the ensemble. We also show the effectiveness of our approach as a (distributed) knowledge representation, reasoning, argumentation, and learning mechanism by applying it to the well-known test beds found in the literature [87, 121]. Our approach paves the way for modular, integrated computation and learning of distributed, nonclassical knowledge, with a broad range of applications from practical reasoning to evolving multiagent systems.

Technical aspects of this work will be presented throughout the book as the need arises. No assumption is made that the reader has prior knowledge of nonclassical logic or neural networks. Connectionist modal logic, a (one-dimensional) ensemble of neural networks [66], is used to represent modalities such as *necessity* and *possibility*. In CTLK, a two-dimensional network ensemble is used to represent the evolution of knowledge through time. In both cases, each network ensemble can be seen as representing a possible world that contains information about the knowledge held by an agent in a distributed system. Learning in the CML system is achieved by training each network in the ensemble independently, corresponding to the evolution of an agent's knowledge within a possible world. It is important that these logics are investigated within the neural-computation paradigm. For instance, applications in artificial intelligence and computer science have made extensive use of decidable modal logics, including the analysis and model checking of distributed and multiagent systems, program verification and specification, and hardware model checking.[2] In the case of temporal and epistemic logics, these logics have found a large number of applications, notably in game theory and in models of knowledge and interaction in multiagent systems [87, 89, 103, 207].

From a machine-learning perspective, the merging of theory (background knowledge) and data learning (learning from examples) in neural networks has provided learning systems that are more effective than purely symbolic or purely connectionist systems [246, 250]. In order to achieve this merging, first one translates the background knowledge into a neural network's initial architecture, and then one trains the network with examples using, for example, backpropagation. In the case of CML, for instance, learning is achieved by training each individual network, each of which is a standard network.

Another long-term aim is to contribute to the challenge of representing expressive symbolic formalisms within learning systems. We are thus proposing a methodology for the representation of several nonclassical logics in artificial neural networks. We believe that connectionist approaches should take these logics into account by means of adequate computational models catering for reasoning, knowledge representation, and learning. This is necessary because real-world applications, such as failure diagnosis, fraud prevention, and bioinformatics applications, will require the use of languages more expressive than propositional logic. Bioinformatics, in particular, requires very much the ability to represent and reason about relations such as those used in predicate logic [6]. In summary, knowledge is represented by a symbolic language, whilst deduction and learning are carried out by a connectionist engine.

---

[2] It is well known that modal logic corresponds, in terms of expressive power, to the two-variable fragment of first-order logic [264]. Further, as the two-variable fragment of predicate logic is decidable, this explains why modal logic is so robustly decidable and amenable to multiple applications.

1.3 Structure of the Book

This research monograph is divided into the following chapters. Chapter 1 (the present chapter) introduces the subject and overviews developments in the area of connectionist models for integrated reasoning and learning. Chapter 2 introduces the basic concepts of logic and knowledge representation. Chapter 3 introduces the concepts of neural networks. Chapter 4 introduces the foundations of neural-symbolic integration. Chapter 5 introduces connectionist modal logic, covering some foundational results and introductory examples. Chapter 6 presents CTLK and its applications in distributed temporal knowledge representation and learning. Chapter 7 introduces intuitionistic reasoning and learning in neural networks. Chapter 8 describes some applications of connectionist nonclassical reasoning. Chapter 9 introduces the idea of combining (fibring) networks, for example CTLK and intuitionism. Chapter 10 describes the combination networks to represent and learn relations in a first-order setting with variables. Chapter 11 establishes a close relatioship between connectionist models and argumentation frameworks, and uses argumentation as an application of fibring. Chapter 12 introduces symbolic reasoning under uncertainty in neural networks and illustrates its feasibility using well-known test beds, including the Monty Hall puzzle [121]. Chapter 13 concludes the book and indicates directions for further research.

An extensive list of references cited is provided at the end of the book. The list is by no means complete, as the literature in this field is vast.

Chapter 2
Logic and Knowledge Representation

This chapter introduces the basics of knowledge representation and of logic used throughout this book. The material on logic presented here follows the presentation given in [100]. Several books contain introductions to (logic-based) knowledge representation and reasoning, including [42, 87, 100, 106].

Classical logic is a powerful language for certain forms of reasoning, and much can be done with it. However, it does not capture all that the natural reasoning methods of humans do. For example, we might not know for certain that an atomic sentence was true, but know that there was a 75% chance that it was – this cannot be captured by classical propositional logic. As a further illustration, let the atoms p and q represent two different coins which can be exchanged for an item r. This could be stated by $p \land q \Rightarrow r$. However, stating that the amount represented by p and q is used up in the exchange cannot be done by classical reasoning. When we use an implication $A \Rightarrow B$, we assume that no change is undergone by A when it is used to conclude B. This does not carry over into a number of problems in computer science. Note that attempts to express the changes to p and q are doomed to failure: $p \land q \Rightarrow r \land \neg p \land \neg q$ reduces to $\neg(p \land q)$.

Many nonclassical logics have been devised to handle these and other problems which exceed the capabilities of classical logic. There are alternatives to classical logic which add more connectives to the language, and other alternatives which vary the meaning of the existing connectives. Amongst the most important of the latter are *many-valued* logics, *intuitionistic* logic, *modal* and *temporal* logics, and *resource* (*relevance* and *linear*) logics. For an introduction to the subject, we refer the reader to [42, 100]. A thorough state-of-the-art analysis of nonclassical logics can be found in the multivolume collection [102].

In this book, several nonclassical logics will be of interest, such as the modal, temporal, and intuitionistic logics. They will be introduced when an account of the motivation behind them and definitions are needed, providing the reader with an integrated presentation of the connectionist models of nonclassical reasoning described in the book. Before presenting each nonclassical connectionist model, however, we give the reader a taste of (classical and nonclassical) logic and knowledge representation, which will serve as background.

A.S. d'Avila Garcez et al., *Neural-Symbolic Cognitive Reasoning*, Cognitive Technologies,   9

2.1 Preliminaries

We need to assert some basic concepts of set and order theory that will be used throughout this book (see [54,117,213] for details). These concepts are useful when defining semantic models for several logics and knowledge representation languages. In what follows, $\mathbb{N}$ and $\mathbb{R}$ will denote the sets of natural and real numbers, respectively.

Definition 1. A *partial order* is a reflexive, transitive, and antisymmetric binary relation on a set.

Definition 2. A partial order $\preceq$ on a set X is *total* iff for every $x, y \in X$, either $x \preceq y$ or $y \preceq x$. Sometimes $\preceq$ is also called a *linear order*, or simply a *chain*.

As usual, $x \prec y$ is an abbreviation for $x \preceq y$ and $x \neq y$.

Definition 3. In a partially ordered set $[X, \preceq]$, x is the *immediate predecessor* of y if $x \prec y$ and there is no element z in X such that $x \prec z \prec y$. The inverse relation is called the *immediate successor*.

Definition 4. Let X be a set and $\preceq$ an ordering on X. Let $x \in X$.

- x is *minimal* if there is no element $y \in X$ such that $y \prec x$.
- x is a *minimum* if for all elements $y \in X, x \preceq y$. If $\preceq$ is also antisymmetric and such an x exists, then x is unique and will be denoted by $inf(X)$.
- x is *maximal* if there is no element $y \in X$ such that $x \prec y$.
- x is a *maximum* if for all elements $y \in X, y \preceq x$. If $\preceq$ is also antisymmetric and such an x exists, then x is unique and will be denoted by $sup(X)$.

A maximum (or minimum) element is also maximal (or minimal, respectively) but is, in addition, comparable to every other element. This property and antisymmetry lead directly to the demonstration of the uniqueness of $inf(X)$ and $sup(X)$.

Definition 5. Let $[X, \preceq]$ be a partially ordered set and let $Y \subseteq X$.

- An element $x \in X$ is an *upper bound* of Y if $y \preceq x$ for all $y \in Y$ (a *lower bound* is defined dually).
- x is called the *least upper bound* (*lub*) of Y if x is an upper bound of Y and $x \preceq z$ for all upper bounds z of Y (the *greatest lower bound* (*glb*) is defined dually).
- If any two elements x and y in X have a least upper bound, denoted by $x \vee y$ and read as "x *join* y", and a greatest lower bound, denoted by $x \wedge y$ and read as "x *meet* y", then X is called a *lattice*.
- If $lub(Y)$ and $glb(Y)$ exist for all $Y \subseteq X$ then X is called a *complete lattice*.
- A lattice L is *distributive* if $x \vee (y \wedge z) = (x \vee y) \wedge (x \vee z)$ and $x \wedge (y \vee z) = (x \wedge y) \vee (x \wedge z)$, for all $x, y, z \in L$.

Definition 6. Let U be a set and $f : U \times U \rightarrow \mathbb{R}$ be a function satisfying the following conditions:

- $f(x,y) \geq 0$,
- $f(x,y) = 0 \leftrightarrow x = y$,
- $f(x,y) = f(y,x)$, and
- $f(x,y) \leq f(x,z) + f(z,y)$.

f is called a *metric* on U.[1] A *metric space* is a tuple $\langle U, f \rangle$. A metric f on U is *bounded* iff for some constant $k \in \mathbb{R}, f(x,y) \leq k$ for all $x, y \in U$.

2.2 Classical Logic

This section introduces the basic definitions of propositional and first-order predicate logic. The presentation is based on definitions in [100], which offers a comprehensive introduction to logic in computation and artificial intelligence.

Propositional logic is weaker in terms of *expressive power* than first-order predicate logic. The smallest semantic units which can receive truth values in propositional logic are *sentences*. Yet we are often concerned with the various pieces of information which make up a sentence. For example, the utterance, seen as a sentence in propositional logic, 'a hero is someone admired by everyone' contains several items of data which cannot be represented distinctly in propositional logic. We would be reduced to using a single proposition, p say, to represent the entire sentence.

To increase the expressive power of (propositional) logic, we need to add a means to talk about the semantic units contained within sentences – this entails using a predicate logic. In the definitions below, the differences between these logics become very clear.

2.2.1 Propositional Logic

We now formally define the notion of a well-formed formula (wff) of classical propositional logic and the truth values given to the various operators.

Definition 7. (Classical Propositional Logic) [100].

1. The language of classical propositional logic contains a set $\mathcal{L}_p$ of atomic propositions with typical members $\{p, q, r, s, q_1, q_2, q_3, \ldots\}$ and a set of connectives $\{\wedge, \vee, \neg, \rightarrow\}$.
2. The notion of a well-formed formula (wff) is defined inductively by the following conditions:

---

[1] f is sometimes called a *distance function*.

(a) Any atom $p \in \mathcal{L}_p$ is a wff. We say it is built up from $\{p\}$.

(b) If A and B are wffs, then so are $\neg(A), (A)\wedge(B), (A)\vee(B), (A)\rightarrow(B)$. If A is built up from the atoms $\{p_1,\ldots,p_n\}$ and B is built up from the atoms $\{q_1,\ldots,q_k\}$, then $\neg(A)$ is built up from the same atoms as A, and $(A) \wedge (B)$, $(A) \vee (B)$, and $(A) \rightarrow (B)$ are built up from $\{p_1,\ldots,p_n,q_1,\ldots,q_k\}$.

(c) Let A be a formula built up from $q_1,\ldots,q_k$. We indicate this fact by writing $A(q_1,\ldots,q_k)$. Let $B_1,\ldots,B_k$ be wffs. We define by structural induction the result of substituting into A the formulas B_i for the atom q_i, for $i = 1,\ldots,k$. We denote this substitution by $A(q_1/B_1,\ldots,q_k/B_k)$ and refer to it as a substitution instance of A.

- For atomic $A(q) = q$, we let $A(q/B) = B$.
- $(\neg(A))(q_1/B_1,\ldots,q_k/B_k) = \neg(A)(q_1/A_1,\ldots,q_k/B_k)$.
- $((A) \rightarrow (B))(q_1/B_1,\ldots,q_k/B_k) = A(q_1/B_1,\ldots,q_k/B_k) \rightarrow B(q_1/B_1,\ldots,q_k/B_k)$, and similarly for $(A) \wedge (B)$ and $(A) \vee (B)$.

3. An *interpretation* (or *assignment*) is any function h that assigns truth values to the atomic propositions. h is a function from $\mathcal{L}_p$ into $\{\top,\bot\}$, i.e. $h : \mathcal{L}_p \mapsto \{\top,\bot\}$.

4. We can extend the definition of h from atomic propositions to any wff A by induction, as follows:

(a) $h(\neg(A)) = \top$ if $h(A) = \bot$, otherwise the value is $\bot$.

(b) $h((A)\wedge(B)) = \top$ if $h(A) = \top$ and $h(B) = \top$, otherwise the value is $\bot$.

(c) $h((A)\vee(B)) = \top$ if $h(A) = \top$ or $h(B) = \top$ or both, otherwise the value is $\bot$.

(d) $h((A)\rightarrow(B)) = \top$ if $h(A) = \bot$ or $h(B) = \top$ or both, otherwise the value is $\bot$.

The above definition of $h(A)$ agrees with our understanding of the meaning of the connectives as presented in the truth tables.

5. We may find it convenient to assume that our language contains as atomic propositions the constant atoms $\top$ and $\bot$. $\top$ is always *true* and $\bot$ is always *false*.

2.2.2 First-Order Logic

Definition 8 (Syntax of Predicate Logic) [100]. The formulas of the predicate language $\mathcal{L}$ are built up from the following symbols:

- a set $\mathcal{L}_{pred}$ of predicate symbols, each with an associated arity, which is a positive integer;
- a set $\mathcal{L}_{cons}$ of constant symbols;
- a set $\mathcal{L}_{var}$ of variable symbols;
- a set $\mathcal{L}_{func}$ of function symbols, each with an associated arity, which is a positive integer;
- quantifiers $\forall, \exists$;
- classical connectives $\neg$ and $\rightarrow$. The other classical connectives are definable from these connectives.

The set of terms $\mathcal{L}_{\text{term}}$ is given by the following rules:

- any member of $\mathcal{L}_{\text{cons}}$ is a term in $\mathcal{L}_{\text{term}}$, with no variables;
- any member x of $\mathcal{L}_{\text{var}}$ is a term in $\mathcal{L}_{\text{term}}$, with variable x (itself);
- if f is a member of $\mathcal{L}_{\text{func}}$ with arity n, and $t_1,\ldots,t_n$ are terms in $\mathcal{L}_{\text{term}}$, then $t = f(t_1,\ldots,t_n)$ is a term in $\mathcal{L}_{\text{term}}$. The set of variables of t is the union of all the sets of variables of $t_1,\ldots,t_n$.

We can now define the wffs of $\mathcal{L}$ by the following rules:

- $\bot$ is a wff of $\mathcal{L}$, with no free variables;
- if p is a member of $\mathcal{L}_{\text{pred}}$ with arity n, and $t_1,\ldots,t_n$ are terms in $\mathcal{L}_{\text{term}}$, then $p(t_1,\ldots,t_n)$ is a wff in $\mathcal{L}$, with the free variables being all the variables of $t_1,\ldots,t_n$;
- if φ is a wff in $\mathcal{L}$, then so is $\neg(\varphi)$;
- if φ and ψ are wffs in $\mathcal{L}$, then so is $\varphi \to \psi$, with the free variables being the union of those free in φ and ψ;
- if v is a variable in $\mathcal{L}_{\text{var}}$ and φ is a wff in $\mathcal{L}$, then $\exists v.\varphi$ is a wff in $\mathcal{L}$. The free variables of $\exists v.\varphi$ are those of φ less the variable v.
- if v is a variable in $\mathcal{L}_{\text{var}}$ and φ is a wff in $\mathcal{L}$, then $\forall v.\varphi$ is a wff in $\mathcal{L}$. The free variables of $\forall v.\varphi$ are those of φ less the variable v.

Definition 9 (Semantics of Predicate Logic). The formulas are given truth values with respect to an interpretation or a model $\mathcal{M} = \langle \mathcal{D}, \pi_{\text{cons}}, \pi_{\text{func}}, \pi_{\text{pred}} \rangle$, with the following four components:

- $\mathcal{D}$, a nonempty domain of objects;
- π_{cons}, a mapping from members of $\mathcal{L}_{\text{cons}}$ to $\mathcal{D}$;
- π_{func}, which maps each member of $\mathcal{L}_{\text{func}}$ to a function mapping $\mathcal{D}^n$ to $\mathcal{D}$, for each $p \in \mathcal{L}_{\text{func}}$ $\pi_{\text{func}}(p) : \mathcal{D}^n \mapsto \mathcal{D}$, where n is the arity of the member of $\mathcal{L}_{\text{func}}$; and
- π_{pred}, which maps each member of $\mathcal{L}_{\text{pred}}$ to $\mathcal{D}^n \mapsto \{\top, \bot\}$, where n is the arity of the member of $\mathcal{L}_{\text{pred}}$.

We also need to interpret the free variables in the formulas. This is done by defining a *variable assignment* V, which is a mapping from $\mathcal{L}_{\text{var}}$ to $\mathcal{D}$. We also need the notation $V_{[v \mapsto d]}$ to mean the assignment V' satisfying $V'(x) = V(x)$, for $x \neq v$ and $V'(v) = d$. Given this, we can interpret all the terms of $\mathcal{L}$ by means of a term mapping π_{term}, based on V, π_{cons}, and π_{func}, which maps all members of $\mathcal{L}_{\text{term}}$ to $\mathcal{D}$. For t in $\mathcal{L}_{\text{term}}$:

- for all members c of $\mathcal{L}_{\text{cons}}$, $\pi_{\text{term}}(c) = \pi_{\text{cons}}(c)$;
- for all members v of $\mathcal{L}_{\text{var}}$, $\pi_{\text{term}}(v) = V(v)$;
- for all members f of $\mathcal{L}_{\text{func}}$ with arity n, $\pi_{\text{term}}(f(t_1,\ldots,t_n)) = \pi_{\text{func}}(f)(\pi_{\text{term}}(t_1),\ldots,\pi_{\text{term}}(t_n))$;
- $\pi_{\text{term}}(t)$ is called the value of t in the model, under the assignment V.

Finally, we can define the truth of a wff φ of $\mathcal{L}$, with respect to an interpretation $\mathcal{M}$ and a variable assignment V. This is written as $\langle \mathcal{M}, V \rangle \models \varphi$, read as '$\varphi$ holds in $\langle \mathcal{M}, V \rangle$' or '$\langle \mathcal{M}, V \rangle$ is a model of φ', and given by

$$\langle \mathcal{M}, V \rangle \not\models \bot,$$
$$\langle \mathcal{M}, V \rangle \models p(t_1, \ldots, t_n) \text{ iff } \pi_{\text{pred}}(p)(\pi_{\text{term}}(t_1), \ldots, \pi_{\text{term}}(t_n)) = \top,$$
$$\langle \mathcal{M}, V \rangle \models \varphi \rightarrow \psi \quad \text{iff } \langle \mathcal{M}, V \rangle \models \varphi \text{ implies } \langle \mathcal{M}, V \rangle \models \psi,$$
$$\langle \mathcal{M}, V \rangle \models \exists v.\ \varphi \quad \text{iff there exists } d \in \mathcal{D} \text{ and } \langle \mathcal{M}, V_{[v \mapsto d]} \rangle \models \varphi,$$
$$\langle \mathcal{M}, V \rangle \models \forall v.\ \varphi \quad \text{iff for all } d \in \mathcal{D}, \langle \mathcal{M}, V_{[v \mapsto d]} \rangle \models \varphi.$$

Let $\varphi(x_1, \ldots, x_n)$ be a formula with free variables $x_1, \ldots, x_n$. It is common to use the notation $\mathcal{M} \models \varphi(a_1, \ldots, a_n)$ to represent the satisfiability relation $\langle \mathcal{M}, V_{[x_i \mapsto a_i | i=1, \ldots, n]} \rangle \models \varphi$.

If the formula contains no free variables, then an arbitrary mapping (sometimes called an *empty* mapping) can be used as the initial variable assignment. We use the notation $[\,]$ for such a mapping and we write $\langle \mathcal{M}, [\,] \rangle \models \varphi$.

We write $\models \varphi$ to indicate that 'φ holds in all models $\langle \mathcal{M}, V \rangle$'.

2.3 Nonclassical Logics

Logic has had a rich and fruitful history, particularly over the last century. Developments in computer science, artificial intelligence, philosophy, and the natural sciences have led to the development of new forms of (formal) reasoning, considering dimensions such as time, space, knowledge, belief, probability, and uncertainty. Logic has been called the 'calculus of computer science' by analogy with the crucial role calculus has historically played in physics [122, 170]. These developments have led to several developments in *nonclassical logics* [42, 100, 214].

Nonclassical logics are ubiquitous in artificial intelligence and computer science. These logics have been developed as alternatives to classical logic and have been applied extensively to research areas in which the use of classical mathematical logic has proved to be of restricted or limited use [42, 100, 214]. In particular, modal, temporal, conditional, epistemic, fuzzy, linear, intuitionistic, and nonmonotonic logics have had a noticeable and effective impact on computer science.

More recently, developments in quantum computation have been influenced by and have influenced developments in quantum logic [147], showing that logic has a role to play in physics. On the other hand, developments in computer science have influenced research on (nonclassical) logical systems because the notions of an algorithm and of a constructive proof are strongly related, as shown in [172] for example. In addition, the development of nonmonotonic logics, particularly in the 1980s, has also led to new developments in the logical modelling of forms of commonsense reasoning including belief revision, conditional reasoning through conditional logics (the study of conditional sentences, or *if sentences*), and abductive and epistemic reasoning (aimed at formalising the notion of the *knowledge* of a cognitive agent).

Nonclassical logics are distinguished semantically from their classical counterparts. One notion widely used in nonclassical logics is the notion of *possible-world semantics*. In this brief introduction, we provide only the basic intuition underlying its foundations. This semantic technique has been successfully used in several nonclassical logical systems, including modal, temporal, conditional, intuitionistic, and epistemic logics. Possible worlds can be used to model an agent's knowledge or beliefs about the world, i.e. the different ways in which an agent sees possibilities about the state of the world he or she is reasoning about, acting in or observing. They can also be used in a temporal perspective considering linear or branching time, where time points may correspond to states of a (computational) system.

Intuitively, under this semantics, a proposition is *necessarily true* in a possible world ω_1 if it is true in *all* possible worlds accessible from ω_1. A proposition is *possibly true* in a given world ω_2 if it is true in *some* world accessible from ω_2. These notions of necessity and possibility are called *modalities*. In the case of temporal reasoning, several modalities may be useful. For instance, one may refer to formulas that are *always true in the future, true sometime in the past, true at the previous time point*, and *true at the next time point*, amongst other possibilities. Of course, the choice of the appropriate modalities will depend on the expressive power needed in the applications at hand, which demands a proper adoption of a nonclassical logical system. In the forthcoming chapters, we shall formally present the possible-worlds semantic model as introduced by Kripke and Hintikka in the early 1960s [129, 156]. We shall introduce the other logics formally as the need arises throughout the book.

In order to illustrate the difference between classical and nonclassical logics, let us consider temporal logic as described in [100]. Let us regard the assignment of truth values to propositions as being a description of the world or situation with respect to a particular time t. In temporal logic, the value assigned to a proposition (statement) can vary with the flow of time. This is not the case in classical logic: once a statement (a proposition) is proved, its truth value is definite. However, in artificial intelligence and computer science, as opposed to classical mathematics, time is an extremely relevant dimension as we are frequently working with several states, statements about particular time points or intervals, and several interpretations of these states. Under a modal interpretation of time, one could refer to the truth values of a proposition on a linear timeline (considering both past and future), or a branching-time interpretation with several futures, using modalities such as *always true in the future/past* and *sometimes true in the future/past*, among several other possibilities. This turns temporal logic into an expressive nonclassical logical system, which perhaps explains the success of this logic in computer science, artificial intelligence, and cognitive science [33, 42, 85, 89, 122, 157].

In summary, nonclassical logics are fundamental in computer science today. Research in computer science is now often a multidisciplinary endeavour. Nonclassical logics offer an adequate language for and formalisation of several dimensions that are relevant in the modelling of cognitive abilities, including reasoning, learning, and analogy. In the forthcoming chapters, we shall exploit nonclassical logics in more detail.

2.4 Nonmonotonic Reasoning

The study of nonmonotonic reasoning has had a relevant impact on logic and artificial intelligence, with implications in computer science and philosophical logics (see [102] for a comprehensive historical and philosophical analysis of nonmonotonicity). *Nonmonotonic reasoning* grew out of attempts to capture the essential aspects of commonsense (practical) reasoning. It resulted in a number of important formalisms, the most well known of them being the circumscription method of McCarthy [175], the default theory of Reiter [220], and the autoepistemic logic of Moore [188] (see [7,171] for an introduction to the subject, and [104] for a thorough study).

Nonmonotonicity is used for reasoning with incomplete information in commonsense or practical reasoning. If, later, additional information becomes available, it may turn out that some conclusions are no longer justified, and must be withdrawn. The standard example of this case is that, if we learn that Tweety is a bird, we conclude that it can fly, but if we subsequently find out that Tweety is a penguin, we withdraw that conclusion. This use of logic, called *belief revision*, is clearly nonmonotonic.[2]

One way of studying nonmonotonic logical systems is by analysing which properties their consequence relations satisfy, as suggested by Gabbay [97].[3] A very strong property of inference relations is monotonicity. An inference relation ($\vdash$) is monotonic if it satisfies $\Gamma \vdash \Psi$ implies $\Gamma \cup \delta \vdash \Psi$, where Γ, Ψ are sets of formulas, and δ is a new premise, added to Γ. The negation-as-finite-failure rule [49] and the closed-world assumption (CWA) [220] introduce nonmonotonicity into logic when negative literals are derived, since, for example, $\{p \leftarrow q\}$ entails $\neg p$ whereas $\{p \leftarrow q, q\}$ does not entail $\neg p$.[4] A good example of the use of the CWA is the process of booking a flight. Assume that you want to know whether there is a flight from London to Porto Alegre on 6 August 2012. Assume that the database of your travel agent does not contain such a flight. He will inform you that there is no flight from London to Porto Alegre on that date. In order to be able to jump to this conclusion, the travel agent has to assume that all flights from London to Porto Alegre are listed on his database. If, later, a new flight is entered into the database, then the earlier conclusion has to be withdrawn, but the convention that the database is complete (i.e. the CWA) will remain (see [37, 166]).

---

[2] The postulates of belief revision, put forward by Alchourrón, Gärdenfors, and Makinson, were published in the influential paper [4]. These postulates are now widely known as the AGM postulates.

[3] This field of research underwent several developments in the 1980s and 1990s. The diligent reader is referred to [155, 168] for a complete analysis of the theme.

[4] The notation $p \leftarrow q$ used here is equivalent to the traditional notation for the implication (classical conditional) $q \rightarrow p$. *Logic programming*, however, has adopted a syntactic notation in which the consequent of a conditional (namely, the *head of a clause*) appears to the *left* of the inverted arrow $\leftarrow$ and the antecedents appear to the right of the inverted arrow (these are called the *body of the clause*).

2.5 Logic Programming

The use of logic in computer programming can be traced back to the beginnings of computer science and artificial intelligence [174]. Logic programming – which should not be taken as meaning a particular implementation or language, such as the programming language Prolog – has been a successful declarative programming paradigm since the late 1970s [260]. Several applications of logic programming have been studied over recent decades. The collection [104] contains foundational chapters on logic programming and on its applications in automated reasoning and theorem proving, in knowledge representation and reasoning, and in artificial intelligence in general.

In this section, we use the standard notation and terminology of [163] to introduce some basic concepts of logic programming. We follow the standard notation with the exception that general logic programs are called *normal logic programs* in [163]. As usual, we assume that a logic program $\mathcal{P}$ has already been instantiated and thus all clauses are propositional. This assumption allows us to restrict our consideration to a fixed objective propositional language $\mathcal{L}$. In particular, if the original (uninstantiated) program is function-free, then the resulting objective language $\mathcal{L}$ is finite.

Definition 10. A *definite logic program* $\mathcal{P}$ is a finite set of clauses of the form $A_0 \leftarrow A_1, \ldots, A_n$, where each A_i is a propositional variable. A_0 is called the head (or consequent) of the clause, and $A_1, \ldots, A_n$ is called the body (or antecedent) of the clause.

A propositional variable is also called an *atom*. A *literal* is an atom or the negation of an atom. $B_{\mathcal{P}}$ denotes the set of atoms occurring in $\mathcal{P}$, i.e. the *Herbrand base* of $\mathcal{P}$. An *interpretation* (or *valuation*) is a mapping from propositional variables to $\{\top, \bot\}$. It is extended to literals, clauses, and programs in the usual way. A *model* for $\mathcal{P}$ is an interpretation which maps $\mathcal{P}$ to *true*. $M_{\mathcal{P}}$ denotes the least *Herbrand model* [5] of $\mathcal{P}$.

The following result dates back to 1976 [260]. The interest in this result arises from the fact that for a definite program $\mathcal{P}$, the collection of all Herbrand interpretations forms a complete lattice and there is a monotonic mapping associated with $\mathcal{P}$ defined on this lattice.

Proposition 1 (Model Intersection Property). *Let $\mathcal{P}$ be a definite program and $\{M_i\}$ be a nonempty set of Herbrand models for $\mathcal{P}$. Then $\cap_i M_i$ is also a Herbrand model for $\mathcal{P}$.*

In the following, we recall some concepts and results concerning monotonic mappings and their fixed points.

Definition 11. Let $[L, \preceq]$ be a complete lattice and $T : L \to L$ be a mapping.

- T is *monotonic* iff $x \preceq y \to T(x) \preceq T(y)$.

---

[5] After Jacques Herbrand, French logician (1908–1931).

- Let $Y \subseteq L$. Y is *directed* iff every finite subset of Y has an upper bound in Y.
- T is *continuous* iff for every directed subset Y of L, $T(lub(Y)) = lub(T(Y))$.

Definition 12. Let $[L, \preceq]$ be a complete lattice and $T : L \to L$ be a mapping. $a \in L$ is the *least fixed point* of T iff a is a fixed point of T (i.e. $T(a) = a$) and, for all fixed points b of T, $a \preceq b$. Similarly, $a \in L$ is the *greatest fixed point* of T iff a is a fixed point of T and, for all fixed points b of T, $b \preceq a$.

Proposition 2. *Let L be a complete lattice and $T : L \to L$ be monotonic. T has a least fixed point $(lfp(T))$ and a greatest fixed point $(gfp(T))$.*

Definition 13. Let L be a complete lattice and $T : L \to L$ be monotonic. We then define: $T \uparrow 0 = inf(L)$;

$T \uparrow \alpha = T(T \uparrow (\alpha - 1))$ if α is a successor ordinal;
$T \uparrow \alpha = lub\{T \uparrow \beta \mid \beta \prec \alpha\}$ if α is a limit ordinal;
$T \downarrow 0 = sup(L)$;
$T \downarrow \alpha = T(T \downarrow (\alpha - 1))$ if α is a successor ordinal;
$T \downarrow \alpha = glb\{T \downarrow \beta \mid \beta \prec a\}$ if α is a limit ordinal.

Proposition 3. *Let L be a complete lattice and $T : L \to L$ be continuous. Then $lfp(T) = T \uparrow \omega$, where ω is the smallest limit ordinal.*

Let $\mathcal{P}$ be a definite program. Then $2^{B_\mathcal{P}}$, which is the set of all Herbrand interpretations of $\mathcal{P}$, is a complete lattice under the partial order of set inclusion $\subseteq$. The top element of this lattice is $B_\mathcal{P}$ and the bottom element is $\varnothing$.

Definition 14 (Immediate-Consequence Operator). Let $\mathcal{P}$ be a definite program. The mapping $T_\mathcal{P} : 2^{B_\mathcal{P}} \to 2^{B_\mathcal{P}}$ is defined as follows. Let I be a Herbrand interpretation; then $T_\mathcal{P}(I) = \{A \in B_\mathcal{P} \mid A \leftarrow A_1, \ldots, A_n$ is a ground instance of a clause in $\mathcal{P}$ and $\{A_1, \ldots, A_n\} \subseteq I\}$.

$T_\mathcal{P}$ provides the link between the declarative and the procedural semantics of $\mathcal{P}$. Clearly, $T_\mathcal{P}$ is monotonic. Therefore, Herbrand interpretations that are models can be characterised in terms of $T_\mathcal{P}$.

Proposition 4. *Let $\mathcal{P}$ be a definite program and I a Herbrand interpretation of $\mathcal{P}$. Then the mapping $T_\mathcal{P}$ is continuous, and I is a model of $\mathcal{P}$ iff $T_\mathcal{P}(I) \subseteq I$.*

Proposition 5 (Fixed-Point Characterisation of the Least Herbrand Model). *Let $\mathcal{P}$ be a definite program. $M_\mathcal{P} = lfp(T_\mathcal{P}) = T_\mathcal{P} \uparrow \omega$.*

So far, we have seen that if $\mathcal{P}$ is a definite logic program, then the least Herbrand model of $\mathcal{P}$ exists and its classical (two-valued) semantics can be defined as the least fixed point of a meaning operator $T_\mathcal{P}$. The semantics is obtained by lattice-theoretic considerations which require $T_\mathcal{P}$ to be monotonic. However, if $\mathcal{P}$ is a general logic program, then $T_\mathcal{P}$ may be nonmonotonic and, consequently, the existence of a least fixed point of $T_\mathcal{P}$ cannot be guaranteed. Take, for example, $\mathcal{P} = \{p \leftarrow \sim q\}$; then $\{p\}$ and $\{q\}$ are the only minimal Herbrand models of $\mathcal{P}$, but none of them is the least model of $\mathcal{P}$. In this case, $T_\mathcal{P}$ may even have no fixed point at all, for example when $\mathcal{P} = \{p \leftarrow \sim p\}$.

2.5.1 Stable-Model and Answer Set Semantics

One of the striking features of logic programming (see [163]) is that it can naturally support nonmonotonic reasoning – by means of negative literals. Many concepts introduced in the area of nonmonotonic reasoning have a natural counterpart within logic programming in spite of its limited syntax.

Definition 15. A *general clause* is a rule of the form $A_0 \leftarrow A_1, \ldots, A_m, \sim A_{m+1}, \ldots,$ $\sim A_n$, where A_i ($0 \leq i \leq n$) is an atom and $\sim$ denotes default negation. A *general logic program* is a finite set of general clauses.

There is no general agreement upon the answer to the question of what is the standard model of a general program. However, there are some desired properties of the natural model that can support some plausible answers to the question. The following definitions attempt to formalise this requirement.

Definition 16 (Supported Interpretation). An interpretation I is called *supported* if $A_0 \in I$ implies that for some ground instance $A_0 \leftarrow A_1, \ldots, A_m, \sim A_{m+1}, \ldots, \sim A_n \in \mathcal{P}$ we have that $I \models A_1 \wedge \ldots \wedge A_m \wedge \sim A_{m+1} \wedge \ldots \wedge \sim A_n$. Intuitively, $A_1, \ldots, A_m, \sim A_{m+1}, \ldots, \sim A_n$ is an explanation for A_0.

Proposition 6. *I is a supported model of $\mathcal{P}$ iff $T_{\mathcal{P}}(I) = I$.*

Thus, in view of the above observation about the behaviour of the $T_{\mathcal{P}}$ operator, we see that for some programs no supported models exist, for example when $\mathcal{P} = \{p \leftarrow \sim p\}$. One possible approach is to accept that some programs have no natural supported model and to identify classes of programs for which a natural supported model exists.

Definition 17 (Dependency). Consider a program $\mathcal{P}$. The dependency graph $D_{\mathcal{P}}$ for $\mathcal{P}$ is a directed graph with signed edges. Its nodes are the literals occurring in $\mathcal{P}$. For every clause in $\mathcal{P}$ with p in its head and q as a positive (or negative) literal in its body, there is a positive (or negative, respectively), edge (p, q) in $D_{\mathcal{P}}$.

- We say that p *uses* (or refers to) q positively (or negatively, respectively).
- We say that p *depends* positively (or negatively) on q if there is a path in $D_{\mathcal{P}}$ from p to q with only positive edges (or at least one negative edge, respectively).
- We say that p *depends evenly* (or *oddly*) on q if there is a path in $D_{\mathcal{P}}$ from p to q with an even (or odd, respectively) number of negative edges.

Definition 18 (Locally Stratified Program). A program $\mathcal{P}$ is called *locally stratified* if no cycle with a negative edge exists in its dependency graph [215].

In [115], Gelfond and Lifschitz introduced the notion of *stable models* – nowadays important in answer set programming [190] – by using the intuitive idea of rational beliefs taken from autoepistemic logic.

Definition 19 (Gelfond–Lifschitz Transformation). Let $\mathcal{P}$ be a grounded logic program. Given a set I of atoms from $\mathcal{P}$, let $\mathcal{P}_I$ be the program obtained from $\mathcal{P}$ by deleting (i) each rule that has a negative literal $\sim A$ in its body with $A \in I$, and (ii) all the negative literals in the bodies of the remaining rules.

Clearly, $\mathcal{P}_I$ is a positive program, so that $\mathcal{P}_I$ has a unique minimal Herbrand model. If this model coincides with I, then we say that I is a stable model of $\mathcal{P}$.

Definition 20 (Stable Model). A Herbrand interpretation I of a program $\mathcal{P}$ is called *stable* iff $T_{\mathcal{P}}(I) = I$.

The intuition behind the definition of a stable model is as follows: consider a rational agent with a set of beliefs I and a set of premises $\mathcal{P}$. Then, any clause that has a literal $\sim A$ in its body when $A \in I$ is useless, and may be removed from $\mathcal{P}$. Moreover, any literal $\sim A$ with $A \notin I$ is trivial, and may be deleted from the clauses in $\mathcal{P}$ in which it appears. This yields the simplified (definite) program $\mathcal{P}_I$, and if I happens to be precisely the set of atoms that follows logically from the simplified set of premises, then the set of beliefs I is stable. Hence, stable models are possible sets of belief that a rational agent might hold.

Stable-model semantics allow more than one stable model, or none at all. This reflects some uncertainty about the conclusions that should be drawn from a program. In some cases, a local uncertainty can destroy too much information. For example, if $\mathcal{P}$ is a stratified program in which the variable p does not occur, then $\mathcal{P} \cup \{p \leftarrow \sim p\}$ has no stable model. Thus, the information contained in $\mathcal{P}$ is not reflected in the stable-model semantics of $\mathcal{P} \cup \{p \leftarrow \sim p\}$, even though it is not related to the uncertainty about the truth value of p.

The use of *well-founded semantics* [261] avoids this problem by using a three-valued model. In contrast with three-valued logic (see [91]), a three-valued interpretation of the connectives is not needed to obtain three-valued models. On the other hand, well-founded semantics has the drawback of not inferring all atoms that one would expect to be *true* (see Apt and Bol's survey of logic programming and negation [9] for a comprehensive comparison between different semantics and classes of programs).

2.6 Discussion

This chapter has briefly introduced some basic concepts of logic and knowledge representation. Logic has been fundamental to artificial intelligence since the early stages of the field [174]. Logic-based knowledge representation is the backbone of artificial-intelligence research (see e.g. [42, 87, 106]). Several logical systems have had an impact on artificial intelligence, including not only classical but also nonclassical logics. Research on theorem proving, model checking, formal specification of multiagent systems, game playing, natural-language processing, planning, knowledge representation, expert systems, and learning theory, to name but a few areas, has been directed influenced by results from classical and nonclassical logics. It has been clearly indicated that logical languages, be they classical or nonclassical, are adequate for this important task in artificial intelligence. Logic has also benefited from artificial-intelligence research. For instance, the field of nonmonotonic reasoning has influenced logicians to axiomatise several forms of commonsense reasoning, leading to the creation of new nonclassical logics of human and practical reasoning (see [102]). The advances in research published annually in the proceedings of the major conferences and in the major research journals in the fields of applied logic, knowledge representation, and artificial intelligence corroborate this claim. Of particular interest to us, in this book, is knowledge representation. We shall make use of several logic-based knowledge representation languages in our models. Any reasoning or learning task run in a computational model demands such a language, since in any machine-learning algorithm or procedure, knowledge representation precedes any other task.

Chapter 3
Artificial Neural Networks

This chapter introduces the basics of neural networks used in this book. Artificial neural networks have a long history in computer science and artificial intelligence. As early as the 1940s, papers were written on the subject [177]. Neural networks have been used in several tasks, including pattern recognition, robot control, DNA sequence analysis, and time series analysis and prediction [125]. Differently from (symbolic) machine learning, (numeric) neural networks perform inductive learning in such a way that the statistical characteristics of the data are encoded in their sets of weights, a feature that has been exploited in a number of applications [66]. A good introductory text on neural networks can be found in [127]. A thorough approach to the subject can be found in [125]. The book by Bose and Liang [35] provides a good balance between the previous two.

3.1 Architectures of Neural Networks

An artificial neural network is a directed graph. A unit in this graph is characterised, at time t, by its input vector $I_i(t)$, its input potential $U_i(t)$, its activation state $A_i(t)$, and its output $O_i(t)$. The units (neurons) of the network are interconnected via a set of directed, weighted connections. If there is a connection from unit i to unit j, then $W_{ji} \in \mathbb{R}$ denotes the *weight* associated with such a connection.

We start by characterising the neuron's *functionality* (see Fig. 3.1). The *activation state* of a neuron i at time t $(A_i(t))$ is a bounded real or integer number. The output of neuron i at time t $(O_i(t))$ is given by the *output rule* f_i, such that $O_i(t) = f_i(A_i(t))$. The input potential of neuron i at time t $(U_i(t))$ is obtained by applying the *propagation rule* of neuron i (g_i) such that $U_i(t) = g_i(I_i(t), W_i)$, where $I_i(t)$ contains the input signals $(x_1(t), x_2(t), \ldots, x_n(t))$ to neuron i at time t, and W_i denotes the weight vector $(W_{i1}, W_{i2}, \ldots, W_{in})$ to neuron i. Finally, the neuron's new activation state $A_i(t + \Delta t)$ is given by its *activation rule* h_i, which is a function of the neuron's current activation state and input potential, i.e. $A_i(t + \Delta t) = h_i(A_i(t), U_i(t))$. The neuron's new output value is $O_i(t + \Delta t) = f_i(A_i(t + \Delta t))$.

A.S. d'Avila Garcez et al., *Neural-Symbolic Cognitive Reasoning*, Cognitive Technologies,
© Springer-Verlag Berlin Heidelberg 2009

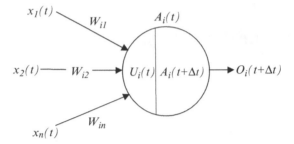

Fig. 3.1 The processing unit, or neuron

There are three basic kinds of *activation function* (h_i): linear, nonlinear, and semi-linear (also known as *sigmoid*). Neurons with linear, nonlinear (binary), and semi-linear activation functions are called linear, nonlinear (binary), and semilinear neurons, respectively. In Fig. 3.2, θ_i is known as the *threshold* of the neuron's activation function.

In general, h_i does not depend on the previous activation state of the unit, that is, $A_i(t + \Delta t) = h_i(U_i(t))$, the propagation rule g_i is a weighted sum, such that $U_i(t) = \sum_j W_{ij} x_j(t)$, and the output rule f_i is given by the identity function, i.e. $O_i(t) = A_i(t)$. In addition, most neural models also have a *learning rule*, responsible for changing the weights of the network, and thus allowing it to perform inductive learning.

The units of a neural network can be organised into layers. An *n-layer feed-forward network* N is an acyclic graph. N consists of a sequence of layers and connections between successive layers, containing one input layer, $n - 2$ hidden layers, and one output layer, where $n \geq 2$. When $n = 3$, we say that N is a *single-hidden-layer network*. When each unit occurring in the *i-th* layer is connected to each unit occurring in layer $i + 1$, we say that N is a *fully connected network* (see Fig. 3.3).

The most interesting properties of a neural network arise not from the functionality of each neuron, but from the collective effect resulting from the interconnection of units. Let r and s be the numbers of units occurring in the input and the output layer, respectively. A multilayer feedforward network N computes a function $f : \mathbb{R}^r \to \mathbb{R}^s$ as follows. The input vector is presented to the input layer at time t_1 and propagated through the hidden layers to the output layer. At each time point, all units update their input potential and activation state synchronously. At time t_n, the output vector is read off from the output layer.

In this book, we shall concentrate on single-hidden-layer networks. We do so because of the following relevant result.

Theorem 7 ([52]). *Let $h : \mathbb{R} \to \mathbb{R}$ be a continuous, semilinear function. Let $\varepsilon \in \mathbb{R}^+$ and $n \in \mathbb{R}$. Given a continuous, real-valued function g on $\mathbb{I}^n = [0,1]^n$, there exist a finite K and parameters $\alpha_j \in \mathbb{R}, \theta_j \in \mathbb{R}$, and $y_j \in \mathbb{R}^n (1 \leq j \leq K)$ such that if $f(x) = \sum_{j=1}^{K} \alpha_j \cdot h(y_j x + \theta_j), x \in \mathbb{I}^n$, then $|f(x) - g(x)| < \varepsilon$ for all $x \in \mathbb{I}^n$.*

In other words, by making α_j the weight from the *j*-th hidden neuron to the output neuron, single-hidden-layer feedforward networks can approximate any (Borel)

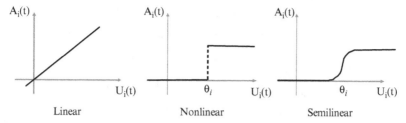

| Linear | Nonlinear | Semilinear |

Fig. 3.2 Activation functions

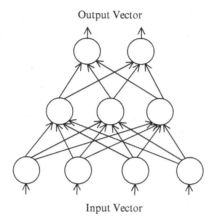

Output Vector

Input Vector

Fig. 3.3 A typical feedforward neural network

measurable function arbitrarily well, regardless of the dimension of the input space n. A similar result was proved independently in [140]. In this sense, single-hidden-layer networks are *universal approximators* of virtually any function of interest (see [140]).

We use *bipolar* semilinear activation functions $h(x) = 2/(1 + e^{-\beta x}) - 1$ and inputs in $\{-1, 1\}$. The reason for using these instead of the standard sigmoid function shown in Fig. 3.2 is that, for standard functions with inputs in $\{0, 1\}$, a *zero* input value would produce no variation of the set of weights during the learning process [35]. If we were to map the truth value *false* to *zero* in our experiments we would have a rather ineffective learning of logical statements. Instead, we shall map the truth value *false* to -1, and (as usual) the truth value *true* to 1. In practice, we associate intervals $(A_{min}, 1)$ with *true*, $A_{min} \in \mathbb{R}^+$, $(-1, -A_{min})$ with *false*, and $[-A_{min}, A_{min}]$ with *unknown*, as discussed later. The following systems of equations describe the dynamics of the networks that we use:

$$n_1 = h(W_{11}^1 i_1 + W_{12}^1 i_2 + \cdots + W_{1p}^1 i_p - \theta_{n_1}), \qquad (3.1)$$
$$n_2 = h(W_{21}^1 i_1 + W_{22}^1 i_2 + \cdots + W_{2p}^1 i_p - \theta_{n_2}),$$
$$\vdots$$
$$n_r = h(W_{r1}^1 i_1 + W_{r2}^1 i_2 + \cdots + W_{rp}^1 i_p - \theta_{n_r}),$$

$$o_1 = h(W_{11}^2 n_1 + W_{12}^2 n_2 + \cdots + W_{1r}^2 n_r - \theta_{o_1}), \qquad (3.2)$$
$$o_2 = h(W_{21}^2 n_1 + W_{22}^2 n_2 + \cdots + W_{2r}^2 n_r - \theta_{o_2}),$$
$$\vdots$$
$$o_q = h(W_{q1}^2 n_1 + W_{q2}^2 n_2 + \cdots + W_{qr}^2 n_r - \theta_{o_q}),$$

where $\mathbf{i} = (i_1, i_2, \ldots, i_p)$ is the network's input vector $(i_{j(1 \leq j \leq p)} \in \{-1, 1\})$, $\mathbf{o} = (o_1, o_2, \ldots, o_q)$ is the network's output vector $(o_{j(1 \leq j \leq q)} \in [-1, 1])$, $\mathbf{n} = (n_1, n_2, \ldots, n_r)$ is the hidden-layer vector $(n_{j(1 \leq j \leq r)} \in [-1, 1])$, $\theta_{n_j(1 \leq j \leq r)}$ is the threshold of the j-th hidden neuron $(\theta_{n_j} \in \mathbb{R})$, $\theta_{o_j(1 \leq j \leq q)}$ is the threshold of the j-th output neuron $(\theta_{o_j} \in \mathbb{R})$, $-\theta_{n_j}$ (and $-\theta_{o_j}$) is called the bias of the j-th hidden neuron (and of the j-th output neuron, respectively), $W_{ij(1 \leq i \leq r, 1 \leq j \leq p)}^1$ is the weight of the connection from the j-th neuron in the input layer to the i-th neuron in the hidden layer $(W_{ij}^1 \in \mathbb{R})$, $W_{ij(1 \leq i \leq q, 1 \leq j \leq r)}^2$ is the weight of the connection from the j-th neuron in the hidden layer to the i-th neuron in the output layer $(W_{ij}^2 \in \mathbb{R})$, and, finally, $h(x) = 2/(1 + e^{-\beta x}) - 1$ is the standard bipolar (semilinear) activation function. Notice that for each output $o_j (1 \leq j \leq q)$ in $\mathbf{o}$ we have $o_j = h(\sum_{i=1}^{r}(W_{ji}^2 . h(\sum_{k=1}^{p}(W_{ik}^1 . i_k) - \theta_{n_i})) - \theta_{o_j}).$[1]

3.2 Learning Strategy

A neural network's *learning* process (or *training*) is carried out by successively changing its weights in order to approximate the function f computed by it to a desired function g. In *supervised learning*, one attempts to estimate the unknown function g from *examples* (input and output patterns) presented to the network. The idea is to *minimise the error* associated with the set of examples by making small changes to the network's weights.

In the case of *backpropagation* [224], the learning process occurs as follows. Given a set of input patterns $\mathbf{i}^i$ and corresponding target vectors $\mathbf{t}^i$, the network's outputs $\mathbf{o}^i = f(\mathbf{i}^i)$ may be compared with the targets $\mathbf{t}^i$, and an error such as

$$Err(\mathbf{W}) = \sum_i (\mathbf{o}^i - \mathbf{t}^i)^2 \qquad (3.3)$$

can be computed. This error depends on the set of examples $((\mathbf{i}, \mathbf{t})$ pairs) and may be minimised by *gradient descent*, i.e. by the iterative application of changes

$$\Delta \mathbf{W} = -\eta \cdot \nabla_{\mathbf{W}} \cdot Err(\mathbf{W}) \qquad (3.4)$$

to the weight vector $\mathbf{W}$.

---

[1] Whenever it is unnecessary to differentiate between the hidden and output layers, we refer to the weights in the network as W_{ij} only. Similarly, we refer to the network's thresholds as θ_i only in general.

The computation of $\nabla_{\mathbf{W}}$ is not obvious for a network with hidden units. However, in their famous paper 'learning internal representations by error propagation' [224], Rumelhart, Hinton, and Williams presented a simple and efficient way of computing such derivatives.[2] They showed that a backward pass of $\mathbf{o}^i - \mathbf{t}^i$ through the network, analogous to the forward propagation of $\mathbf{i}^i$, allows the recursive computation of $\nabla_{\mathbf{W}}$. The idea is that in the forward pass through the network, one should also calculate the derivative of $h_k(x)$ for each neuron k, $dk = h_k'(U_k(t))$. For each output neuron o, one simply calculates $\partial o = (\mathbf{o}^i - \mathbf{t}^i)do$. One can then compute weight changes for all connections that feed into the output layer. For each connection W_{oj}, $\Delta W_{oj} = -\eta \cdot \partial o \cdot O_j(t)$. After this is done, $\partial j = (W_{oj} \cdot \partial o) \cdot dj$ can be calculated for each hidden neuron j. This propagates the errors back one layer, and for each connection W_{ji} from input neuron i to neuron j, $\Delta W_{ji} = -\eta \cdot \partial j \cdot O_i(t)$. Of course, the same process could be repeated for many hidden layers. This procedure is called the *generalised delta rule*, and it is very useful because the backward pass has the same computational complexity as the forward pass.

In the above procedure, η is called the *learning rate*. True gradient descent requires infinitesimal steps to be taken ($\eta \approx 0$). On the other hand, the larger the constant η, the larger the change in the weights, and thus a good choice of η will lead to faster convergence. The design challenge here is how to choose the learning rate to be as large as possible without leading to oscillation. A variation of standard backpropagation allows the adaptation of this parameter during learning. In this case, η is typically large at the beginning of learning, and decreases as the network approaches a minimum of the error surface.

Backpropagation training may lead to a local rather than a global minimum of the error surface. In an attempt to ameliorate this problem and also improve training time, a *term of momentum* can be added to the learning process. The term of momentum allows a network to respond not only to the local gradient, but also to recent trends in the error surface, acting as a low-pass filter.

Momentum is added to backpropagation by making the weight changes equal to the sum of a fraction of the last weight change and the new change suggested by the backpropagation rule. Equation 3.5 shows how backpropagation with momentum is expressed mathematically:

$$\Delta \mathbf{W}(i) = -\eta \cdot \nabla_{\mathbf{W}(i)} \cdot Err(\mathbf{W}(i)) + \alpha \Delta \mathbf{W}(i-1), \qquad (3.5)$$

where $\alpha \Delta W(i-1)$ is the term of momentum and $0 < \alpha < 1$ is the momentum constant. Typically, $\alpha = 0.9$.

Another difficulty with learning is known as the *problem of symmetry*. 'If all weights start out with equal values and if the solution requires that unequal weights be developed, the system can never learn' [224]. This is so because the error backpropagated is proportional to the actual values of the weights. Symmetry breaking is achieved by starting the system with small random weights.

---

[2] The term "backpropagation" appears to have evolved after 1985. However, the basic idea of backpropagation was first described by Werbos in his PhD thesis [268].

If the application at hand contains too many degrees of freedom and too few training data, backpropagation can merely 'memorise' the data. This behaviour is known as *overfitting*. The ultimate measure of success, therefore, should not be how closely the network approximates the training data, but how well it accounts for yet unseen cases, i.e. how well the network generalises to new data. In order to evaluate the network's *generalisation*, the set of examples is commonly partitioned into a *training set* and a *testing set*.

Finally, it should be noted that a network's learning capability and its activation functions are closely related. Linear neurons possess less learning capability than nonlinear ones, because their hidden layers act only as a multiplier of the input vector. As a result, complex functions cannot be learned (see [53, 113, 235]). On the other hand, semilinear activation functions are continuous and differentiable, which is an important property for the use of backpropagation.

Summarising, there are three major issues one must address when applying neural networks in a given domain: the *representation* problem (model, architecture, and size), the *learning* problem (time and training method), and the *generalisation* problem (performance).

As an example, consider the network of Fig. 3.4. This network was trained using input values $\{-1, 1\}$, $f(x) = x$ as the activation function of neurons a and b, and $\tanh(x) = (e^{2x} - 1)/(e^{2x} + 1)$, $e = 2.718$, as the activation function of neurons h, k, and o. In the figure, 1.5 is the bias of neuron o, 2.0 is the bias of h, and 1.0 is the bias of k, where bias $= -$threshold. Consider the training example $(a = 0.5, b = -1.0, t = -0.5)$, where t is the target output for neuron o. We need to compute a weight change (ΔW) for each of the network's weights (including the biases). First, we compute the output of the network for the input vector $(a = 0.5, b = -1.0)$. Let us use a learning rate $\eta = 0.1$. Remember that $\tanh'(x) = 1 - \tanh^2(x)$ and $\Delta W_{ij} = -\eta . \partial_i . o_j$, where ∂_i is the *local gradient* of neuron i, and o_j is the output of neuron j.

Let $Act(x)$ denote the activation state of neuron x. We have $Act(h) = \tanh(2a - 4b + 2)$, $Act(k) = \tanh(2.5a + 3.5b + 1)$, and $Act(o) = \tanh(3h + k + 1.5)$. For

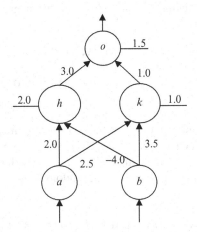

Fig. 3.4 A set of weights for the backpropagation example considered in the text

$a = 0.5, b = -1$, we thus obtain activation values $Act(h) = 0.99$, $Act(k) = -0.85$, and then $Act(o) = 0.99$. We also need to calculate the derivatives $\tanh'(x)$ of the activation values of each hidden and output neuron. We obtain $\tanh'(h) = 0.0199$, $\tanh'(k) = 0.2775$, and $\tanh'(o) = 0.0199$. We then compute the error $e = o - t = 1.49$.

The weight change ΔW_{oh} for the weight between neuron h and the output neuron o is given by $-\eta \cdot \partial o \cdot h$, where $\partial o = e \cdot \tanh'(o) = 0.02965$. Thus, $\Delta W_{oh} = -0.1 \cdot 0.02965 \cdot 0.99$. Similarly, $\Delta W_{ok} = -0.1 \cdot 0.02965 \cdot -0.85$.

For hidden neurons h and k, $\partial h = \tanh'(h) \cdot \partial o \cdot W_{ho} = 0.0199 \cdot 0.02965 \cdot 3.0 = 0.00177$ and $\partial k = \tanh'(k) \cdot \partial o \cdot W_{ko} = 0.2775 \cdot 0.02965 \cdot 1.0 = 0.00823$. Then, the weight change ΔW_{ha} for the weight between input neuron a and hidden neuron h is given by $-\eta \cdot \partial h \cdot a = -0.1 \cdot 0.00177 \cdot 0.5$. Similarly, the weight change ΔW_{hb} for the weight between input neuron b and hidden neuron h is given by $-\eta \cdot \partial h \cdot b = -0.1 \cdot 0.00177 \cdot -1.0$. Further, the weight change ΔW_{ka} for the weight between input neuron a and hidden neuron k is given by $-\eta \cdot \partial k \cdot a = -0.1 \cdot 0.00823 \cdot 0.5$, and the weight change ΔW_{kb} for the weight between input neuron b and hidden neuron k is given by $-\eta \cdot \partial k \cdot b = -0.1 \cdot 0.00823 \cdot -1.0$. The calculations for the variations $\Delta \theta_h$, $\Delta \theta_k$, $\Delta \theta_o$ of the biases are identical to those for the hidden neurons, but using an input 1.0.

3.3 Recurrent Networks

A limitation of feedforward neural networks when compared with symbolic computation is their inability to deal with time or artificial-intelligence applications endowed with a temporal dimension. Recurrent neural networks deal with this problem. A simple form of recurrent network will be used in this book, allowing for the computation of recursive functions. As we shall see, although it is recurrent, the network will be such that standard backpropagation can be used. In this section, we recall recurrent networks as defined by Jordan [145] and Elman [85].

A *recurrent architecture* is needed for a neural network to be able to generalise temporal sequences. In other words, the network is required to have cycles such as the ones shown in Fig. 3.5. The backpropagation algorithm has been extended to deal with such networks by performing the propagation of the error in the direction opposite to the original connections. As expected, the main difficulty of *recurrent backpropagation* is in how to deal with chaotic behaviour resulting from the cycles. This may require some form of synchronisation and may result in complications similar to those found in the training of *symmetric networks* [139]. We shall not use recurrent backpropagation in this book, but it might be an interesting future exercise to compare the results of such learning algorithms and backpropagation in the context of neural-symbolic systems. The details of the algorithms can be found in [127].

A simpler way of generalising temporal sequences in neural networks is to somehow control recurrency by carefully defining the feedback connections using *partially recurrent networks*. In such networks, most of the connections are

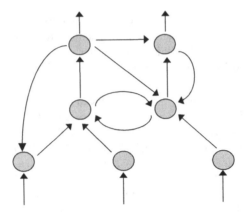

Fig. 3.5 A recurrent network

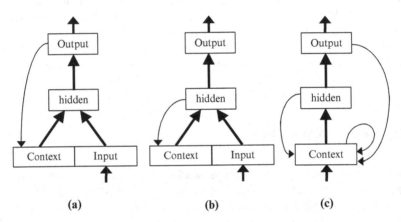

(a)   **(b)**   **(c)**

Fig. 3.6 Architectures of partially recurrent networks

feedforward, and only certain feedback connections are allowed. The idea of this is to obtain the expressive power needed for generalising temporal sequences, without the extra complexity of learning in an underconstrained architecture. In most cases, the feedback connections are also given fixed weights (i.e. no learning takes place in the feedback connections). This allows the standard backpropagation algorithm to be used without changes.

Figure 3.6 shows some typical architectures of partially recurrent networks. In each case, there is always a special set of neurons – called *context units* – that receive the feedback signals in a layer or part of a layer. The feedback signals need to be synchronised so that, at time t, the activations computed in a feedforward manner by the network at time $t-1$ can reach the context units, defining the network's current context. The other signals in the network do not need to be synchronised. One can see the context units as *remembering* some aspect of the network's computation in the recent past. In this way, at each time point, the network's output may now depend upon the network's current input and also upon its context (e.g. a previous network output). In Fig. 3.6(a), first proposed in [145], the input layer contains the neurons that receive values from the outside and the neurons that create the context. The latter simply record, at time t, the activation states of the neurons in the output layer at time $t - 1$. The connections that might have their weights changed by learning are all feedforward. Hence, backpropagation can be applied, with the training examples being presented to the network at each time interval t and with the context units being treated as input units for training purposes. Figure 3.6(b) shows the architecture proposed by Elman [85], which differs from that of Fig. 3.6(a) by having the activation of the hidden neurons feeding the context units. Here, it is the internal structure and behaviour of the network that define its context. Since it is that internal structure and behaviour that define the output of the network, similar results may be obtained either way, by having either the output or the hidden layer feed the context. Ultimately, the choice may depend on the application. Figure 3.6(c) shows an architecture where feedback is allowed from the context units themselves, from the hidden layer, and from the output layer. In this setting, the network combines, in its context units, any input signals with the feedback signals, into a weighted-sum input value that is propagated forward in the normal way.

In what follows, we shall use a slight variation of Jordan's network together with standard backpropagation. We shall also use groups of such networks, which we shall refer to loosely as *network ensembles*. As we shall see, this will be suficient for most of our purposes in relation to knowledge representation and reasoning. We shall also consider briefly a kind of *recursive network* in a setting we call *network fibring* [67]. Networks of this kind are more powerful than the networks above, and may prove to be a more adequate architecture for fully integrated reasoning and learning, and for first-order-logic reasoning. Differently from recurrent networks, the neurons in a recursive network may be networks in their own right, and in this structure, a computation in one network may trigger a learning process in another network in the ensemble. But these are features that we shall introduce as we go along and as they are needed in the text.

All the networks described in this book were trained using standard backpropagation with momentum, the most commonly used and generally most successful learning algorithm. The reader is referred to [47, 224] for the backpropagation algorithm and its variations and improvements, to [161] for a discussion of the problem of overfitting, and to [145, 151] for details of recurrent networks.

3.4 Evaluation of Learning Models

Learning, one of the basic attributes of intelligence, can be defined as a change of behaviour motivated by changes in the environment in order to perform better in different knowledge domains [182]. Learning strategies can be classified into: learning from instruction, learning by deduction, learning by analogy, learning from examples, and learning by observation and discovery; the latter two are forms of inductive learning. Reference [225] is a good introductory text on machine learning, and [184] contains some new hybrid models of learning, in addition to the traditional, purely symbolic paradigm.

The task of inductive learning is to find hypotheses that are consistent with background knowledge to explain a given set of examples. In general, these hypotheses are definitions of concepts described in some logical language, the examples are descriptions of instances and noninstances of the concept to be learned, and the background knowledge gives additional information about the examples and the domain knowledge related to the concepts (see [159]). A general formulation of inductive learning is as follows: given background knowledge or an initial set of beliefs ($\mathcal{B}$) and a set of positive (e^+) and negative (e^-) examples of some concept, find a hypothesis (h) in some knowledge representation language ($\mathcal{L}$) such that $\mathcal{B} \cup h \vdash_{\mathcal{L}} e^+$ and $\mathcal{B} \cup h \nvdash_{\mathcal{L}} e^-$.

Studies of inductive learning date back to the 1960s (see [142]). One of the most successful areas is called *case-based reasoning* (CBR), which is best instantiated in Quinlan's ID3 algorithm [216] and Michalski et al.'s [183]. More recently, the importance of adding background knowledge to help in the learning process, depending on the application at hand, has been highlighted (see e.g. [72, 131, 201]), and the area of *inductive logic programming* (ILP) has flourished (a comprehensive introductory survey of ILP can be found in [189]). In [159], CBR and ILP were integrated by means of the LINUS system, which translates a fragment of first-order logic into attribute-value examples in order to apply, for instance, a decision-tree-generation learning algorithm such as ID3. The result of learning can then be translated back onto the original language.

If a learning algorithm fails to extract any pattern from a set of examples, one cannot expect it to be able to extrapolate (or generalise) to examples it has not seen. Finding a pattern means being able to describe a large number of cases in a concise way. A general principle of inductive learning, often called *Ockham's razor*,[3] is thus as follows: *the most likely hypothesis is the simplest one that is consistent with all observations.* Unfortunately, finding the smallest representation (e.g. the smallest decision tree) is an intractable problem, and usually the use of some heuristics is needed. In [110], some conditions for the applicability of Ockham's razor were discussed. In a more general perspective, [253, 263] discuss the general theory of learning.

We normally evaluate the performance of a learning system with the use of *cross-validation*, a testing methodology in which the set of examples is permuted and divided into n sets. One division is used for testing and the remaining $n-1$ divisions are used for training. The testing division is never seen by the learning algorithm during the training process. The procedure is repeated n times so that every division is used once for testing. We call the average classification rate of the learning system over the test sets its *test set performance*. We call one pass through the training set a learning *epoch*. For a predefined number of epochs, we call the average classification rate of the system over the training sets its *training-set performance*.

For example, in [66] we experimented with two real-world problems in the domain of DNA sequence analysis: the *promoter recognition*[4] and the *splice-junction*

---

[3] Also spelled *Occam's razor*.

[4] Promoters are short DNA sequences that precede the beginning of genes.

determination[5] problems [191]. For the first problem, there were 106 examples available (53 promoter and 53 nonpromoter sequences), and we used *leaving-one-out* cross-validation, in which each example is successively left out of the training set. Hence, this required 106 training networks in which the training set had 105 examples and the testing set had one example. Leaving-one-out becomes computationally expensive as the number of available examples grows. For the splice-junction problem, for example, there were 3190 examples available, and therefore, following [191], we selected 1000 examples randomly from the original set, to which we applied a 10-fold cross-validation process (i.e. 10 networks were created, each using 900 examples for training and 100 examples for testing). Cross-validation is primarily a statistical evaluation methodology. It can also be used, for example, for model selection (i.e. to estimate the number of hidden neurons that a network should have in a given application). Alternatively, one may create a model that includes all the networks used in the evaluation (e.g. by taking as the "network output" the average of the outputs of all the 10 networks used for splice-junction determination).

3.5 Discussion

This chapter has introduced the basic concepts of neural networks used in this book. As mentioned above, neural networks have a long history in computer science and artificial intelligence, with applications in the engineering, physical, natural, and social sciences. Our interest in neural networks is based not only on their learning capabilities, but also on their computational power. If one aims to build sound (cognitive) computational models, several aspects of cognition must be investigated. In the case of connectionist models, these include explanation capabilities, knowledge representation, and expressivity. The coming chapters will analyse these in the context of neural-symbolic models.

---

[5] Splice junctions are points on a DNA sequence at which the noncoding regions are removed during the process of protein synthesis.

Chapter 4
Neural-Symbolic Learning Systems

This chapter introduces the basics of neural-symbolic systems used thoughout the book. A brief bibliographical review is also presented. Neural-symbolic systems have become a very active area of research in the last decade. The integration of neural networks and symbolic knowledge was already receiving considerable attention in the 1990s. For instance, in [250], Towell and Shavlik presented the influential model KBANN (Knowledge-Based Artificial Neural Network), a system for rule insertion, refinement, and extraction from neural networks. They also showed empirically that knowledge-based neural networks, trained using the backpropagation learning algorithm (see Sect. 3.2), provided a very efficient way of learning from examples and background knowledge. They did so by comparing the performance of KBANN with other hybrid, neural, and purely symbolic inductive learning systems (see [159, 189] for a comprehensive description of a number of symbolic inductive learning systems, including inductive logic programming systems).

Briefly, the rules-to-network algorithm of KBANN builds AND/OR trees. Firstly, it creates a hierarchy in the set of rules and rewrites certain rules in order to eliminate disjuncts with more than one term. In this process, a set of rules $R = \{c \land d \to a, d \land e \to a, a \land \neg f \to b\}$ becomes $R' = \{c \land d \to a', a' \to a, d \land e \to a'', a'' \to a, a \land \neg f \to b\}$. Then, KBANN sets weights and thresholds such that the network behaves as a set of AND/OR neurons. Figure 4.1 shows a KBANN network derived from a set of rules R'.

KBANN served as an inspiration for the construction of the *Connectionist Inductive Learning and Logic Programming* (CILP) system [66]. CILP builds upon KBANN so as to provide a sound theoretical foundation for reasoning in artificial neural networks, and uses logic programming as a knowledge representation language. In the following, we present the foundations of CILP and some illustrative examples that will prove useful in the rest of the book.

4.1 The CILP System

CILP [66, 80] is a massively parallel computational model based on a feedforward artificial neural network that integrates inductive learning from examples and background knowledge with deductive reasoning using logic programming.

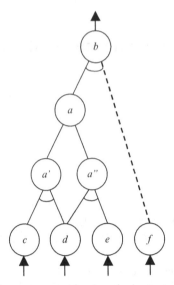

Fig. 4.1 A KBANN network. a', a'', and b are AND neurons, and a is an OR neuron. Each neuron has a semilinear activation function

A Translation Algorithm maps a general logic program[1] $\mathcal{P}$ into a single-hidden-layer neural network $\mathcal{N}$ such that $\mathcal{N}$ computes the least fixed-point of $\mathcal{P}$. In addition, $\mathcal{N}$ can be trained by examples using backpropagation [224] (the learning algorithm most successfully applied in real-world problems, e.g. in bioinformatics and pattern recognition [14, 26, 27]), treating $\mathcal{P}$ as background knowledge. The knowledge acquired by training can then be extracted [65], closing the learning cycle, as was done in [250] (see Fig. 4.2).

A typical application of CILP's explanation module is in safety-critical domains, such as fault diagnosis systems, where the neural network can detect a fault quickly, triggering safety procedures, while the knowledge extracted from it can justify the fault later on. If the diagnosis is mistaken, the information can be used to fine-tune the learning system.

In a nutshell, the CILP system can be divided into three parts (Fig. 4.2):

- *knowledge refinement in a neural network: phases 1, 2, and 3 of* CILP;
- *knowledge extraction from a trained network: phase 5 of* CILP;
- *theory revision in a neural network: phase 4 of* CILP.

The first part of CILP is based on Hölldobler and Kalinke's work [135, 136] and on that of Towell and Shavlik [231, 249, 250]. We chose the above approaches carefully, because Hölldobler and Kalinke used a neat, simple model of neural networks to compute one of the standard semantics of logic programming, and Towell and Shavlik's KBANN and its subsequent developments (e.g. [169, 195, 196])

---

[1] Recall that a general clause is a rule of the form $L_1, \ldots, L_k \rightarrow A$, where A is an atom and L_i ($1 \leq i \leq k$) is a literal (an atom or the negation of an atom). A general logic program is a finite set of general clauses [163].

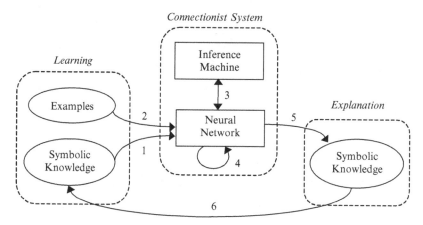

Fig. 4.2 Neural-symbolic integration

have been empirically shown to be superior to some of the main neural, symbolic, and hybrid learning systems, and have provided one of the most effective hybrid systems to date.

These important contributions are detailed in [66], where extensive analyses of their capabilities for knowledge representation and learning were reported. Theoretical results about CILP regarding phases 1, 2, and 3 of the system were also extensively studied in [66]. CILP's efficiency as a hybrid learning system and its applications to real-world problems compared with some of the main competitors, including KBANN, were also studied in [66]. The results show that CILP networks can be very effective in a number of domains.

Let us exemplify how CILP's Translation Algorithm works. Each clause (r_l) of $\mathcal{P}$ is mapped from the input layer to the output layer of $\mathcal{N}$ through one neuron (N_l) in the single hidden layer of $\mathcal{N}$. Intuitively, the Translation Algorithm from $\mathcal{P}$ to $\mathcal{N}$ has to implement the following conditions: **(C1)** the input potential of a hidden neuron (N_l) can only exceed N_l's threshold (θ_l), activating N_l, when all the positive antecedents of r_l are assigned the truth value *true* while all the negative antecedents of r_l are assigned *false*; and **(C2)** the input potential of an output neuron (A) can only exceed A's threshold (θ_A), activating A, when at least one hidden neuron N_l that is connected to A is activated.

Example 1. Consider the logic program $\mathcal{P} = \{B; B \wedge C \wedge \sim D \rightarrow A; E \wedge F \rightarrow A\}$. The Translation Algorithm derives the network $\mathcal{N}$ of Fig. 4.3, setting weights (W') and thresholds (θ') in such a way that the conditions **(C1)** and **(C2)** above are satisfied. Note that if $\mathcal{N}$ ought to be fully connected, any other link (not shown in Fig. 4.3) should receive weight zero initially.

Notice that, in Example 1, following [135], each input and output neuron of $\mathcal{N}$ is associated with an atom of $\mathcal{P}$. As a result, each input and output vector of $\mathcal{N}$ can be associated with an interpretation for $\mathcal{P}$. Notice also that each hidden neuron N_l corresponds to a clause r_l of $\mathcal{P}$. In order to compute a fixed-point semantics of $\mathcal{P}$,

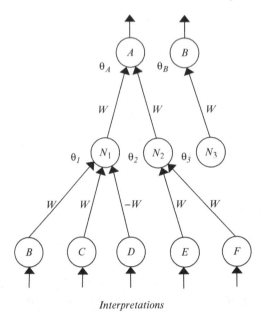

Interpretations

Fig. 4.3 Sketch of a neural network for the logic program $\mathcal{P}$ in Example 1

output neuron B should feed input neuron B such that $\mathcal{N}$ is used to iterate $T_\mathcal{P}$, the fixed-point operator[2] of $\mathcal{P}$. $\mathcal{N}$ will eventually converge to a stable state which is identical to the stable model of $\mathcal{P}$.

Notation   Given a general logic program $\mathcal{P}$, let:

q denote the number of clauses r_l ($1 \leq l \leq q$) occurring in $\mathcal{P}$;

υ denote the number of literals occurring in $\mathcal{P}$;

A_{min} denote the minimum activation for a neuron to be *active* (or, analogously, for its associated literal to be assigned a truth value *true*), $A_{min} \in (0,1)$;

A_{max} denote the maximum activation when a neuron is not active (or when its associated literal is *false*), $A_{max} \in (-1,0)$;

$h(x) = 2/(1+e^{-\beta x}) - 1$, the bipolar semilinear activation function;[3]

$g(x) = x$, the standard linear activation function;

$s(x) = y$, the standard nonlinear activation function ($y = 1$ if $x > 0$, and $y = 0$ otherwise), also known as the step function;

W and $-W$ denote the weights of connections associated with positive and negative literals, respectively;

θ_l denote the threshold of the hidden neuron N_l associated with clause r_l;

θ_A denote the threshold of the output neuron A, where A is the head of clause r_l;

k_l denote the number of literals in the body of clause r_l;

---

[2] Recall that the mapping $T_\mathcal{P}$ is defined as follows. Let I be a Herbrand interpretation; then $T_\mathcal{P}(I) = \{A_0 \mid L_1,\ldots,L_n \to A_0$ is a ground clause in $\mathcal{P}$ and $\{L_1,\ldots,L_n\} \subseteq I\}$.

[3] We use the bipolar semilinear activation function for convenience (see Sect. 3.1). Any monotonically increasing activation function could have been used here.

p_l denote the number of positive literals in the body of clause r_l;

n_l denote the number of negative literals in the body of clause r_l;

μ_l denote the number of clauses in $\mathcal{P}$ with the same atom in the head, for each clause r_l;

$MAX_{r_l}(k_l, \mu_l)$ denote the greater element of k_l and μ_l for clause r_l; and

$MAX_{\mathcal{P}}(k_1, \ldots, k_q, \mu_1, \ldots, \mu_q)$ denote the greatest element of all k's and μ's of $\mathcal{P}$.

We also use $\overrightarrow{k}$ as a shorthand for $(k_1, \ldots, k_q)$, and $\overrightarrow{\mu}$ as a shorthand for $(\mu_1, \ldots, \mu_q)$.

For instance, for the program $\mathcal{P}$ of Example 1, $q = 3$, $v = 6$, $k_1 = 3$, $k_2 = 2$, $k_3 = 0$, $p_1 = 2$, $p_2 = 2$, $p_3 = 0$, $n_1 = 1$, $n_2 = 0$, $n_3 = 0$, $\mu_1 = 2$, $\mu_2 = 2$, $\mu_3 = 1$, $MAX_{r_1}(k_1, \mu_1) = 3$, $MAX_{r_2}(k_2, \mu_2) = 2$, $MAX_{r_3}(k_3, \mu_3) = 1$, and $MAX_{\mathcal{P}}(k_1, k_2, k_3, \mu_1, \mu_2, \mu_3) = 3$.

In the Translation Algorithm below, we define A_{min}, W, θ_l, and θ_A such that the conditions (**C1**) and (**C2**) above are satisfied. Equations 4.1, 4.2, 4.3, and 4.4 below are obtained from the proof of Theorem 8 [80]. We assume, for mathematical convenience and without loss of generality, that $A_{max} = -A_{min}$. In this way, we associate the truth value *true* with values in the interval $(A_{min}, 1)$, and the truth value *false* with values in the interval $(-1, -A_{min})$.

Theorem 8 guarantees that values in the interval $[-A_{min}, A_{min}]$ do not occur in the network with weights W and thresholds θ, but, informally, this interval may be associated with a third truth value *unknown*[4]. The proof of Theorem 8 presented in [66] is reproduced here for the sake of completeness, as several proofs presented in the book will make reference to it.

We start by calculating $MAX_{\mathcal{P}}(\overrightarrow{k}, \overrightarrow{\mu})$ such that

$$A_{min} > \frac{MAX_{\mathcal{P}}(\overrightarrow{k}, \overrightarrow{\mu}) - 1}{MAX_{\mathcal{P}}(\overrightarrow{k}, \overrightarrow{\mu}) + 1}. \tag{4.1}$$

CILP Translation Algorithm

1. Calculate the value of W such that the following is satisfied:

$$W \geq \frac{2}{\beta} \cdot \frac{\ln(1 + A_{min}) - \ln(1 - A_{min})}{MAX_{\mathcal{P}}(\overrightarrow{k}, \overrightarrow{\mu})(A_{min} - 1) + A_{min} + 1}. \tag{4.2}$$

2. For each clause r_l of $\mathcal{P}$ of the form $L_1, \ldots, L_k \to A$ ($k \geq 0$):

   (a) Create input neurons $L_1, \ldots, L_k$ and an output neuron A in $\mathcal{N}$ (if they do not exist yet).

   (b) Add a neuron N_l to the hidden layer of $\mathcal{N}$.

---

[4] If a network obtained by the Translation Algorithm is then trained by examples with the use of a learning algorithm that does not impose any constraints on the weights, values in the interval $[-A_{min}, A_{min}]$ may occur and should be interpreted as unknown by following a three-valued interpretation.

(c) Connect each neuron L_i ($1 \le i \le k$) in the input layer to the neuron N_l in the hidden layer. If L_i is a positive literal, then set the connection weight to W; otherwise, set the connection weight to $-W$.

(d) Connect the neuron N_l in the hidden layer to the neuron A in the output layer and set the connection weight to W.

(e) Define the threshold (θ_l) of the neuron N_l in the hidden layer as

$$\theta_l = \frac{(1+A_{min})(k_l-1)}{2} W. \tag{4.3}$$

a. Define the threshold (θ_A) of the neuron A in the output layer as

$$\theta_A = \frac{(1+A_{min})(1-\mu_l)}{2} W. \tag{4.4}$$

3. Set $g(x)$ as the activation function of the neurons in the input layer of $\mathcal{N}$. In this way, the activation of the neurons in the input layer of $\mathcal{N}$ given by each input vector $\mathbf{i}$ will represent an interpretation for $\mathcal{P}$.

4. Set $h(x)$ as the activation function of the neurons in the hidden and output layers of $\mathcal{N}$. In this way, a gradient descent learning algorithm, such as backpropagation, can be applied to $\mathcal{N}$.

5. If $\mathcal{N}$ needs to be fully connected, set all other connections to zero.

Theorem 8. *[66] For each propositional general logic program $\mathcal{P}$, there exists a feedforward artificial neural network $\mathcal{N}$ with exactly one hidden layer and semilinear neurons such that $\mathcal{N}$ computes the fixed-point operator $T_{\mathcal{P}}$ of $\mathcal{P}$.*

Proof. ($\leftarrow$) '$A \ge A_{min}$ if $L_1,\ldots,L_k$ is satisfied by $\mathbf{i}$'. Assume that the p_l positive literals in $L_1,\ldots,L_k$ are *true*, and the n_l negative literals in $L_1,\ldots,L_k$ are *false*. Consider the mapping from the input layer to the hidden layer of $\mathcal{N}$. The input potential (I_l) of N_l is minimum when all the neurons associated with a positive literal in $L_1,\ldots,L_k$ are at A_{min}, while all the neurons associated with a negative literal in $L_1,\ldots,L_k$ are at $-A_{min}$. Thus, $I_l \ge p_lA_{min}W + n_lA_{min}W - \theta_l$ and, assuming $\theta_l = ((1+A_{min})(k_l-1)/2)W$, $I_l \ge p_lA_{min}W + n_lA_{min}W - ((1+A_{min})(k_l-1)/2)W$.

If $h(I_l) \ge A_{min}$, i.e. $I_l \ge -\frac{1}{\beta}ln((1-A_{min})/(1+A_{min}))$, then N_l is active. Therefore, Equation 4.5 must be satisfied:[5]

$$p_lA_{min}W + n_lA_{min}W - \frac{(1+A_{min})(k_l-1)}{2} W \ge$$

$$-\frac{1}{\beta}ln\left(\frac{1-A_{min}}{1+A_{min}}\right). \tag{4.5}$$

Solving Equation 4.5 for the connection weight (W) yields Equations 4.6 and 4.7, given that $W > 0$:

---

[5] Throughout, we use the word 'Equation', as in 'Equation 4.5', even though 'Equation 4.5' is an inequality.

$$W \geq -\frac{2}{\beta} \cdot \frac{\ln\left(1-A_{min}\right)-\ln\left(1+A_{min}\right)}{k_l\left(A_{min}-1\right)+A_{min}+1}, \tag{4.6}$$

$$A_{min} > \frac{k_l - 1}{k_l + 1}. \tag{4.7}$$

Consider now the mapping from the hidden layer to the output layer of $\mathcal{N}$. By Equations 4.6 and 4.7, at least one neuron N_l that is connected to A is 'active'. The input potential (I_l) of A is minimum when N_l is at A_{min}, while the other $\mu_l - 1$ neurons connected to A are at -1. Thus, $I_l \geq A_{min}W - (\mu_l - 1)W - \theta_l$ and, assuming $\theta_l = (1 + A_{min})(1 - \mu_l)/2W$, $I_l \geq A_{min}W - (\mu_l - 1)W - (1 + A_{min})(1 - \mu_l)/2W$.

If $h(I_l) \geq A_{min}$, i.e. $I_l \geq -\frac{1}{\beta}\ln\left((1-A_{min})/(1+A_{min})\right)$, then A is active. Therefore, Equation 4.8 must be satisfied:

$$A_{min}W - (\mu_l - 1)W - \frac{(1+A_{min})(1-\mu_l)}{2}W \geq$$

$$-\frac{1}{\beta}\ln\left(\frac{1-A_{min}}{1+A_{min}}\right). \tag{4.8}$$

Solving Equation 4.8 for the connection weight W yields Equations 4.9 and 4.10, given that $W > 0$:

$$W \geq -\frac{2}{\beta} \cdot \frac{\ln\left(1-A_{min}\right)-\ln\left(1+A_{min}\right)}{\mu_l\left(A_{min}-1\right)+A_{min}+1}, \tag{4.9}$$

$$A_{min} > \frac{\mu_l - 1}{\mu_l + 1}. \tag{4.10}$$

($\rightarrow$) '$A \leq -A_{min}$ if $L_1, \ldots, L_k$ is not satisfied by $\mathbf{i}$'. Assume that at least one of the p_l positive literals in $L_1, \ldots, L_k$ is $false$ or one of the n_l negative literals in $L_1, \ldots, L_k$ is $true$. Consider the mapping from the input layer to the hidden layer of $\mathcal{N}$. The input potential (I_l) of N_l is maximum when only one neuron associated with a positive literal in $L_1, \ldots, L_k$ is at $-A_{min}$ or when only one neuron associated with a negative literal in $L_1, \ldots, L_k$ is at A_{min}. Thus, either $I_l \leq (p_l - 1)W - A_{min}W + n_lW - \theta_l$ or $I_l \leq (n_l - 1)W - A_{min}W + p_lW - \theta_l$ and, assuming $\theta_l = ((1 + A_{min})(k_l - 1)/2)W$, $I_l \leq (k_l - 1 - A_{min})W - ((1 + A_{min})(k_l - 1)/2)W$.

If $-A_{min} \geq h(I_l)$, i.e. $-A_{min} \geq 2/(1 + e^{-\beta(I_l)}) - 1$, then $I_l \leq -(1/\beta)\ln((1+A_{min})/(1-A_{min}))$, and so N_l is not active. Therefore, Equation 4.11 must be satisfied:

$$(k_l - 1 - A_{min})W - \frac{(1+A_{min})(k_l - 1)}{2}W \leq$$

$$-\frac{1}{\beta}\ln\left(\frac{1-A_{min}}{1+A_{min}}\right). \tag{4.11}$$

Solving Equation 4.11 for the connection weight W yields Equations 4.12 and 4.13, given that $W > 0$:

$$W \geq \frac{2}{\beta} \cdot \frac{\ln(1 + A_{min}) - \ln(1 - A_{min})}{k_l(A_{min} - 1) + A_{min} + 1}, \qquad (4.12)$$

$$A_{min} > \frac{k_l - 1}{k_l + 1}. \qquad (4.13)$$

Consider now the mapping from the hidden layer to the output layer of $\mathcal{N}$. By Equations 4.12 and 4.13, all neurons N_l that are connected to A are 'not active'. The input potential (I_l) of A is maximum when all the neurons connected to A are at $-A_{min}$. Thus, $I_l \leq -\mu_l A_{min} W - \theta_l$ and, assuming $\theta_l = ((1 + A_{min})(1 - \mu_l)/2)W$, $I_l \leq -\mu_l A_{min} W - ((1 + A_{min})(1 - \mu_l)/2)W$.

If $-A_{min} \geq h(I_l)$, i.e. $-A_{min} \geq 2/(1 + e^{-\beta(I_l)}) - 1$, then $I_l \leq -(1/\beta)\ln((1 + A_{min})/(1 - A_{min}))$, and so A is not active. Therefore, Equation 4.14 must be satisfied:

$$-\mu_l A_{min} W - \frac{(1 + A_{min})(1 - \mu_l)}{2} W \leq$$
$$-\frac{1}{\beta} \ln\left(\frac{1 + A_{min}}{1 - A_{min}}\right). \qquad (4.14)$$

Solving Equation 4.14 for the connection weight W yields Equations 4.15 and 4.16, given that $W > 0$:

$$W \geq \frac{2}{\beta} \cdot \frac{\ln(1 + A_{min}) - \ln(1 - A_{min})}{\mu_l(A_{min} - 1) + A_{min} + 1}, \qquad (4.15)$$

$$A_{min} > \frac{\mu_l - 1}{\mu_l + 1}. \qquad (4.16)$$

Notice that Equations 4.6 and 4.9 are equivalent to Equations 4.12 and 4.15, respectively. Hence, the theorem holds if, for each clause C_l in $\mathcal{P}$, Equations 4.6 and 4.7 are satisfied by W and A_{min} from the input layer to the hidden layer of $\mathcal{N}$, and Equations 4.9 and 4.10 are satisfied by W and A_{min} from the hidden layer to the output layer of $\mathcal{N}$.

In order to unify the weights of $\mathcal{N}$ for each clause C_l of $\mathcal{P}$, given the definition of $MAX_{C_l}(k_l, \mu_l)$, it is sufficient that Equations 4.17 and 4.18 below are satisfied by W and A_{min}, respectively:

$$W \geq \frac{2}{\beta} \cdot \frac{\ln(1 + A_{min}) - \ln(1 - A_{min})}{MAX_{C_l}(k_l, \mu_l)(A_{min} - 1) + A_{min} + 1}, \qquad (4.17)$$

$$A_{min} > \frac{MAX_{C_l}(k_l, \mu_l) - 1}{MAX_{C_l}(k_l, \mu_l) + 1}. \qquad (4.18)$$

Finally, in order to unify all the weights of $\mathcal{N}$ for a program $\mathcal{P}$, given the definition of $MAX_{\mathcal{P}}(k_1,\ldots,k_q,\mu_1,\ldots,\mu_q)$, it is sufficient that Equations 4.19 and 4.20 are satisfied by W and A_{min}, respectively:

$$W \geq \frac{2}{\beta} \frac{\ln(1+A_{min}) - \ln(1-A_{min})}{MAX_{\mathcal{P}}(k_1,\ldots,k_q,\mu_1,\ldots,\mu_q)(A_{min}-1)+A_{min}+1}, \quad (4.19)$$

$$A_{min} > \frac{MAX_{\mathcal{P}}(k_1,\ldots,k_q,\mu_1,\ldots,\mu_q)-1}{MAX_{\mathcal{P}}(k_1,\ldots,k_q,\mu_1,\ldots,\mu_q)+1}. \quad (4.20)$$

As a result, if Equations 4.19 and 4.20 are satisfied by W and A_{min}, respectively, then $\mathcal{N}$ computes $T_{\mathcal{P}}$. This is indeed the case in CILP's Translation Algorithm. ∎

4.2 Massively Parallel Deduction in CILP

Recall that $T_{\mathcal{P}}^n \overset{def}{=} T_{\mathcal{P}}(T_{\mathcal{P}}^{n-1})$, with $T_{\mathcal{P}}^0 \overset{def}{=} T_{\mathcal{P}}(\{\varnothing\})$. We say that $\mathcal{P}$ is *well behaved* if, after a finite number m of iterations, $T_{\mathcal{P}}^m = T_{\mathcal{P}}^{m-1}$. It is not difficult to see that if $\mathcal{P}$ is well behaved and we use $\mathcal{N}$ to iterate $T_{\mathcal{P}}$, then $\mathcal{N}$ will converge to $T_{\mathcal{P}}^m$, as follows. Consider a feedforward neural network $\mathcal{N}$ with p input neurons $(i_1,\ldots,i_p)$ and q output neurons $(o_1,\ldots,o_q)$. Assume that each input and output neuron in $\mathcal{N}$ is labelled by an atom A_k associated with it. Let us use $name(i_i) = name(o_j)$ to denote the fact that the literal associated with neuron i_i is the same as the literal associated with neuron o_j.

Let

$$valuation(Act(x)) = \begin{cases} 1, & \text{if } Act(x) > A_{min}, \\ -1, & \text{otherwise}, \end{cases}$$

where $Act(x)$ is the activation state of neuron x.

We say that the computation of $\mathcal{P}$ by $\mathcal{N}$ *terminates* when $valuation(Act(i_i)) = valuation(Act(o_j))$ for every pair of neurons (i_i,o_j) in $\mathcal{N}$ such that $name(i_i) = name(o_j)$.

Now, from Theorem 8 and the definition of $T_{\mathcal{P}}^n$ above, it is clear that, starting from $\{\varnothing\}$ (i.e. $\mathbf{i} = (i_1,\ldots,i_p) = [-1,-1,\ldots,-1]$), if $\mathcal{P}$ is well behaved, then the computation of $\mathcal{P}$ by $\mathcal{N}$ terminates. The computation is as follows (below, we use $\mathbf{o} = \mathcal{N}(\mathbf{i})$ to denote the output vector $\mathbf{o} = (o_1,\ldots,o_q)$ obtained by presenting the input vector $\mathbf{i}$ to the network $\mathcal{N}$):

1. Let $\mathbf{i} = [-1,-1,\ldots,-1]$;
2. Repeat:

   (a) Calculate $\mathbf{o} = \mathcal{N}(\mathbf{i})$;
   (b) For each o_j in $\mathbf{o}$, do: If $name(o_j) = name(i_i)$ Then replace the value of i_i in $\mathbf{i}$ by $valuation(Act(o_j))$;

3. Until $valuation(Act(o_j)) = valuation(Act(i_i))$ for all (i_i, o_j) such that
   $name(i_i) = name(o_j)$.

The set $\bigcup name(x) \subseteq B_{\mathcal{P}}$ of input and output neurons x in $\mathcal{N}$ for which $valuation(Act(x)) = 1$ will denote $T_{\mathcal{P}}^m$. When it is clear from the context, we may write *neuron A_k* to indicate the neuron in $\mathcal{N}$ associated with atom A_k in $\mathcal{P}$.

In [135], Hölldobler and Kalinke showed that autoassociative networks with a nonlinear activation function can be used for the computation of $T_{\mathcal{P}}$. Theorem 8 generalises their result to heteroassociative networks with semilinear neurons (i.e. networks that can use backpropagation).

Example 2. (Example 1 continued) To construct the network of Fig. 4.3, firstly we calculate $MAX_{\mathcal{P}}(\overrightarrow{k}, \overrightarrow{\mu}) = 3$ and $A_{min} > 0.5$. Then, $\theta_1 = (1 + A_{min})W$, $\theta_2 = (1 + A_{min})W/2$, $\theta_3 = -(1 + A_{min})W/2$, $\theta_A = -(1 + A_{min})W/2$, and $\theta_B = 0$. Now, suppose $A_{min} = 0.6$; we obtain $W \geq 6.931/\beta$. Alternatively, suppose $A_{min} = 0.7$; then $W \geq 4.336/\beta$. Let us take $A_{min} = 0.7$ and take $h(x)$ as the standard bipolar semilinear activation function ($\beta = 1$). Then, if $W = 4.5$,[6] $\mathcal{N}$ will compute the operator $T_{\mathcal{P}}$ of $\mathcal{P}$. The computation of $\mathcal{P}$ by $\mathcal{N}$ terminates with $T_{\mathcal{P}}^m = \{B\}$ when $m = 2$.

4.3 Inductive Learning in CILP

One of the main features of artificial neural networks is their learning capability. The program $\mathcal{P}$, viewed as background knowledge, may now be refined with examples in a learning process in $\mathcal{N}$.

Hornik, Stinchcombe, and White [140] and Cybenco [52] have proved that standard feedforward neural networks with as few as one hidden layer can approximate any (Borel measurable) function from one finite-dimensional space to another, to any desired degree of accuracy, provided sufficiently many hidden units are available. Hence, we can train single-hidden-layer neural networks to approximate the operator $T_{\mathcal{P}}$ associated with a logic program $\mathcal{P}$. Powerful neural learning algorithms have been established theoretically and applied extensively in practice. These algorithms may be used to learn the operator $T_{\mathcal{P}'}$ of a previously unknown program $\mathcal{P}'$, and therefore to learn the program $\mathcal{P}'$ itself. Moreover, DasGupta and Schnitger [53] have proved that neural networks with continuously differentiable activation functions are capable of computing a family of n-ary Boolean functions using two neurons (i.e. constant size), whereas networks composed of binary threshold functions require size of at least $O(\log(n))$ neurons. Hence, analogue neural networks have more computational power than discrete neural networks, even when computing Boolean functions.

The network's recurrent connections contain fixed weights $W_r = 1$, with the sole purpose of ensuring that the output feeds the input in the next learning or recall

---

[6] Note that a sound translation from $\mathcal{P}$ to $\mathcal{N}$ does not require all the weights in $\mathcal{N}$ to have the same absolute value. We have unified the weights ($|W|$) for the sake of simplicity.

phase. Since the network does not learn in its recurrent connections,[7] the standard backpropagation algorithm can be applied directly [127] (see also [125, 145]). Hence, in order to perform inductive learning with examples on $\mathcal{N}$, four simple steps should be followed: (i) add neurons to the input and output layers of $\mathcal{N}$, according to the training set (the training set may contain concepts not represented in the background knowledge, and vice versa); (ii) add neurons to the hidden layer of $\mathcal{N}$, if it is so required for the convergence of the learning algorithm; (iii) add connections with weight zero, in which $\mathcal{N}$ will learn new concepts; and (iv) perturb the connections by adding small random numbers to its weights in order to avoid the problem of symmetry.[8]

4.4 Adding Classical Negation

According to Lifschitz and McCarthy, commonsense knowledge can be represented more easily when *classical negation* ($\neg$), sometimes called *explicit negation,* is available. In [116], Gelfond and Lifschitz extended the notion of stable models to programs with classical negation. *Extended logic programs* can be viewed as a fragment of default theories (see [171]), and thus are of interest with respect to the relation between logic programming and nonmonotonic formalisms. In this section, we extend CILP to incorporate classical negation. The extended CILP system computes the *answer set semantics* [116] of extended logic programs. As a result, it can be applied in a broader range of domains.

General logic programs provide negative information implicitly, by the closed-world assumption, whereas extended programs include explicit negation, allowing the presence of incomplete information in the database. 'In the language of extended programs, we can distinguish between a query which fails in the sense that it does not succeed, and a query which fails in the stronger sense that its negation succeeds' [116]. The following example, due to John McCarthy, illustrates such a difference: a school bus may cross railway tracks unless there is an approaching train. This would be expressed in a general logic program by the rule $cross \leftarrow \sim train$, in which case the absence of *train* in the database is interpreted as the absence of an approaching train, i.e. using the closed-world assumption. Such an assumption is unacceptable if one reasons with incomplete information. However, if we use classical negation and represent the above knowledge as the extended program $cross \leftarrow \neg train$, then *cross* will not be derived until the fact $\neg train$ is added to the database.

Therefore, it is essential to differentiate between $\neg A$ and $\sim A$ in a logic program whenever the closed-world assumption is not applicable to A. Nevertheless, the closed-world assumption can be explicitly included in extended programs by adding rules of the form $\neg A \leftarrow \sim A$ whenever the information about A in the database is

---

[7] The recurrent connections represent an external process between the output and input of the network for neurons having the same name, for example neuron B in Fig. 4.3.

[8] The perturbation should be small enough not to have an adverse effect on the computation of the background knowledge.

assumed to be complete. Moreover, for some literals, the opposite assumption $A \leftarrow \sim \neg A$ may be appropriate.

The semantics of extended programs, called the answer set semantics, is an extension of the stable-model semantics for general logic programs. "A 'well-behaved' general program has exactly one stable model, and the answer that it returns for a ground query (A) is *yes* or *no*, depending on whether A belongs or not to the stable model of the program. A 'well-behaved' extended program has exactly one answer set, and this set is consistent. The answer that an extended program returns for a ground query (A) is *yes*, *no* or *unknown*, depending on whether its answer set contains A, $\neg A$ or neither" [116]. If a program does not contain classical negation, then its answer sets are exactly the same as its stable models.

Definition 21. [116] An *extended logic program* is a finite set of clauses of the form $L_0 \leftarrow L_1, \ldots, L_m, \sim L_{m+1}, \ldots, \sim L_n$, where L_i $(0 \le i \le n)$ is a literal (an atom or the classical negation of an atom, denoted by $\neg$).

Definition 22. [116] Let $\mathcal{P}$ be an extended program. We denote by *Lit* the set of ground literals in the language of $\mathcal{P}$. For any set $\mathcal{S} \subset Lit$, let $\mathcal{P}^+$ be the extended program obtained from $\mathcal{P}$ by deleting (i) each clause that has a formula $\sim L$ in its body when $L \in \mathcal{S}$, and (ii) all formulas of the form $\sim L$ present in the bodies of the remaining clauses.

Following [40], we say that $\mathcal{P}^+ = \mathbf{R}_{\mathcal{S}}(\mathcal{P})$, which should be read as '$\mathcal{P}^+$ is the *Gelfond–Lifschitz reduction* of $\mathcal{P}$ with respect to $\mathcal{S}$'.

By the above definition, $\mathcal{P}^+$ does not contain default negation $(\sim)$, and its answer set can be defined as follows.

Definition 23. [116] The answer set of $\mathcal{P}^+$ is the smallest subset $\mathcal{S}^+$ of *Lit* such that (i) for any rule $L_0 \leftarrow L_1, \ldots, L_m$ of $\mathcal{P}^+$, if $L_1, \ldots, L_m \in \mathcal{S}^+$, then $L_0 \in \mathcal{S}^+$, and (ii) if $\mathcal{S}^+$ contains a pair of complementary literals, then $\mathcal{S}^+ = Lit.^9$

Finally, the answer set of an extended program $\mathcal{P}$ that contains default negation $(\sim)$ can be defined as follows.

Definition 24. [116] Let $\mathcal{P}$ be an extended program and let $\mathcal{S} \subset Lit$. Let $\mathcal{P}^+ = \mathbf{R}_{\mathcal{S}}(\mathcal{P})$ and let $\mathcal{S}^+$ be the answer set of $\mathcal{P}^+$. $\mathcal{S}$ is the answer set of $\mathcal{P}$ iff $\mathcal{S} = \mathcal{S}^+$.

For example, the program $\mathcal{P} = \{r \leftarrow \sim p; \neg q \leftarrow r\}$ has $\{r, \neg q\}$ as its only answer set, since no other subset of the literals in $\mathcal{P}$ has the same fixed-point property. The answers that $\mathcal{P}$ gives to the queries p, q, and r are, respectively, *unknown*, *false*, and *true*. Note that the answer set semantics assigns different meanings to the rules $\neg q \leftarrow r$ and $\neg r \leftarrow q$, i.e. it is not contrapositive with respect to $\leftarrow$ and $\neg$. For instance, the answer set of $\mathcal{P}' = \{r \leftarrow \sim p; \neg r \leftarrow q\}$ is $\{r\}$, differently from the answer set of (the classically equivalent) $\mathcal{P}$.

If $\mathcal{P}$ does not contain classical negation $(\neg)$, then its answer sets do not contain negative literals. As a result, the answer sets of a general logic program are identical

---

^{9} $\mathcal{S}^+ = Lit$ works as though the schema $X \leftarrow L, \sim L$ were present for all L and X in $\mathcal{P}_{\mathcal{S}}^+$.

to its stable models. However, the absence of an atom A in the stable model of a general program means that A is *false* (by default), whereas the absence of A (and $\neg A$) in the answer set of an extended program means that nothing is known about A.[10]

An extended logic program $\mathcal{P}$ that has a consistent answer set can be reduced to a general logic program $\mathcal{P}^*$ as follows. For any negative literal $\neg A$ occurring in $\mathcal{P}$, let A' be a positive literal that does not occur in $\mathcal{P}$. A' is called the *positive form* of $\neg A$. $\mathcal{P}^*$ is obtained from $\mathcal{P}$ by replacing all the negative literals of each rule of $\mathcal{P}$ by their positive forms; $\mathcal{P}^*$ is called the positive form of $\mathcal{P}$. For example, the program $\mathcal{P} = \{a \leftarrow b \wedge \neg c; c \leftarrow\}$ can be reduced to its positive form; $\mathcal{P}^* = \{a \leftarrow b \wedge c'; c \leftarrow\}$.

Definition 25. [116] For any set $\mathcal{S} \subset Lit$, let $\mathcal{S}^*$ denote the set of the positive forms of the elements of $\mathcal{S}$.

Proposition 9. *[116] A consistent set $\mathcal{S} \subset Lit$ is an answer set of $\mathcal{P}$ if and only if $\mathcal{S}^*$ is a stable model of $\mathcal{P}^*$.*

The mapping from $\mathcal{P}$ to $\mathcal{P}^*$ reduces extended programs to general programs, although $\mathcal{P}^*$ alone does not indicate that A' represents the negation of A.

By Proposition 9, in order to translate an extended program ($\mathcal{P}$) into a neural network ($\mathcal{N}$), we can use the same approach as the one for general programs (see Sect. 4.1, for a description of the Translation Algorithm), with the only difference being that input and output neurons should be labelled as literals, instead of atoms. In the case of general logic programs, a concept A is represented by a neuron, and its weights indicate whether A is a positive or a negative literal in the sense of default negation, that is, the weights differentiate between A and $\sim A$. In the case of extended logic programs, we must also be able to represent the concept $\neg A$ in the network. We do so by explicitly labelling input and output neurons as $\neg A$, while the weights differentiate between $\neg A$ and $\sim \neg A$. Notice that, in this case, the neurons A and $\neg A$ might both be present in the same network.

Analogously to Theorem 8, the following proposition ensures that the translation of extended programs into a neural network is sound.

Proposition 10. *[66] For any extended logic program $\mathcal{P}$, there exists a feedforward artificial neural network $\mathcal{N}$ with exactly one hidden layer and semilinear neurons such that $\mathcal{N}$ computes $T_{\mathcal{P}^*}$, where $\mathcal{P}^*$ is the positive form of $\mathcal{P}$.*

Example 3. Consider the extended program $\mathcal{P} = \{A \leftarrow B \wedge \neg C; \neg C \leftarrow B \wedge \sim \neg E; B \leftarrow \sim D\}$. The CILP Translation Algorithm applied over the positive form $\mathcal{P}^*$ of $\mathcal{P}$ obtains the network $\mathcal{N}$ of Fig. 4.4 such that $\mathcal{N}$ computes the fixpoint operator $T_{\mathcal{P}^*}$ of $\mathcal{P}^*$.

---

[10] Gelfond and Lifschitz think of answer sets as incomplete theories rather than three-valued models. Intuitively, the answer sets of a program $\mathcal{P}$ are possible sets of beliefs that a rational agent may hold on the basis of the incomplete information expressed by $\mathcal{P}$. 'When a program has several answer sets, it is incomplete also in another sense – it has several different interpretations, and the answer to a query may depend on the interpretation' [116].

As before, the network of Fig. 4.4 can be transformed into a partially recurrent network by connecting neurons in the output layer (e.g. *B*) to their corresponding neurons in the input layer, with weight $W_r = 1$, so that $\mathcal{N}$ computes the upward powers of $T_{\mathcal{P}^*}$.

Corollary 11. *[66] Let $\mathcal{P}$ be a well-behaved extended program. Let $\mathcal{P}^*$ be the positive form of $\mathcal{P}$. There exists a recurrent neural network $\mathcal{N}$ with semilinear neurons such that, starting from an arbitrary input, $\mathcal{N}$ converges to the unique fixpoint of $\mathcal{P}^*$, which is identical to the unique answer set of $\mathcal{P}$.*

Example 4. (Example 3 continued) Given any initial activation in the input layer of $\mathcal{N}$ (in Fig. 4.4), the network always converges to the following stable state: $A = true, B = true, \neg C = true$, which represents the answer set of $\mathcal{P}$, $\mathcal{S}_{\mathcal{P}} = \{A, B, \neg C\}$. The truth values of D and E are unknown.

Let us now briefly discuss the case of inconsistent extended programs. Consider, for example, the contradictory program $\mathcal{P} = \{B \leftarrow A; \neg B \leftarrow A; A \leftarrow\}$. As it is well behaved, despite being contradictory, its associated network always converges to the stable state that represents the set $\{A, B, \neg B\}$. At this point, we have to make a choice. Either we adopt Gelfond and Lifschitz's definition of answer sets and assume that the answer set of $\mathcal{P}$ is the set *Lit* of all literals in the language, or we use a *paraconsistent* approach (see [29]). We believe that the second option is more appropriate, owing to the following argument:

> Inconsistencies can be read as signals to take external actions, such as 'ask the user', or as signals for internal actions that activate some rules and deactivate other rules. There is a need to develop a framework in which inconsistency can be viewed according to context, as a trigger for actions, for learning, and as a source of directions in argumentation. [105]

In [66], neural networks were used to resolve inconsistencies through learning. In Chap. 11, we deal with value-based argumentation frameworks, and the methodology proposed there, we believe, can deal with inconsistencies in general. We propose the use of learning as a way of resolving inconsistencies or deadlocks (indicated by loops in the network computation; we say that loops are a trigger for learning).

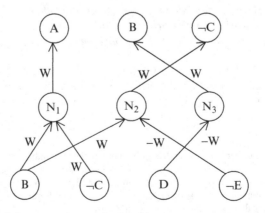

Fig. 4.4 From extended programs to neural networks

4.5 Adding Metalevel Priorities

So far, we have seen that a single-hidden-layer network can represent either a general or an extended logic program. In both cases, the network does not contain negative connections from the hidden layer to the output. What would then be the meaning of negative weights from the hidden to the output layer of the network? One interpretation is that such negative weights are used to block an output neuron's activation, serving as a form of prioritisation (or, in other words, implementing a preference relation between rules). Below, we use $r_j \succ r_i$ to indicate that rule r_j has a higher priority than rule r_i. We start with an example.

Example 5. Consider the following program: $P = \{r_1 : fingerprints, r_2 : alibi,$ $r_3 : fingerprints \rightarrow guilty, r_4 : alibi \rightarrow \neg guilty\}$. Take a priority relation $r_3 \succ r_4$, indicating that $fingerprints \rightarrow guilty$ is stronger evidence than $alibi \rightarrow \neg guilty$. A neural network that encodes the program P but not the relation $r_3 \succ r_4$ will compute the inconsistent answer set $\{fingerprints, alibi, guilty, \neg guilty\}$. Alternatively, the metalevel priority relation could be incorporated into the object level by changing the rule $alibi \rightarrow \neg guilty$ to $alibi \wedge \sim fingerprints \rightarrow \neg guilty$. The new program would compute the answer set $\{fingerprints, alibi, guilty\}$, which contains the intended answers for P given $r_3 \succ r_4$.

How could we represent the above priority explicitly in the neural network? In the same way that negative weights from input to hidden neurons are interpreted as negation by default because they contribute to blocking the activation of the hidden neurons, negative weights from hidden to output neurons could be seen as the implementation of the metalevel priority [64]. A negative weight from hidden neuron r_3 to the output neuron $\neg guilty$ would implement $r_3 \succ r_4$ provided that whenever r_3 is activated, r_3 then *blocks* (or *inhibits*) the activation of $\neg guilty$, which is the conclusion of r_4. Figure 4.5 illustrates the idea.

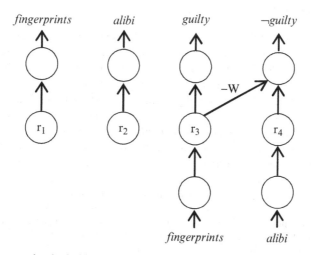

Fig. 4.5 Adding metalevel priorities ($r_3 \succ r_4$)

In the above example, $r_3 \succ r_4$ means that whenever the conclusion of r_3 holds, the conclusion of r_4 does not hold. Hence, $\succ (r_i, r_j)$ defines priorities among rules that can allow the conclusion of one rule to override the conclusion of another. It is thus similar to the *superiority relation* defined by Nute [193, 194] and later investigated by Antoniou et al. [8].

In the following, we recall some of the basic definitions of Nute's superiority relation. A superiority (binary) relation $\succ$ is a strict partial order, i.e. an irreflexive and transitive relation on a set. Rule r_1 is said to be superior to rule r_2 if $r_1 \succ r_2$. When the antecedents of two rules are derivable, the superiority relation is used to adjudicate the conflict. If either rule is superior to the other, then the superior rule is applied. In other words, $\succ$ provides information about the relative strength of the rules. Following [8], we shall define superiority relations over rules with contradictory conclusions only. More precisely, for all r_i, r_j, if $\succ (r_i, r_j)$, then r_i and r_j have complementary literals (x and $\neg x$) as consequents.[11] A cycle in the superiority relation (e.g. $r_1 \succ r_2$ and $r_2 \succ r_1$) is counterintuitive from a knowledge representation perspective, and thus $\succ$ is also required to be an acyclic relation, i.e. we assume that the transitive closure of $\succ$ is irreflexive.

It has been proved [8] that the above superiority relation does not add to the expressive power of *defeasible logic* [194]. In fact, (object-level) default negation and (metalevel) superiority relations are interchangeable (see [146]). The translation is as follows:

1. Replace the clause $L_1, \ldots, L_p, \sim L_{p+1}, \ldots, \sim L_q \to L_{q+1}$ by the clause $r : L_1, \ldots, L_p \to L_{q+1}$;
2. Add to $\mathcal{P}$, j clauses of the form $r_{i(1 \le i \le j)} : L_j \to \neg L_{q+1}$, where $p+1 \le j \le q$;
3. Define a preference relation between r_i and r. In general, $r_i \succ r$ for $1 \le i \le j$.

Example 6. Let $P = \{p; \ p \to b; \ b \wedge \sim p \to f\}$. P can be translated to the following logic program without negation as failure: $P' = \{r_1 : \to p; \ r_2 : p \to b; \ r_3 : b \to f; \ r_4 : p \to \neg f\}$, $r_4 \succ r_3$, such that $\mathcal{S}(P') \approx \mathcal{S}(P)$, i.e. the answer set semantics of P and P' are equivalent.

Nute's superiority relation adds, however, to the epistemic power of defeasible logic because it allows one to represent information in a more natural way. For example, the Nixon diamond *problem* can be expressed as follows: $r_1 : quaker(Nixon) \rightsquigarrow pacifist(Nixon)$ and $r_2 : republican(Nixon) \rightsquigarrow \neg pacifist(Nixon)$, where $\rightsquigarrow$ should be read as 'normally implies'. The definition of an adequate priority relation between r_1 and r_2 would then resolve the inconsistency regarding the pacifism of Nixon, when both $quaker(Nixon)$ and $republican(Nixon)$ are *true*. Also, for epistemological reasons, in many cases it is useful to have both default negation and metalevel priorities. This facilitates the expression of (object-level)

---

[11] In [8], Antoniou et al. argue that 'It turns out that we only need to define the superiority relation over rules with contradictory conclusions'. In [211], however, Prakken and Sartor present examples in which priorities have to be given between noncontradictory pieces of information, which propagate in order to solve an inconsistency. Otherwise, they claim, the result obtained is counterintuitive. For the sake of simplicity, we restrict $\succ (r_i, r_j)$ to conflicting rules.

priorities in the sense of default reasoning and (metalevel) priorities in the sense that a given conclusion should be overridden by another with higher priority.[12]

Of course, preference relations can represent much more than a superiority relation between conflicting consequents. Brewka's preferred subtheories [38] and Prakken and Sartor's argument-based extended logic programming with defeasible priorities [211] are only two examples in which a preference relation establishes a partial ordering between rules that describes the relative degree of belief in some beliefs in general, and not only between conflicting conclusions. From a more philosophical point of view, the AGM theory [4] defines a priority relation as representative of the *epistemic entrenchment* of a set of beliefs, in which formulas are analysed assuming that they are closed under logical consequence. In [221], a preference relation is defined as a preorder, and in this case, one can differentiate between two incomparable beliefs and two beliefs with the same priority. We shall investigate the links between neural networks and argumentation in detail in Chap. 11.

In this section, however, we are interested in finding out what is the preference relation that fits easily into a single-hidden-layer neural network. For this reason, we shall stick to Nute's superiority relation $\succ$. It would be interesting, though, to try to implement some of the above more sophisticated preference relations. Owing to the limitations of $\succ$, it might be more appropriate to see it as *inconsistency handling* rather than *preference handling*.[13]

Hence, the superiority relation that we discuss here essentially makes explicit the priorities encoded in the object level. As a result, a network $N_\succ$ encoding a program $P_\succ$ with explicit priorities is expected to behave exactly like the network N that encodes the equivalent extended program P without priorities. The following definition clarifies what we mean by the equivalence between $P_\succ$ and P in terms of T_P.

Definition 26. Let $P_\succ = \{r_1, r_2, \ldots, r_n\}$ be an extended program with an explicit superiority relation $\succ$. Let P be the same extended program $P_\succ$ without the superiority relation $\succ$. For any two rules r_i, r_j in $P_\succ$ such that $r_j \succ r_i$, let $P' = P - r_i$, i.e. P' is the program P without rule r_i. We define $T_{P_\succ} := T_{P'}$ if r_j fires, and $T_{P_\succ} := T_P$ otherwise.

The following example illustrates how we can encode metalevel priorities in a neural network by adding a very simple and straightforward step to the translation algorithm.

Example 7. Consider the following *labelled* logic program $P = \{r_1 : a \land b \land \sim c \to x,$ $r_2 : d \land e \to \neg x\}$. P can be encoded in a neural network by using the Translation Algorithm of Sect. 4.1. If we have also the information that, say, $r_1 \succ r_2$, then we know that the consequent of r_1 (x) is preferred over the consequent of r_2 $(\neg x)$. We can represent this in the network by ensuring that whenever x is activated, the activation of $\neg x$ is blocked. We might do so by simply connecting the hidden neuron r_1

---

[12] In a trained neural network, both representations (P and P') might be encoded simultaneously, so that the network is more robust.

[13] In [40], Brewka and Eiter differentiated between the use of priorities to resolve conflicts that emerge from rules with opposite conclusions, and the use of priorities for choosing a rule out of a set of (not necessarily conflicting) rules for application. Whereas Brewka and Eiter's preferred answer set semantics uses the latter, this section offers a neural implementation of the former.

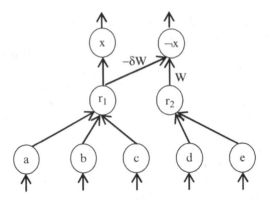

Fig. 4.6 Adding metalevel priorities ($r_1 \succ r_2$)

(remember that each hidden neuron represents a rule of the background knowledge) to the output neuron $\neg x$ with a negative weight (see Fig. 4.6). The idea is (a) that, from the Translation Algorithm, when x is activated, r_1 also is, and in this case r_1 should inhibit $\neg x$, regardless of the activation of r_2. Hence, we need to set the weight $-\delta W$ ($\delta, W \in \Re^+$) from r_1 to $\neg x$ accordingly. We also need to guarantee that (b) the addition of such a new weight does not change the behaviour of the network when r_1 is not activated. In this example, to satisfy (a) above, if the weight from r_2 to $\neg x$ is W, then $h(W - A_{min}\delta W - \theta_{\neg x}) < -A_{min}$ has to be satisfied. To satisfy (b), we need to guarantee that when r_1 is not activated, $\neg x$ is activated if and only if r_2 is activated. Therefore, $h(A_{min}W + \delta W - \theta_{\neg x}) > A_{min}$ and $h(-A_{min}W + A_{min}\delta W - \theta_{\neg x}) < -A_{min}$ have to be satisfied. This imposes a constraint on $\theta_{\neg x}$.[14] If, for example, $W = 6.0$ and $A_{min} = 0.8$, then $3.4 < \theta_{\neg x} < 86.0$ and, if we take $\theta_{\neg x} = 5$, then $0.666 < \delta < 1.267$ is such that the intended meaning of $r_1 \succ r_2$ is obtained.

4.6 Applications of CILP

In [66], the CILP system was applied to two real-world problems of DNA classification, which have become benchmark data sets for testing the accuracy of machine-learning systems. That publication also presents a comparison of CILP with other neural, symbolic, and hybrid inductive learning systems. Briefly, the test-set performance of CILP is at least as good as that of KBANN and of backpropagation, and better than that of any other system investigated, and CILP's training-set performance is considerably superior to that of KBANN and of back-propagation. We also applied CILP to fault diagnosis, using a simplified version of a real power generation plant. In this application, we used a system extended with classical negation. We then compared CILP with backpropagation, using three different architectures. The results corroborate the importance of learning with background knowledge in the presence of noisy data sets.

---

[14] Recall that we originally had (by Equation 4.4) $\theta_{\neg x} = 0$ in this example.

4.7 Discussion

Many different systems that combine background knowledge and learning from examples – ranging from Bayesian networks [184] to neuro-fuzzy systems [51] – have been proposed in the last decade. Among those that combine fragments of predicate logic [86, 100] and connectionist models [125], the work of Pinkas [204, 205] and of Hölldobler [133, 134, 137] is particularly relevant. In an attempt to show the capabilities and limitations of neural networks in performing logical inference, Pinkas defined a bidirectional mapping between symmetric neural networks[15] and fragments of predicate logic. He presented a theorem showing equivalence between the problem of satisfiability of propositional logic and minimising the energy function associated with a symmetric network: for every well-formed formula (wff), a quadratic energy function can be found efficiently, and for every energy function there exists a wff (found inefficiently) such that the global minima of the function are exactly equal to the satisfying models of the formula. Hölldobler presented a parallel unification algorithm and an automated reasoning system for first-order Horn clauses, implemented in a feedforward neural network, called the *Connectionist Horn Clause Logic* (CHCL) system.

The relations between neural networks and nonmonotonicity can be traced back to [16], in which Balkenius and Gärdenfors showed that symmetric neural networks can compute a form of nonmonotonic inference relation, satisfying some of the most fundamental postulates for nonmonotonic logic. Gärdenfors went on to produce his theory of conceptual representations [112], according to which a bridge between the symbolic and connectionist approaches to cognitive science could be built from geometric structures based on a number of quality dimensions such as temperature, weight, and brightness, as well as the spatial dimensions. The only nonmonotonic neural-symbolic learning systems are, to the best of our knowledge, the CILP system and Boutsinas and Vrahatis' *artificial nonmonotonic neural networks* (ANNN) [36], which uses a multiple inheritance scheme with exceptions to learn inheritance networks. Although Pinkas's work [205] dealt with the representation of *penalty logic*, a kind of nonmonotonic logic, in symmetric neural networks, the task of learning (penalties) from examples in such networks was not investigated to the same extent as the task of representation. Finally, neural networks have been combined with *explanation-based learning* (EBL) systems [185] into *Explanation-based neural networks* (EBNN) [245], and EBL has been combined with *inductive logic programming* (ILP) [187] (see [159, 189] for introductions to ILP), whereas the relations between ILP and neural networks have only begun to be unravelled (see [19, 252] and Chap. 10).

Recent decades have also seen much work in the field of hybrid (learning and reasoning) systems. In particular, many neuro-fuzzy systems have been developed. The main difficulties in comparing these systems with CILP are with regard to the employment for each system of different testing methodologies and very specific

---

[15] A neural network is called *symmetric* if $W_{ij} = W_{ji}$ for all neurons i, j (e.g. Hopfield networks [139]).

learning techniques. For example, in [95], Fu described the *Knowledge-Based Conceptual Neural Network* (KBCNN), a hybrid system similar to KBANN. The results obtained with KBCNN in the domain of the promoter recognition problem (98.1% accuracy) were marginally better than those obtained with CILP (97.2% accuracy),[16] as discussed in [66]. However, it seems that Fu did not use the method of cross-validation in his experiments with KBCNN. To further complicate things, KBCNN seems closely tied to its particular learning algorithm.

The overall performance of CILP is very satisfactory. CILP's effectiveness is a result of three of the system's features:

- CILP is based on *backpropagation*,
- CILP uses *background knowledge*, and
- CILP provides an *accurate, compact translation*.

In this chapter, we have presented the Connectionist Inductive Learning and Logic Programming System (CILP) – a massively parallel computational model based on artificial neural networks that integrates inductive learning from examples and background knowledge with deductive learning from logic programming. We have also illustrated how an extension of CILP can be used as a massively parallel model for extended logic programming. Consequently, some facts of commonsense knowledge can be represented more easily when classical negation is available.

In a rather satisfying way, following [135], the algorithm for translation of $\mathcal{P}$ into $\mathcal{N}$ associates each hidden neuron of $\mathcal{N}$ with a rule of $\mathcal{P}$. Such a representation has led to an extension of CILP in which negative connections from hidden to output layers are used to inhibit the presence of a neuron in the answer set of $\mathcal{P}$, thereby acting as a metalevel priority. To summarise, we have shown that single-hidden-layer neural networks can represent, in a very natural way, the class of extended logic programs augmented with metalevel priorities given by a superiority relation. The question of whether this is the language that single-hidden layer networks can learn still remains without an answer.

---

[16] KBCNN was not applied to the splice-junction determination problem.

Chapter 5
Connectionist Modal Logic

This chapter introduces connectionist modal logic (CML). CML can be seen as a general model for the development of connectionist nonclassical reasoning based on modal logics [79]. CML uses ensembles of neural networks to represent possible worlds, which underpin the semantics of several modal logics. In what follows, we introduce the theoretical foundations of CML and show how to build an integrated model for computing and learning modal logics.

It is now common knowledge that modal logic has become one of the outstanding logical languages used in computer science, enjoying success across the science's spectrum, from the theoretical foundations [42, 87, 143] to state-of-the-art hardware [50] and multiagent technologies [89]. The toolbox of any AI researcher now includes modal logic, as it has been found appropriate for research in several areas of AI [24, 42, 87, 106]. Areas such as knowledge representation, planning, and theorem proving have also been making extensive use of modal logic, be it temporal, epistemic, conditional, intuitionistic, doxastic, or many-dimensional modal logic, including, for instance, combinations of time and knowledge, time and belief, or space and time, to name a few [24, 42, 106, 218].

In this chapter, we propose a new approach to the representation and learning of propositional modal logic in a connectionist framework by introducing *connectionist modal logic* (CML). We use the language of modal logic programming [226], extended to allow modalities such as necessity and possibility in the head of clauses [197].[1]

We shall present an algorithm to set up an ensemble of Connectionist Inductive Learning and Logic Programming (CILP) networks [66]. A theorem then shows that the resulting ensemble computes a fixed-point semantics of the original modal program. In other words, the network ensemble can be seen as a massively parallel system for representation and reasoning in modal logic. We validate the system by applying it to the muddy children puzzle, a well-known problem in the domain of distributed knowledge representation and reasoning [87, 143]. We then proceed to

---

[1] Note that Sakakibara's modal logic programming [226] is referred to as Modal Prolog in the well-known survey of temporal and modal logic programming by Orgun and Ma [197].

A.S. d'Avila Garcez et al., *Neural-Symbolic Cognitive Reasoning,* Cognitive Technologies, 55
© Springer-Verlag Berlin Heidelberg 2009

learning experiments to validate the proposed connectionist model. The experiments indicate that the merging of background knowledge and data learning (learning from examples) in neural networks can provide an effective learning system [66, 250].

Learning in connectionist modal logic is achieved by training each individual neural network, which in turn corresponds to the current knowledge of an agent within a possible world; we use backpropagation. Learning will be exemplified by the system learning the knowledge of an agent in the muddy children puzzle using neural networks.

The CML framework presented here thus provides neural-symbolic learning systems with a better balance between expressive power and computational feasibility, owing to the use of a more expressive, yet computationally tractable, knowledge representation language. The well-established translation between propositional modal logic and the two-variable fragment of first-order logic [264] indicates that neural-symbolic learning systems may go beyond propositional logic.[2]

As argued in [71, 72], we believe that the combination of modal and nonclassical logics and connectionist models may provide the way forward towards the provision of an integrated system of expressive, sound reasoning and robust learning.

In what follows, we briefly present the basic concepts of modal logic used throughout this chapter. Then, we present a Connectionist Modal Algorithm that shows how to compute extended modal programs in artificial neural networks. The network obtained is an ensemble of simple CILP networks, each representing a (learnable) possible world. We then show that the network computes a fixed-point semantics of the given modal theory, thus proving the soundness of the Connectionist Modal Algorithm. We also prove termination of the Connectionist Modal Algorithm. Finally, we apply the system to the muddy children puzzle.

5.1 Modal Logic and Extended Modal Programs

In this section, we present some basic concepts of modal logic that will be used throughout the chapter. Modal logic began with an analysis of concepts such as necessity and possibility from a philosophical perspective [42, 46, 106, 141, 162]. A main feature of modal logic is the use of *possible-world semantics* (proposed by Kripke and Hintikka), which has significantly contributed to the development of new nonclassical logics, many of which have had a great impact in computing science. In modal logic, a proposition is necessary in a world if it is true in all worlds which are possible in relation to that world, whereas it is possible in a world if it is true in

---

[2] In [264], p. 2, Vardi states that '(propositional) modal logic, in spite of its apparent propositional syntax, is essentially a first-order logic, since the necessity and possibility modalities quantify over the set of possible worlds'. And, in [264], p. 7, 'the states in a Kripke structure correspond to domain elements in a relational structure, and modalities are nothing but a limited form of quantifiers'. A comprehensive treatment of this subject, including a study of the correspondence between propositional modal logic and (fragments of) first-order logic, can be found in [106] and in the work of van Benthem [256, 257].

at least one world which is possible in relation to that same world. This is expressed in the formalisation of the semantics by a (binary) relation between possible worlds.

Modal logic was found to be appropriate for studying mathematical necessity (in the logic of provability), time, knowledge, belief, obligation, and other concepts and modalities [42, 46, 106]. In artificial intelligence and computing, modal logic is one of the formalisms most frequently employed to analyse and represent reasoning in multiagent systems and concurrency properties [87]. The basic definitions related to modal logic that we shall use in this chapter are as follows. As usual, the language of propositional modal logic extends the language of propositional logic with the *necessity* ($\Box$) and *possibility* ($\Diamond$) operators. Moreover, we assume that any clause is grounded over a finite domain (i.e. the clauses contain no variables).

Definition 27. A *modal atom* is of the form MA, where $M \in \{\Box, \Diamond\}$ and A is an atom. A *modal literal* is of the form ML, where L is a literal.

Definition 28. A *modal program* is a finite set of clauses of the form $\alpha_1 \wedge \ldots \wedge \alpha_n \rightarrow \alpha_{n+1}$, where α_i ($1 \leq i \leq n$) is either an atom or a modal atom, and α_{n+1} is an atom.

We define *extended modal programs* as modal programs with single modalities $\Box$ and $\Diamond$ in the head of clauses, and default negation $\sim$ in the body of clauses [49], thus extending Sakakibara's modal logic programming [197, 226]. In addition, each clause is labelled by the possible world in which it holds, similarly to Gabbay's labelled deductive systems [42, 99]. Finally, the use of classical negation $\neg$ in the body of clauses is allowed, as done in [116], by renaming each literal of the form $\neg A$ as a new literal A^* not present in the language.

Definition 29. An *extended modal program* is a finite set of clauses C of the form $\omega_i : \beta_1 \wedge \ldots \wedge \beta_n \rightarrow \beta_{n+1}$, where ω_i is a label representing a world in which the associated clause holds, β_i ($1 \leq i \leq n$) is either a literal or a modal literal, and β_{n+1} is either an atom or a modal atom, together with a finite set of relations $\mathcal{R}(\omega_i, \omega_j)$ between the worlds ω_i and ω_j in C.

For example, $\mathcal{P} = \{\omega_1 : r \rightarrow \Box q; \omega_1 : \Diamond s \rightarrow r; \omega_2 : s; \omega_3 : q \rightarrow \Diamond p; \mathcal{R}(\omega_1, \omega_2), \mathcal{R}(\omega_1, \omega_3)\}$ is an extended modal program. Formulas in modal logic will be interpreted in Kripke models, which are defined as follows.

Definition 30 (Kripke Model). Let $\mathcal{L}$ be a modal language. A *Kripke model* for $\mathcal{L}$ is a tuple $\mathcal{M} = \langle \Omega, \mathcal{R}, v \rangle$, where Ω is a set of possible worlds, v is a mapping that assigns a subset of Ω to each propositional letter of $\mathcal{L}$, and $\mathcal{R}$ is a binary relation over Ω.

A modal formula φ is said to be true in a possible world ω of a model $\mathcal{M}$, written $(\mathcal{M}, \omega) \models \varphi$, if the following satisfiability condition holds.

Definition 31 (Satisfiability of Modal Formulas). Let $\mathcal{L}$ be a modal language, and let $\mathcal{M} = \langle \Omega, \mathcal{R}, v \rangle$ be a Kripke Model. The satisfiability relation $\models$ is uniquely defined as follows:

(i) $(\mathcal{M}, \omega) \models p$ iff $\omega \in v(p)$ for a propositional letter p;
(ii) $(\mathcal{M}, \omega) \models \neg\varphi$ iff $(\mathcal{M}, \omega) \not\models \varphi$;
(iii) $(\mathcal{M}, \omega) \models \varphi \wedge \psi$ iff $(\mathcal{M}, \omega) \models \varphi$ and $(\mathcal{M}, \omega) \models \psi$;
(iv) $(\mathcal{M}, \omega) \models \varphi \vee \psi$ iff $(\mathcal{M}, \omega) \models \varphi$ or $(\mathcal{M}, \omega) \models \psi$;
(v) $(\mathcal{M}, \omega) \models \varphi \rightarrow \psi$ iff $(\mathcal{M}, \omega) \not\models \varphi$ or $(\mathcal{M}, \omega) \models \psi$;
(vi) $(\mathcal{M}, \omega) \models \Box\varphi$ iff, for all $\omega_1 \in \Omega$, if $\mathcal{R}(\omega, \omega_1)$ then $(\mathcal{M}, \omega_1) \models \varphi$;
(vii) $(\mathcal{M}, \omega) \models \Diamond\varphi$ iff there exists an ω_1 such that $\mathcal{R}(\omega, \omega_1)$ and $(\mathcal{M}, \omega_1) \models \varphi$.

A variety of proof procedures for modal logic have been developed over the years (e.g. [42, 90]). In some of these, formulas are labelled by the worlds in which they hold, thus facilitating the modal reasoning process (see [42] for a discussion of this topic). In the natural-deduction-style rules below, the notation $\omega : \varphi$ means that the formula φ holds in the possible world ω. Moreover, the explicit reference to the accessibility relation also helps in deriving what formula holds in the worlds which are related by $\mathcal{R}$. The rules that we shall represent in CML are similar to the ones presented in [42], which we reproduce in Table 5.1.

The $\Diamond E$ rule can be seen (informally) as a *Skolemisation* of the existential quantifier over possible worlds, which is semantically implied by the formula $\Diamond\varphi$ in the premise. The term $f_\varphi(\omega)$ defines a particular possible world that is uniquely associated with the formula φ, and inferred to be accessible from the possible world ω (i.e. $\mathcal{R}(\omega, f_\varphi(\omega))$). In the $\Box I$ rule, the (temporary) assumption $[\mathcal{R}(\omega, g_\varphi(\omega))]$ should be read as 'given an arbitrary accessible world $g_\varphi(\omega)$, if one can derive $g_\varphi(\omega) : \varphi$, then it is possible to show that $\Box\varphi$ holds in ω.' The rule for $\Diamond I$ represents the assertion that if we have a relation $\mathcal{R}(\omega_1, \omega_2)$, and if φ holds in ω_2, then it must be the case that $\Diamond\varphi$ holds in ω_1. The rule $\Box E$ represents the assertion that if $\Box\varphi$ holds in a world ω_1, and ω_1 is related to ω_2, then we can infer that φ holds in ω_2.

5.1.1 Semantics for Extended Modal Logic Programs

In what follows, we define a model-theoretic semantics for extended modal programs. According to the rules for modality given above, we shall deal with $\Diamond$ by

Table 5.1 Reasoning rules for modality operators

$$
\begin{array}{ll}
\begin{array}{c}
[R(\omega, g_\varphi(\omega))] \\
\vdots \\
\dfrac{g_\varphi(\omega) : \varphi}{\omega : \Box\varphi} \, \Box I
\end{array}
&
\dfrac{\omega_1 : \Box\varphi, R(\omega_1, \omega_2)}{\omega_2 : \varphi} \, \Box E
\\[4ex]
\dfrac{\omega : \Diamond\varphi}{f_\varphi(\omega) : \varphi, R(\omega, f_\varphi(\omega))} \, \Diamond E
&
\dfrac{\omega_2 : \varphi, R(\omega_1, \omega_2)}{\omega_1 : \Diamond\varphi} \, \Diamond I
\end{array}
$$

making a choice of the world ω_j in which to have A when $\Diamond A$ is true in ω_i and $\mathcal{R}(\omega_i, \omega_j)$. In this chapter, we choose an arbitrary world (i.e. one that is uniquely associated with A). In practice, one may opt to manage several neural networks, one for each choice,[3] in the same way that one may opt to manage several graphs, for example as in the (modal) tableau prover LoTREC [45]. In this case, each choice could possibly lead to different fixed points of a given extended modal program, but once the choice is made, if the program is well behaved (e.g. in the sense of Fitting's metric methods [92]), we should be able to prove that the computation terminates with our neural network converging to a fixed point of the meaning operator.

When computing the fixed point, we have to consider the consequences derived locally and the consequences derived from the interaction between worlds. Locally, fixed points are computed as in the stable-model semantics for logic programming, by simply renaming each modal literal ML_i as a new literal L_j not in the language $\mathcal{L}$, and applying the Gelfond–Lifschitz transformation [40]. When we are considering interacting worlds, there are four more cases to be addressed, according to the rules in Table 5.1.

Hence, we proceed as follows. Given an extended modal program, for each literal of the form $\Diamond L$ in the head of a clause, we choose a world and *connect* (in a sense that will become clear soon) $\Diamond L$ to the literal L in this world. We also connect each literal of the form $\Box L$ to literals L in every world related to that of $\Box L$, and similarly for the other rules. The definition of the modal consequence operator below captures this.

Definition 32 (Modal Immediate-Consequence Operator). Let $\mathcal{P} = \{\mathcal{P}_1, \ldots, \mathcal{P}_k\}$ be an extended modal program, where each $\mathcal{P}_i$ is the set of modal clauses that hold in a world ω_i $(1 \leq i \leq k)$. Let $B_{\mathcal{P}}$ denote the set of atoms occurring in $\mathcal{P}$ (i.e. the Herbrand base of $\mathcal{P}$), and let I be a Herbrand interpretation for $\mathcal{P}$. Let α be either an atom or a modal atom. The mapping $MT_{\mathcal{P}} : 2^{B_{\mathcal{P}}} \to 2^{B_{\mathcal{P}}}$ is defined as follows: $MT_{\mathcal{P}}(I) = \{\alpha \in B_{\mathcal{P}} \mid \text{either } (i) \text{ or } (ii) \text{ or } (iii) \text{ or } (iv) \text{ or } (v) \text{ below holds}\}.$

(i) $\beta_1, \ldots, \beta_n \to \alpha$ is a clause in $\mathcal{P}$ and $\{\beta_1, \ldots, \beta_n\} \subseteq I$;

(ii) α is of the form $\omega_i : A$, ω_i is of the type $f_A(\omega_k)$ (i.e. ω_i is a particular possible world uniquely associated with A), there exists a world ω_k such that $\mathcal{R}(\omega_k, \omega_i)$, and $\omega_k : \beta_1, \ldots, \beta_m \to \Diamond A$ is a clause in $\mathcal{P}$ with $\{\beta_1, \ldots, \beta_m\} \subseteq I$;

(iii) α is of the form $\omega_i : \Diamond A$, there exists a world ω_j such that $\mathcal{R}(\omega_i, \omega_j)$, and $\omega_j : \beta_1, \ldots, \beta_m \to A$ is a clause in $\mathcal{P}$ with $\{\beta_1, \ldots, \beta_m\} \subseteq I$;

(iv) α is of the form $\omega_i : \Box A$ and, for each world ω_j such that $\mathcal{R}(\omega_i, \omega_j)$, $\omega_j : \beta_1, \ldots, \beta_o \to A$ is a clause in $\mathcal{P}$ with $\{\beta_1, \ldots, \beta_o\} \subseteq I$;

(v) α is of the form $\omega_i : A$, there exists a world ω_k such that $\mathcal{R}(\omega_k, \omega_i)$, and $\omega_k : \beta_1, \ldots, \beta_o \to \Box A$ is a clause in $\mathcal{P}$ with $\{\beta_1, \ldots, \beta_o\} \subseteq I$.

Following [21], one can construct the semantics of extended modal programs by considering extended modal ground formulas in order to compute a fixed point. As a result, one can associate with every extended modal program a modal ground

---

[3] Such a choice is computationally similar to the approach adopted by Gabbay in [98], in which one chooses a point in the future for execution and then backtracks if it is judged necessary (and is at all possible).

program (the modal closure of the program) so that both programs have the same models. Hence, the classical results about the fixed-point semantics of logic programming can be applied to the modal ground closure of a program.

5.2 Connectionist Modal Logic

In this section, we introduce CML. We shall use ensembles of CILP networks as the underlying CML architecture to represent modal theories. We then present an efficient translation algorithm from extended modal programs to neural-network ensembles.

Let us start with a simple example. It briefly illustrates how an ensemble of CILP networks can be used for modelling nonclassical reasoning with modal logic. Input and output neurons may represent $\Box L$, $\Diamond L$, or L, where L is a literal.

Example 8. Figure 5.1 shows an ensemble of three CILP networks $(\omega_1, \omega_2, \omega_3)$, which might *communicate* in many different ways. The idea is to see ω_1, ω_2, and ω_3 as *possible worlds,* and to incorporate modalities into the language of CILP. For example, (i) 'If $\omega_1 : \Box A$ then $\omega_2 : A$' could be communicated from ω_1 to ω_2 by connecting $\Box A$ in ω_1 to A in ω_2 such that, whenever $\Box A$ is activated in ω_1, A is activated in ω_2. Similarly, (ii) 'If $(\omega_2 : A) \lor (\omega_3 : A)$ then $\omega_1 : \Diamond A$' could be implemented by connecting the neurons A of ω_2 and ω_3 to the neuron $\Diamond A$ of ω_1 through

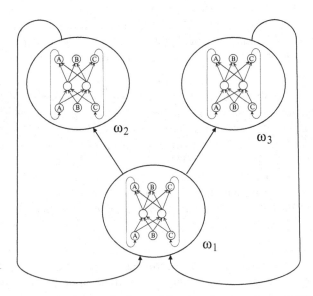

Fig. 5.1 An ensemble of CILP networks that models uncertainty by using modalities and possible worlds (ω_2 and ω_3 may be seen as alternative models)

a number of hidden neurons. Examples (i) and (ii) simulate, in a finite universe, the rules of □ *Elimination* and ◊ *Introduction* (see Table 5.1).

Owing to the simplicity of each CILP network in the ensemble, performing inductive learning within each possible world is straightforward. The main problem to be tackled when it comes to learning in the new neural model is how to set up the connections that establish the necessary communication between networks, for example ω_1 and ω_2. In the case of modal logic, such connections are defined by the modal rules of natural deduction (Table 5.1). The Connectionist Modal Algorithm presented in Sect. 5.2.1 implements those rules.

5.2.1 Computing Modalities in Neural Networks

In this section, we present the computational machinery of CML. We use the *CILP Translation Algorithm* presented in Chap. 4 for creating each network of the ensemble, and the *Connectionist Modal Algorithm* described below for interconnecting and reasoning with the various networks. The Connectionist Modal Algorithm translates natural-deduction modal rules into the networks. Intuitively, the accessibility relation is represented by connections between (sub)networks. As depicted in Fig. 5.2, where $\mathcal{R}(\omega_1,\omega_2)$ and $\mathcal{R}(\omega_1,\omega_3)$, connections from ω_1 to ω_2 and ω_3 represent either □E or ◊E. Connections from ω_2 and ω_3 to ω_1 represent either □I or ◊I.

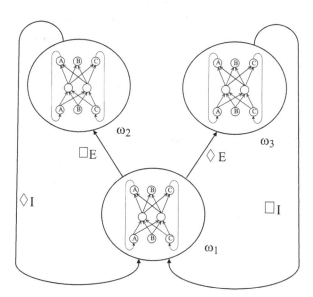

Fig. 5.2 An ensemble of networks representing the natural-deduction-style rules for the □ and ◊ modalities

Let $\mathcal{P}$ be an extended modal program with clauses of the form $\omega_i : ML_1, \ldots,$ $ML_k \rightarrow MA$, where each L_j is a literal, A is an atom, and $M \in \{\Box, \Diamond\}$, $1 \leq i \leq n$, $0 \leq j \leq k$. As in the case of individual CILP networks, we start by calculating $MAX_{\mathcal{P}}(\overrightarrow{k}, \overrightarrow{\mu}, n)$ of $\mathcal{P}$ and A_{min} such that

$$A_{min} > \frac{MAX_{\mathcal{P}}(\overrightarrow{k}, \overrightarrow{\mu}, n) - 1}{MAX_{\mathcal{P}}(\overrightarrow{k}, \overrightarrow{\mu}, n) + 1}, \tag{5.1}$$

but now we also need to take into account the number n of networks (i.e. possible worlds) in the ensemble, and thus we use $MAX_{\mathcal{P}}(\overrightarrow{k}, \overrightarrow{\mu}, n)$ instead of simply $MAX_{\mathcal{P}}(\overrightarrow{k}, \overrightarrow{\mu})$.

Connectionist Modal Algorithm

1. Let $\mathcal{P}_i \subseteq \mathcal{P}$ be the set of clauses labelled by ω_i in $\mathcal{P}$. Let $W^M \in \mathbb{R}$.
2. For each $\mathcal{P}_i$, do:

   (a) Rename each ML_j in $\mathcal{P}_i$ as a new literal not occurring in $\mathcal{P}$, of the form $L_j^{\Box}$ if $M = \Box$, or $L_j^{\Diamond}$ if $M = \Diamond$.[4]
   (b) Call CILP's Translation Algorithm (Sect. 4.1).
   (c) Let $\mathcal{N}_i$ be the neural network that denotes $\mathcal{P}_i$.

3. For each output neuron $L_j^{\Diamond}$ in $\mathcal{N}_i$, do:

   (a) Add a hidden neuron L_j^M to an arbitrary $\mathcal{N}_k$ ($0 \leq k \leq n$) such that $\mathcal{R}(\omega_i, \omega_k)$.
   (b) Set the step function $s(x)$ as the activation function of L_j^M.
   (c) Connect $L_j^{\Diamond}$ in $\mathcal{N}_i$ to L_j^M and set the connection weight to 1.
   (d) Set the threshold θ^M of L_j^M such that $-1 < \theta^M < A_{min}$.
   (e) Create an output neuron L_j in $\mathcal{N}_k$, if it does not exist yet.
   (f) Connect L_j^M to L_j in $\mathcal{N}_k$, and set the connection weight to $W_{L_j}^M > h^{-1}(A_{min}) + \mu_{L_j} W + \theta_{L_j}$.[5]

4. For each output neuron $L_j^{\Box}$ in $\mathcal{N}_i$, do:

   (a) Add a hidden neuron L_j^M to each $\mathcal{N}_k$ ($0 \leq k \leq n$) such that $\mathcal{R}(\omega_i, \omega_k)$.
   (b) Set the step function $s(x)$ as the activation function of L_j^M.
   (c) Connect $L_j^{\Box}$ in $\mathcal{N}_i$ to L_j^M and set the connection weight to 1.
   (d) Set the threshold θ^M of L_j^M such that $-1 < \theta^M < A_{min}$.

---

[4] This allows us to treat each ML_j as a literal and apply the Translation Algorithm of Chap. 4 directly to $\mathcal{P}_i$ by labelling neurons as $\Box L_j$, $\Diamond L_j$, or L_j.

[5] Recall that μ_L is the number of connections to output neuron L, and that θ_L is the threshold of output neuron L. Note also that μ_L, W, and θ_L are all obtained from CILP's Translation Algorithm.

(e) Create output neurons L_j in each $\mathcal{N}_k$, if they do not exist yet.

(f) Connect L_j^M to L_j in $\mathcal{N}_k$, and set the connection weight to $W_{L_j}^M > h^{-1}(A_{\min}) + \mu_{L_j} W + \theta_{L_j}$.

5. For each output neuron L_j in $\mathcal{N}_k$ such that $\mathcal{R}(\omega_i, \omega_k)$ $(0 \leq i \leq n)$, do:

   (a) Add a hidden neuron $L_j^\vee$ to $\mathcal{N}_i$, if it does not exist yet.
   (b) Set the step function $s(x)$ as the activation function of $L_j^\vee$.
   (c) For each ω_i such that $\mathcal{R}(\omega_i, \omega_k)$, do:
       i. Connect L_j in $\mathcal{N}_k$ to $L_j^\vee$ and set the connection weight to 1.
       ii. Set the threshold $\theta^\vee$ of $L_j^\vee$ such that $-nA_{min} < \theta^\vee < A_{min} - (n-1)$.
       iii. Create an output neuron $L_j^\Diamond$ in $\mathcal{N}_i$, if it does not exist yet.
       iv. Connect $L_j^\vee$ to $L_j^\Diamond$ in $\mathcal{N}_i$, and set the connection weight to $W_{L_j^\Diamond}^M > h^{-1}(A_{\min}) + \mu_{L_j^\Diamond} W + \theta_{L_j^\Diamond}$.

6. For each output neuron L_j in $\mathcal{N}_k$ such that $\mathcal{R}(\omega_i, \omega_k)$ $(0 \leq i \leq n)$, do:

   (a) Add a hidden neuron $L_j^\wedge$ to $\mathcal{N}_i$, if it does not exist yet.
   (b) Set the step function $s(x)$ as the activation function of $L_j^\wedge$.
   (c) For each ω_i such that $\mathcal{R}(\omega_i, \omega_k)$, do:
       i. Connect L_j in $\mathcal{N}_k$ to $L_j^\wedge$ and set the connection weight to 1.
       ii. Set the threshold $\theta^\wedge$ of $L_j^\wedge$ such that $n - (1 + A_{min}) < \theta^\wedge < nA_{min}$.
       iii. Create an output neuron $L_j^\square$ in $\mathcal{N}_i$, if it does not exist yet.
       iv. Connect $L_j^\wedge$ to $L_j^\square$ in $\mathcal{N}_i$, and set the connection weight to $W_{L_j^\square}^M > h^{-1}(A_{\min}) + \mu_{L_j^\square} W + \theta_{L_j^\square}$.[6]

7. For each $\mathcal{P}_i$, recurrently connect each output neuron L_j (and $L_j^\Diamond, L_j^\square$) in $\mathcal{N}_i$ to its corresponding input neuron L_j (and $L_j^\Diamond, L_j^\square$, respectively) in $\mathcal{N}_i$ with weight $W_r = 1$.[7]

Let us now illustrate the use of the Connectionist Modal Algorithm with the following example.

Example 9. Let $\mathcal{P} = \{\omega_1 : r \to \square q, \omega_1 : \Diamond s \to r, \omega_2 : s, \omega_3 : q \to \Diamond p, \mathcal{R}(\omega_1, \omega_2), \mathcal{R}(\omega_1, \omega_3)\}$. We start by applying CILP's Translation Algorithm, which creates three neural networks to represent the worlds ω_1, ω_2, and ω_3 (see Fig. 5.3). Then, we apply the Connectionist Modal Algorithm. Hidden neurons labelled by $\{M, \vee, \wedge\}$ are created using the Connectionist Modal Algorithm. The remaining neurons are all created using the Translation Algorithm. For the sake of clarity, unconnected input and output neurons are not shown in Fig. 5.3. Taking $\mathcal{N}_1$ (which

---

[6] The values of W^M are derived from the proof of Theorem 12.

[7] This essentially allows one to iterate $MT_\mathcal{P}$, thus using the ensemble to compute the extended modal program in parallel.

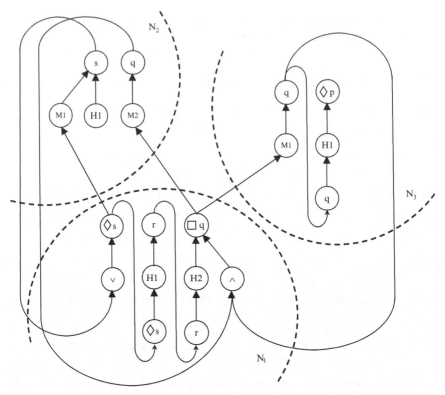

Fig. 5.3 The ensemble of networks $\{\mathcal{N}_1, \mathcal{N}_2, \mathcal{N}_3\}$ representing $\mathcal{P} = \{\omega_1 : r \to \Box q,\ \omega_1 : \Diamond s \to r,$ $\omega_2 : s,\ \omega_3 : q \to \Diamond p,\ \mathcal{R}(\omega_1, \omega_2),\ \mathcal{R}(\omega_1, \omega_3)\}$

represents ω_1), output neurons $L_j^\Diamond$ should be connected to output neurons L_j in an arbitrary network $\mathcal{N}_i$ (which represents ω_i) to which $\mathcal{N}_1$ is related. For example, taking $\mathcal{N}_i = \mathcal{N}_2$, $\Diamond s$ in $\mathcal{N}_1$ is connected to s in $\mathcal{N}_2$. Then, output neurons $L_j^\Box$ should be connected to the output neurons L_j in every network $\mathcal{N}_i$ to which $\mathcal{N}_1$ is related. For example, $\Box q$ in $\mathcal{N}_1$ is connected to q in both $\mathcal{N}_2$ and $\mathcal{N}_3$. Now, taking $\mathcal{N}_2$, the output neurons L_j need to be connected to output neurons $L_j^\Diamond$ and $L_j^\Box$ in every world $\mathcal{N}_j$ related to $\mathcal{N}_2$. For example, s in $\mathcal{N}_2$ is connected to $\Diamond s$ in $\mathcal{N}_1$ via the hidden neuron denoted by $\vee$ in Fig. 5.3, while q in $\mathcal{N}_2$ is connected to $\Box q$ in $\mathcal{N}_1$ via the hidden neuron denoted by $\wedge$. Similarly, q in $\mathcal{N}_3$ is connected to $\Box q$ in $\mathcal{N}_1$ via $\wedge$. Finally, the output neurons $\Diamond s$ and r in $\mathcal{N}_1$ are connected to the input neurons $\Diamond s$ and r, respectively, in $\mathcal{N}_1$, and the output neuron q in $\mathcal{N}_3$ is connected to the input neuron q in $\mathcal{N}_3$, all with weight 1. The algorithm terminates when all output neurons have been connected.

Table 5.2 contains a valid set of weights for the connections shown in Fig. 5.3, obtained from the Connectionist Modal Algorithm and the Translation Algorithm. We use (X_{N_i}, Y_{N_j}) to denote the weight from neuron X in network N_i to neuron Y in network N_j, and (X_{N_i}) to denote the threshold of neuron X in network N_i.

The calculations are as follows. From Equation 5.1, $A_{min} > (MAX_{\mathcal{P}}(1,2,3) - 1)/$ $(MAX_{\mathcal{P}}(1,2,3) + 1)$. Let $A_{min} = 0.6$. From Equation 4.2, taking $\beta = 1$, $W \geq$ $2(\ln(1.6) - \ln(0.4))/(2(-0.4) + 1.6) = 1.1552$. Let $W = 2$. Thus, all feedforward connections internal to a subnetwork will receive a weight 2. Recall that all feedback connections internal to a subnetwork will receive a weight 1. Then, the thresholds of the hidden neurons H are calculated according to Equation 4.3, and the thresholds of all the output neurons are calculated according to Equation 4.4. For example, $(H1_{N_1}) = 2((1 + 0.6) \cdot (1 - 1))/2 = 0$, $(\Box q_{N_1}) = 2((1 + 0.6) \cdot (1 - 1))/2 = 0$, $(H1_{N_2}) = 2((1 + 0.6) \cdot (0 - 1))/2 = -1.6$ and $(\Diamond s_{N_1}) = 2((1 + 0.6) \cdot (1 - 0))/2 = 1.6$. Now, thresholds and weights for the neurons M, $\wedge$, and $\vee$ need to be calculated. From the Connectionist Modal Algorithm, connections between subnetworks, for example $(\Diamond s_{N_1}, M1_{N_2})$, will receive a weight 1, the thresholds θ^M of neurons M must satisfy $-1 < \theta^M < A_{min}$ (e.g. $(M1_{N_2}) = 0.5$), the thresholds $\theta^\vee$ of neurons $\vee$ must satisfy $-nA_{min} < \theta^\vee < A_{min} - (n - 1)$ (e.g. $(\vee_{N_1}) = -1.6$), and the thresholds $\theta^\wedge$ of neurons $\wedge$ must satisfy $n - (1 + A_{min}) < \theta^\wedge < nA_{min}$ (e.g. $(\wedge_{N_1}) = 1.6$).[8] Finally, weights $W_L^M > h^{-1}(0.6) + 2\mu_L + \theta_L$ must be calculated.[9] For example, the output neuron $\Diamond s$ in N_1 has $\mu = 0$ and $\theta = 1.6$, and thus $W^M > 2.986$. Similarly, the output neuron s in N_2 has $\mu = 1$ and $\theta = 0$, and thus $W^M > 3.386$. Although it is not necessary, we choose $W^M = 4$ to unify all of the five remaining weights (see Table 5.2).

Table 5.2 A valid set of weights for the CML network in Example 9

$(\vee_{N_1}, \Diamond s_{N_1}) = 4$	$(M1_{N_2}, s_{N_2}) = 4$	$(M1_{N_3}, q_{N_3}) = 4$
$(\Diamond s_{N_1}, \Diamond s_{N_1}) = 1$	$(H1_{N_2}, s_{N_2}) = 2$	$(q_{N_3}, q_{N_3}) = 1$
$(\Diamond s_{N_1}, H1_{N_1}) = 2$	$(M2_{N_2}, q_{N_2}) = 4$	$(q_{N_3}, H1_{N_3}) = 2$
$(H1_{N_1}, r_{N_1}) = 2$		$(H1_{N_3}, \Diamond p_{N_3}) = 2$
$(r_{N_1}, r_{N_1}) = 1$		
$(r_{N_1}, H2_{N_1}) = 2$		
$(H2_{N_1}, \Box q_{N_1}) = 2$		
$(\wedge_{N_1}, \Box q_{N_1}) = 4$		
$(\Diamond s_{N_1}, M1_{N_2}) = 1$	$(s_{N_2}, \vee_{N_1}) = 1$	$(q_{N_3}, \wedge_{N_1}) = 1$
$(\Box q_{N_1}, M2_{N_2}) = 1$	$(q_{N_2}, \wedge_{N_1}) = 1$	
$(\Box q_{N_1}, M1_{N_3}) = 1$		
$(\vee_{N_1}) = -1.6$	$(M1_{N_2}) = 0.5$	$(M1_{N_3}) = 0.5$
$(\Diamond s_{N_1}) = 1.6$	$(H1_{N_2}) = -1.6$	$(q_{N_3}) = 1.6$
$(H1_{N_1}) = 0$	$(M2_{N_2}) = 0.5$	$(H1_{N_3}) = 0$
$(r_{N_1}) = 0$	$(s_{N_2}) = 0$	$(\Diamond p_{N_3}) = 0$
$(H2_{N_1}) = 0$	$(q_{N_2}) = 1.6$	
$(\wedge_{N_1}) = 1.6$		
$(\Box q_{N_1}) = 0$		

---

[8] Recall that $n = 3$ in this example.

[9] Recall that $W = 2$ in this example; $h^{-1}(A_{min}) = (-1/\beta)\ln((1 - A_{min})/(1 + A_{min}))$.

5.2.2 Soundness of Modal Computation

We are now in a position to show that the ensemble of neural networks $\mathcal{N}$ obtained from the above Connectionist Modal Algorithm is equivalent to the original extended modal program $\mathcal{P}$, in the sense that $\mathcal{N}$ computes the modal immediate-consequence operator $MT_{\mathcal{P}}$ of $\mathcal{P}$ (see Definition 32).

Theorem 12. *For any extended modal program $\mathcal{P}$, there exists an ensemble of feed-forward neural networks $\mathcal{N}$ with a single hidden layer and semilinear neurons, such that $\mathcal{N}$ computes the modal fixed-point operator $MT_{\mathcal{P}}$ of $\mathcal{P}$.*

Proof. We have to show that there exists $W > 0$ such that the network $\mathcal{N}$ obtained by the Connectionist Modal Algorithm computes $MT_{\mathcal{P}}$. Throughout, we assume that $\mathcal{N}_i$ and $\mathcal{N}_j$ are two arbitrary subnetworks of $\mathcal{N}$, representing possible worlds ω_i and ω_j, respectively, such that $\mathcal{R}(\omega_i, \omega_j)$. We distinguish two cases: (a) clauses with modalities $\Box$ and $\Diamond$ in the head, and (b) clauses with no modalities in the head.

(a) Firstly, note that clauses with $\Box$ in the head must satisfy $\Box E$ in Table 5.1, while clauses with $\Diamond$ in the head must satisfy $\Diamond E$. Given input vectors **i** and **j** to $\mathcal{N}_i$ and $\mathcal{N}_j$, respectively, each neuron A in the output layer of $\mathcal{N}_j$ is active ($A > A_{min}$) if and only if (i) there exists a clause of $\mathcal{P}_j$ of the form $ML_1, \ldots, ML_k \rightarrow A$ such that $ML_1, \ldots, ML_k$ are satisfied by interpretation **j**, or (ii) there exists a clause of $\mathcal{P}_i$ of the form $ML_1, \ldots, ML_k \rightarrow \Box A$ such that $ML_1, \ldots, ML_k$ are satisfied by interpretation **i**, or (iii) there exists a clause of $\mathcal{P}_i$ of the form $ML_1, \ldots, ML_k \rightarrow \Diamond A$ such that $ML_1, \ldots, ML_k$ are satisfied by interpretation **i**, and the Connectionist Modal Algorithm (step 3a) has selected $\mathcal{N}_j$ as the arbitrary network $\mathcal{N}_k$.

($\leftarrow$) (i) results directly from Theorem 8. (ii) and (iii) share the same proof, as follows. From Theorem 8, we know that if $ML_1, \ldots, ML_k$ are satisfied by interpretation **i**, then MA is active in $\mathcal{N}_i$ (recall that $M \in \{\Box, \Diamond\}$). Hence, we only need to show that MA in $\mathcal{N}_i$ activates A in $\mathcal{N}_j$. From the Connectionist Modal Algorithm, A^M is a nonlinear hidden neuron in $\mathcal{N}_j$. Thus, if MA is active ($MA > A_{min}$), then A^M presents an activation 1. As a result, the minimum activation of A is $h(W_A^M - \mu_A W - \theta_A)$. Now, since $W_A^M > h^{-1}(A_{min}) + \mu_A W + \theta_A$, we have $h(W_A^M - \mu_A W - \theta_A) > A_{min}$ and, therefore, A is active ($A > A_{min}$).

($\rightarrow$) Directly from the Connectionist Modal Algorithm, since A^M is a nonlinear neuron, this neuron contributes zero to the input potential of A in $\mathcal{N}_j$ when MA is not active in $\mathcal{N}_i$. In this case, the behaviour of A in $\mathcal{N}_j$ is not affected by $\mathcal{N}_i$. Now, from Theorem 8, $\mathcal{N}_j$ computes the fixed-point operator $T_{\mathcal{P}_j}$ of $\mathcal{P}_j$. Thus, if $ML_1, \ldots, ML_k$ are not satisfied by **j**, then A is not active in $\mathcal{N}_j$.

(b) Clauses with no modalities must satisfy $\Box I$ and $\Diamond I$ in Table 5.1. Given input vectors **i** and **j** to $\mathcal{N}_i$ and $\mathcal{N}_j$, respectively, each neuron $\Box A$ in the output layer of $\mathcal{N}_i$ is active ($\Box A > A_{min}$) if and only if (i) there exists a clause of $\mathcal{P}_i$ of the form $ML_1, \ldots, ML_k \rightarrow \Box A$ such that $ML_1, \ldots, ML_k$ are satisfied by interpretation **i**, or (ii) for all $\mathcal{N}_j$, there exists a clause of $\mathcal{P}_j$ of the form $ML_1, \ldots, ML_k \rightarrow A$ such that $ML_1, \ldots, ML_k$ are satisfied by interpretation **j**. Each neuron $\Diamond A$ in the output layer of $\mathcal{N}_i$ is active ($\Diamond A > A_{min}$) if and only if (iii) there exists a clause of $\mathcal{P}_i$ of the form $ML_1, \ldots, ML_k \rightarrow \Diamond A$ such that $ML_1, \ldots, ML_k$ are satisfied by interpretation **i**, or (iv) there exists a clause of $\mathcal{P}_j$ of the form $ML_1, \ldots, ML_k \rightarrow A$ such that $ML_1, \ldots, ML_k$ are satisfied by interpretation **j**.

($\leftarrow$) (i) and (iii) result directly from Theorem 8. (ii) and (iv) are proved in what follows. From Theorem 8, we know that if $ML_1, \ldots, ML_k$ are satisfied by interpretation **j**, then A is active in $\mathcal{N}_j$. (ii) We need to show that if A is active in every network $\mathcal{N}_j$ $(0 \leq j \leq n)$ to which $\mathcal{N}_i$ relates, $\Box A$ is active in $\mathcal{N}_i$. From the Connectionist Modal Algorithm, $A^\wedge$ is a nonlinear hidden neuron in $\mathcal{N}_i$. If A is active $(A > A_{min})$ in $\mathcal{N}_j$, the minimum input potential of $A^\wedge$ is $nA_{min} - \theta^\wedge$. Now, since $\theta^\wedge < nA_{min}$ (Connectionist Modal Algorithm, step 6(c)ii), the minimum input potential of $A^\wedge$ is greater than zero and, therefore, $A^\wedge$ presents an activation 1. (iv) We need to show that if A is active in at least one network $\mathcal{N}_j$ $(0 \leq j \leq n)$ to which $\mathcal{N}_i$ relates, $\Diamond A$ is active in $\mathcal{N}_i$. From the Connectionist Modal Algorithm, $A^\vee$ is a nonlinear hidden neuron in $\mathcal{N}_i$. If A is active $(A > A_{min})$ in $\mathcal{N}_j$, the minimum input potential of $A^\vee$ is $A_{min} - \theta^\vee$. Now, since $\theta^\vee < A_{min} - (n-1)$ (Connectionist Modal Algorithm, step 5(c)ii), and $n \geq 1$, the minimum input potential of $A^\vee$ is greater than zero and, therefore, $A^\vee$ presents an activation 1. Finally, if $A^\wedge$ presents an activation 1, the minimum activation of $\Box A$ is $h(W_{\Box A}^M - \mu_{\Box A}W - \theta_{\Box A})$, and, exactly as in item (a) above, $\Box A$ is active in $\mathcal{N}_i$. Similarly, if $A^\vee$ presents an activation 1, the minimum activation of $\Diamond A$ is $h(W_{\Diamond A}^M - \mu_{\Diamond A}W - \theta_{\Diamond A})$, and, exactly as in item (a) above, $\Diamond A$ is active in $\mathcal{N}_i$.

($\rightarrow$) Again, (i) and (iii) result directly from Theorem 8. (ii) and (iv) are proved below: (ii) We need to show that if $\Box A$ is not active in $\mathcal{N}_i$ then at least one A is not active in $\mathcal{N}_j$ to which $\mathcal{N}_i$ relates $(0 \leq j \leq n)$. If $\Box A$ is not active, $A^\wedge$ presents an activation 0. In the worst case, A is active in $n-1$ networks with maximum activation 1, and not active in a single network with minimum activation $-A_{min}$. In this case, the input potential of $A^\wedge$ is $n - 1 - A_{min} - \theta^\wedge$. Now, since $\theta^\wedge > n - (1 + A_{min})$ (Connectionist Modal Algorithm, step 6(c)ii), the maximum input potential of $A^\wedge$ is smaller than zero and, therefore, $A^\wedge$ presents an activation 0. (iv) We need to show that if $\Diamond A$ is not active in $\mathcal{N}_i$, then A is not active in any network $\mathcal{N}_j$ to which $\mathcal{N}_i$ relates $(0 \leq j \leq n)$. If $\Diamond A$ is not active, $A^\vee$ presents an activation 0. In the worst case, A presents an activation $-A_{min}$ in all $\mathcal{N}_j$ networks. In this case, the input potential of $A^\vee$ is $-nA_{min} - \theta^\vee$. Now, since $\theta^\vee > -nA_{min}$ (Connectionist Modal Algorithm, step 5(c)ii), the maximum input potential of $A^\vee$ is smaller than zero and, therefore, $A^\vee$ presents an activation 0. Finally, from Theorem 8, if $A^\wedge$ and $A^\vee$ have activation 0, $\mathcal{N}_i$ computes the fixed-point operator $MT_{\mathcal{P}_i}$ of $\mathcal{P}_i$. This completes the proof. ∎

5.2.3 Termination of Modal Computation

A network ensemble can be used to compute extended modal programs in parallel in the same way that CILP networks are used to compute logic programs. We take a network ensemble $\{\mathcal{N}_1, \ldots, \mathcal{N}_n\}$ obtained from the Connectionist Modal Algorithm, and rename each input and output neuron $L_k^{\{\Box,\Diamond\}}$ in $\mathcal{N}_i$ ($1 \le i \le n$) as $\omega_i : L_k$, where L_k can be either a literal or a modal literal. This basically allows us to have copies of the literal L_k in different possible worlds ($\omega_i, \omega_j, \ldots$), and to treat the occurrence of L_k in $\mathcal{N}_i$ ($\omega_i : L_k$) as different from the occurrence of L_k in $\mathcal{N}_j$ ($\omega_j : L_k$). It is not difficult to see that we are left with a large single-hidden-layer neural network $\mathcal{N}$, in which each input and output neuron is now labelled. This *flattened* network is a recurrent network containing feedback connections from the output layer to the input layer, and sometimes from the output to the hidden layer. Any feedback connection from output neurons ($o_j, o_k, \ldots$) to a hidden neuron (h_i) may be replaced equivalently by feedback from the output to the input layer only, if we create new input neurons $i_j, i_k, \ldots$ and connect output o_j to input i_j, output o_k to input i_k, and so on, and then connect inputs $i_j, i_k, \ldots$ to the hidden neuron h_i. As a result, as in the case of CILP networks, if $\mathcal{P}$ is well behaved, the computation of $\mathcal{P}$ by $\mathcal{N}$ should terminate.

For example, in Fig. 5.3, since $\Diamond s$ and r in $\mathcal{N}_1$ and q in $\mathcal{N}_3$ are recursively connected, the ensemble computes $\{\Diamond s, r, \Box q\}$ in ω_1, $\{s, q\}$ in ω_2, and $\{q, \Diamond s\}$ in ω_3. As expected, these are logical consequences of the original program $\mathcal{P}$ given in Example 9. Although the computation is done in parallel in $\mathcal{N}$, following it by starting from facts (such as s in ω_2) may help verify this.

Notice how the idea of labelling the neurons, allowing multiple copies of neurons L_j to occur in the neural network simultaneously, allows us to give a modal interpretation to CILP networks as a corollary (below) of Theorem 12. Let $MT_{\mathcal{P}}^n \overset{def}{=} MT_{\mathcal{P}}(MT_{\mathcal{P}}^{n-1})$ with $MT_{\mathcal{P}}^0 \overset{def}{=} MT_{\mathcal{P}}(\{\varnothing\})$. We say that an extended modal program $\mathcal{P}$ is *well behaved* if, after a finite number m of iterations, $MT_{\mathcal{P}}^m = MT_{\mathcal{P}}^{m-1}$.

Corollary 13. *Let $\mathcal{P}$ be an extended modal program. There exists an ensemble of neural networks $\mathcal{N}$ with semilinear neurons such that, if $\mathcal{P}$ is well behaved, the computation of $\mathcal{P}$ by $\mathcal{N}$ terminates. The set $\bigcup name(x) \subseteq B_{\mathcal{P}}$ of input and output neurons x in $\mathcal{N}$ for which $valuation(Act(x)) = 1$ will denote $MT_{\mathcal{P}}^m$.*

5.3 Case Study: The Muddy Children Puzzle

In this section, we apply CML to the muddy children puzzle, a classic example of reasoning in multiagent environments. In contrast to the also well-known wise men puzzle [87, 143], in which the reasoning process is sequential, here it is clear that a distributed (simultaneous) reasoning process occurs, as follows. There is a group of n children playing in a garden. A certain number of children k ($k \le n$) have mud on their faces. Each child can see if the others are muddy, but cannot see if they themselves are muddy. Consider the following situation.[10]

A caretaker announces that at least one child is muddy ($k \ge 1$) and asks 'do you know if you have mud on your face?' To help in the understanding of the puzzle, let us consider the cases where $k = 1$, $k = 2$, and $k = 3$.

---

[10] We follow the description of the muddy children puzzle presented in [87]. We must also assume that all the agents involved in the situation are truthful and intelligent.

If $k = 1$ (only one child is muddy), the muddy child answers *yes* in the first instance, since she cannot see any other muddy child. (For convenience, we assume that all of the children are female here.) All the other children answer *no* in the first instance.

If $k = 2$, suppose children 1 and 2 are muddy. In the first instance, all children can only answer *no*. This allows 1 to reason as follows: 'If 2 had said *yes* the first time round, she would have been the only muddy child. Since 2 said *no*, she must be seeing someone else muddy, and since I cannot see anyone else muddy apart from 2, I myself must be muddy!' Child 2 can reason analogously, and also answers *yes* the second time round.

If $k = 3$, suppose children 1, 2, and 3 are muddy. Each child can only answer *no* in the first two rounds. Again, this allows 1 to reason as follows: 'If 2 or 3 had said *yes* in the second round, they would have been the only two muddy children. Thus, there must be a third person with mud. Since I can see only 2 and 3 with mud, this third person must be me!' Children 2 and 3 can reason analogously to conclude as well that *yes*, they are muddy.

The above cases clearly illustrate the need to distinguish between an agent's individual knowledge and *common knowledge* about the world in a particular situation. For example, when $k = 2$, after everybody has said *no* in the first round, it becomes common knowledge that at least two children are muddy. Similarly, when $k = 3$, after everybody has said *no* twice, it becomes common knowledge that at least three children are muddy, and so on. In other words, when it is common knowledge that there are at least $k - 1$ muddy children, after the announcement that nobody knows if they are muddy or not, it then becomes common knowledge that there are at least k muddy children, for if there were $k - 1$ muddy children all of them would have known that they had mud on their faces. Notice that this reasoning process can only start once it is common knowledge that at least one child is muddy, as announced by the caretaker.[11]

5.3.1 Distributed Knowledge Representation in CML

Let us now formalise the muddy children puzzle in our CML framework. Typically, the way to represent the knowledge of a particular agent is to express the idea that an agent knows a fact α if the agent considers/thinks that α is true in every world the agent sees as possible. In such a formalisation, a modality $\mathbf{K}_j$ that represents the

---

[11] The question of how to represent common knowledge in neural networks is an interesting one. In this book, we do this implicitly – as will become clearer in what follows – by connecting neurons appropriately as the reasoning progresses (for example, as we find out in round two that at least two children should be muddy). The representation of common knowledge explicitly at the object level would require the use of neurons that are activated when 'everybody knows' something (serving to implement in a finite domain the common-knowledge axioms of [87]), but this would complicate the formalisation of the puzzle given in this chapter. This explicit form of representation and its ramifications are worth investigating, though, and should be treated in their own right in future work.

knowledge of an agent j is used analogously to the modality $\square$ defined in Sect. 5.1. In addition, we use p_i to denote that proposition p is *true* for agent i, so that $\mathbf{K}_j p_i$ means that agent j knows that p is *true* for agent i. We shall omit the subscript j of $\mathbf{K}$ whenever this is clear from the context. We use p_i to say that child i is muddy, and q_k to say that at least k children are muddy ($k \leq n$). Let us consider the case in which three children are playing in the garden ($n = 3$). Clause r_1^1 below states that when child 1 knows that at least one child is muddy and that neither child 2 nor child 3 is muddy, then child 1 knows that she herself is muddy. Similarly, clause r_2^1 states that if child 1 knows that there are at least two muddy children and she knows that child 2 is not muddy, then she must also be able to know that she herself is muddy, and so on. The clauses for children 2 and 3 are interpreted analogously.

Clauses for agent (child) 1:

r_1^1: $\mathbf{K}_1 q_1 \wedge \mathbf{K}_1 \neg p_2 \wedge \mathbf{K}_1 \neg p_3 \rightarrow \mathbf{K}_1 p_1$
r_2^1: $\mathbf{K}_1 q_2 \wedge \mathbf{K}_1 \neg p_2 \rightarrow \mathbf{K}_1 p_1$
r_3^1: $\mathbf{K}_1 q_2 \wedge \mathbf{K}_1 \neg p_3 \rightarrow \mathbf{K}_1 p_1$
r_4^1: $\mathbf{K}_1 q_3 \rightarrow \mathbf{K}_1 p_1$

Clauses for agent (child) 2:

r_1^2: $\mathbf{K}_2 q_1 \wedge \mathbf{K}_2 \neg p_1 \wedge \mathbf{K}_2 \neg p_3 \rightarrow \mathbf{K}_2 p_2$
r_2^2: $\mathbf{K}_2 q_2 \wedge \mathbf{K}_2 \neg p_1 \rightarrow \mathbf{K}_2 p_2$
r_3^2: $\mathbf{K}_2 q_2 \wedge \mathbf{K}_2 \neg p_3 \rightarrow \mathbf{K}_2 p_2$
r_4^2: $\mathbf{K}_2 q_3 \rightarrow \mathbf{K}_2 p_2$

Clauses for agent (child) 3:

r_1^3: $\mathbf{K}_3 q_1 \wedge \mathbf{K}_3 \neg p_1 \wedge \mathbf{K}_3 \neg p_2 \rightarrow \mathbf{K}_3 p_3$
r_2^3: $\mathbf{K}_3 q_2 \wedge \mathbf{K}_3 \neg p_1 \rightarrow \mathbf{K}_3 p_3$
r_3^3: $\mathbf{K}_3 q_2 \wedge \mathbf{K}_3 \neg p_2 \rightarrow \mathbf{K}_3 p_3$
r_4^3: $\mathbf{K}_3 q_3 \rightarrow \mathbf{K}_3 p_3$

Each set of clauses r_m^l ($1 \leq l \leq n$, $m \in \mathbb{N}$) was implemented in a CILP network. Figure 5.4 shows the implementation of clauses r_1^1 to r_4^1 (for agent 1).[12] In addition, it contains p_1 and $\mathbf{K} q_1$, $\mathbf{K} q_2$, and $\mathbf{K} q_3$, all represented as facts.[13] This is indicated by the grey highlighting in Fig. 5.4. This setting complies with the presentation of the puzzle given in [143], in which *snapshots* of the evolution of knowledge from round to round are taken in order to logically deduce the solution of the problem without the addition of a time variable. Here, p_1 and $\mathbf{K} q_k$ ($1 \leq k \leq 3$) are obtained from the network's input, which denotes a snapshot in the computation (i.e. a particular round), whereas $\mathbf{K} \neg p_2$ and $\mathbf{K} \neg p_3$ are obtained from the other networks in the ensemble (representing agents 2 and 3, respectively, whenever agent 1 does not see mud on their foreheads). A complete solution to the puzzle would require the replication of the ensemble presented here for all time points according to the various

---

[12] Note that $\mathbf{K} p_i$ and $\mathbf{K} \neg p_i$ should be represented by two different input neurons [62]. Negative weights in the network then allow one to differentiate between $\mathbf{K} p_i$ and $\sim \mathbf{K} p_i$, and between $\mathbf{K} \neg p_i$ and $\sim \mathbf{K} \neg p_i$, respectively. This can easily be verified by renaming $\mathbf{K} \neg p_i$ as a new literal $\mathbf{K} p_i'$.

[13] Note the difference between p_1 (child 1 is muddy) and $\mathbf{K} p_1$ (child 1 knows she is muddy).

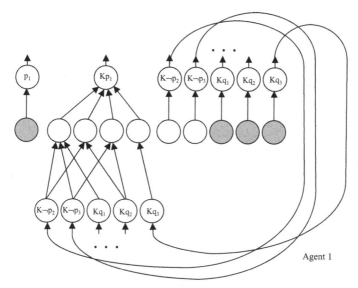

Fig. 5.4 Implementation of the rules $\{r_1^1, \ldots, r_4^1\}$

rounds of computation. This would produce a two-dimensional network ensemble, where in one dimension we have *agents* (as depicted here) and in the other we have *time*, so that we can represent the evolution of the agents' knowledge across the time points explicitly [70]. We shall consider the full version of the puzzle with a time variable in Chap. 6.

Figure 5.5 illustrates the interaction between three agents in the muddy children puzzle. The arrows connecting CILP networks implement the fact that when a child is muddy, the other children can see her. For the sake of clarity, the clauses r_m^1, corresponding to the neuron $\mathbf{K}_1 p_1$, are shown only in Fig. 5.4. The clauses r_m^2 and r_m^3 for $\mathbf{K}_2 p_2$ and $\mathbf{K}_3 p_3$ would be represented analogously in similar CILP networks. This is indicated in Fig. 5.5 by neurons highlighted in black. In addition, Fig. 5.5 shows only positive information about the problem. Recall that negative information such as $\neg p_1$, $\mathbf{K} \neg p_1$, and $\mathbf{K} \neg p_2$ is to be added explicitly to the network, as shown in Fig. 5.4.

5.3.2 Learning in CML

As discussed in the introduction to this chapter, one of our objectives when developing neural-symbolic learning systems is to retain good learning capability while seeking to develop systems that can deal with more expressive languages such as modal logic.

In the work described in this section, we used the Connectionist Modal Algorithm given in Sect. 5.2.1 to perform a translation from the modal background knowledge

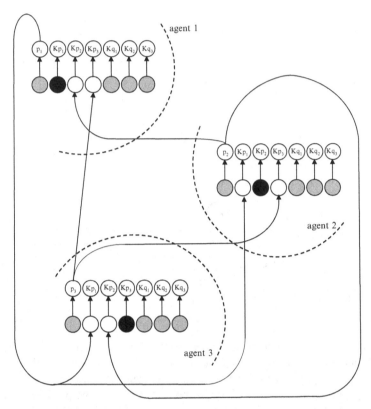

Fig. 5.5 Interaction between agents in the muddy children puzzle

to the initial architecture of the ensemble. We then used standard backpropagation to train each network of the ensemble with examples.[14] Our aim was to verify whether a particular agent i can learn from examples whether she is muddy or not, i.e. learn clauses r_1^i to r_4^i above.

We performed two sets of experiments using the muddy children puzzle in order to compare learning with background knowledge and without background knowledge. In the first set of experiments, we created networks with random weights, to which we then presented a number of training examples. In the second set of experiments, we inserted a clause $r_1^i : \mathbf{K}_1 q_1 \wedge \mathbf{K}_1 \neg p_2 \wedge \mathbf{K}_1 \neg p_3 \rightarrow \mathbf{K}_1 p_1$ as background knowledge before training the networks with examples.[15] Each training example stated whether agent i was muddy or not, according to the truth values of literals $\mathbf{K}_i q_1, \mathbf{K}_i q_2, \mathbf{K}_i q_3, \mathbf{K}_i p_1, \mathbf{K}_i \neg p_1, \mathbf{K}_i p_2, \mathbf{K}_i \neg p_2, \mathbf{K}_i p_3, \mathbf{K}_i \neg p_3$ (represented as input neurons).

---

[14] Recall that each network in the ensemble is a CILP network and, therefore, can be trained with examples using standard backpropagation.

[15] Note that the rule r_1^i works as a base rule for induction in the muddy children puzzle.

We evaluated the networks using cross-validation (see Sect. 3.4 for a definition). In both experiments, we used eightfold cross-validation over a set of 32 examples. In addition, we used a learning rate $\eta = 0.2$, a term of momentum $\xi = 0.1$, $h(x) = 2/1 + e^{-\beta x} - 1$ as the activation function, and bipolar inputs in $\{-1, 1\}$.

The training sets were presented to the networks for $10\,000$ epochs and the weights were updated, as usual, after every epoch. For each experiment, this resulted in eight networks being trained with 28 examples, with four examples reserved for testing. All 16 networks reached a training-set error $Err(\mathbf{W})$ (according to Equation 3.3) smaller than 0.01 before $10\,000$ epochs had elapsed. In other words, all the networks were trained successfully. Recall that learning takes place locally in each network. The connections between networks in the ensemble are defined by the rules of natural deduction for modalities presented in Sect. 5.1 and are fixed.

As for the networks' *generalisation* performance, the results corroborated the importance of exploiting any available background knowledge (assuming that the background knowledge is correct, of course). In the first experiment, in which the connectionist modal system was trained with no background knowledge, the networks presented an average test set accuracy of 84.37%. In the second experiment, in which the clause r_1^i was added to the networks prior to training, an average test set accuracy of 93.75% was obtained under exactly the same training conditions.

5.4 Discussion

In this chapter, we have presented connectionist modal logics (CML), a connectionist computational model for modal logic. We have introduced algorithms which translate extended modal programs into ensembles of neural networks [66, 80], and proved that these ensembles compute fixed-point semantics of the programs. The computations always terminate when the program is well behaved, and thus the network ensembles can be used as a distributed computational model for modal logic. In addition, the ensembles can learn possible-world representations from examples by using standard learning algorithms such as backpropagation. Finally, we have applied the CML system to the muddy children puzzle, a well-known benchmark for distributed knowledge representation. We have both set up and trained networks to reason about this puzzle.

CML opens up a new area of research in which modal reasoning can be represented and learned using artificial neural networks. There are several avenues of research to be pursued as a result. For instance, an important aspect of neural-symbolic learning systems – not dealt with in this chapter – is *rule extraction* from neural-network ensembles [65, 273]. In the case of CML, rule extraction methods would need to consider a more expressive knowledge representation language. Since we have shown that modalities can be represented by network ensembles, one should expect, when extracting rules from a given trained ensemble, that rules with modalities will offer a better representation formalism for the ensemble, in terms of either rule comprehensibility or rule expressiveness.

Extensions of CML include the study of how to represent other modal logics such as temporal logic (as shown in Chap. 6), and other nonclassical logics such as dynamic logic [124] and conditional logics of normality [41], as well as inference and learning of (fragments of) first-order modal logic [15]. The addition of a time variable to the approach presented here allows the representation of knowledge evolution. This can be implemented using labelled transitions from one knowledge state to the next, with a linear time flow, where each time point is associated with a state of knowledge, i.e. a network ensemble. This point is made clear in Chap. 6.

One could also think of the system presented here as a first step towards a model construction algorithm, which in turn would allow investigations into model checking of distributed reasoning systems in a connectionist setting. Alternatively, CML can be seen as a starting point towards the construction of a connectionist theorem prover for modal logic, which can be implemented in hardware as a neural network. In summary, we believe that CML contributes to addressing the need for integrated distributed knowledge representation, computation, and learning mechanisms in artificial intelligence, computing, and cognitive science.

Chapter 6
Connectionist Temporal Reasoning

In this chapter, following the formalisation of connectionist modal logics (CML) presented in Chap. 5, we show that temporal and epistemic logics can be effectively represented in and combined with artificial neural networks, by means of temporal and epistemic logic programming. This is done by providing a translation algorithm from temporal-logic theories to the initial architecture of a neural network. A theorem then shows that the given temporal theory and the network are equivalent in the usual sense that the network computes a fixed-point semantics of the theory. We then describe a validation of the *Connectionist Temporal Logic of Knowledge* (CTLK) system by applying it to a distributed time and knowledge representation problem, the full version of the *muddy children puzzle* [87]. We also describe experiments on learning in the muddy children puzzle, showing how knowledge evolution can be analysed and understood in a learning model.

As an extension of CML that includes temporal operators, CTLK provides a combined (multimodal) connectionist system of knowledge and time. This allows the modelling of evolving situations such as changing environments or possible worlds, and the construction of a connectionist model for reasoning about the temporal evolution of knowledge. These temporal-logic features, combined with the computational power of neural networks, leads towards a rich neural-symbolic learning system, where various forms of nonclassical reasoning are naturally represented, derived, and learned. Hence, the approach presented here extends the representation power of artificial neural networks beyond the classical level, by dealing with temporal and epistemic logics.

This chapter is organised as follows. In Sect. 6.1, we recall some useful preliminary concepts related to temporal reasoning, present the CTLK system (and introduce the *Temporal Algorithm*, which translates temporal-logic programs into artificial neural networks), and prove that the translation is correct. In Sect. 6.2, we describe the use of CML and CTLK to tackle the muddy children puzzle, and compare the solutions provided by each system. In Sect. 6.3, we conclude and discuss directions for future work.

A.S. d'Avila Garcez et al., *Neural-Symbolic Cognitive Reasoning,* Cognitive Technologies,
© Springer-Verlag Berlin Heidelberg 2009

6.1 Connectionist Temporal Logic of Knowledge

Temporal logic and its combination with other modalities such as knowledge and belief operators have been the subject of intensive investigation [87, 106, 129]. Temporal logic has evolved from philosophical logic to become one of the main logical systems used in computer science and artificial intelligence [87, 89, 103, 207]. It has been shown to be a powerful formalism for the modelling, analysis, verification, and specification of distributed systems [32, 33, 87, 123, 157]. Further, in logic programming, several approaches to dealing with temporal reasoning have been developed, leading to application in databases, knowledge representation, and the specification of systems (see e.g. [88, 197, 199]).

In this chapter, we show how temporal-logic programs can be expressed in a connectionist setting in conjunction with a *knowledge* operator. We do so by extending CML into the *connectionist temporal logic of knowledge* (CTLK), which allows the specification of the evolution of knowledge through time in network ensembles. In what follows, we present a *temporal algorithm*, which translates temporal programs into neural networks, and a theorem showing that the temporal theory and the network ensemble are equivalent, and therefore that the translation is correct. Let us start by presenting a simple example.

Example 10. (**Next-Time Operator**) One of the typical axioms of the temporal logics of knowledge is $K_i \bigcirc \alpha \rightarrow \bigcirc K_i \alpha$ [123], where $\bigcirc$ denotes the next-time (tomorrow) temporal operator. This means that what an agent i knows today (K_i) about tomorrow ($\bigcirc \alpha$), he or she still knows tomorrow ($\bigcirc K_i \alpha$). In other words, this axiom states that an agent does not forget what he or she knew. This can be represented in an ensemble of *CILP* networks with the use of a network that represents the agent's knowledge today, a network that represents the agent's knowledge tomorrow, and the appropriate connections between the networks. Clearly, an output neuron $K \bigcirc \alpha$ of a network that represents agent i at time t needs to be connected to an output neuron $K \alpha$ of a network that represents agent i at time $t + 1$ in such a way that, whenever $K \bigcirc \alpha$ is activated, $K \alpha$ is also activated. This is illustrated in Fig. 6.1, where the black circle denotes a neuron that is always activated, and the activation value of output neuron $K \bigcirc \alpha$ is propagated to output neuron $K \alpha$.

Generally speaking, the idea behind a connectionist temporal logic is to have (instead of a single ensemble) a number n of ensembles, each representing the knowledge held by a number of agents at a given time point. Figure 6.2 illustrates how this dynamic feature can be combined with the symbolic features of the knowledge represented in each network, allowing not only analysis of the current state (the current possible world or time point), but also analysis of how knowledge changes with time.

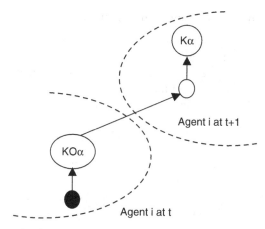

Fig. 6.1 Simple example of connectionist temporal reasoning

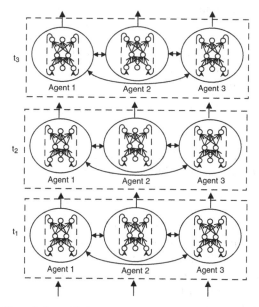

Fig. 6.2 Evolution of knowledge with time

6.1.1 The Language of CTLK

In order to reason over time and represent knowledge evolution, we have combined temporal logic programming [197] and the knowledge operator K_i into the Connectionist Temporal Logic of Knowledge. The implementation of K_i is analogous to that of $\Box$; we treat K_i as a universal modality, as done in [87]. This will become clearer when we apply a temporal operator and K_i to the muddy children puzzle in Sect. 6.2.

Definition 33 (Connectionist Temporal Logic). The language of CTLK contains:

1. A set $\{p, q, r, \ldots\}$ of primitive propositions.
2. A set of agents $\mathcal{A} = \{1, \ldots, n\}$.
3. A set of connectives K_i ($i \in \mathcal{A}$), where $K_i p$ reads 'agent i knows p.'
4. The temporal operator $\bigcirc$ (next time).
5. A set of extended modal-logic clauses of the form $t : ML_1, \ldots, ML_n \to ML_{n+1}$, where t is a label representing a discrete time point at which the associated clause holds, $M \in \{\Box, \Diamond\}$, and L_j ($1 \le j \le n+1$) is a literal.

We consider the case of a linear flow of time. As a result, the semantics of CTLK requires that we build models in which possible states form a linear temporal relationship. Moreover, with each time point, we associate the set of formulas holding at that point by use of a valuation map. The definitions are as follows.

Definition 34 (Timeline). A timeline T is a sequence of ordered points, each corresponding to a natural number.

Definition 35 (Temporal Model). A model M is a tuple $M = (T, R_1, \ldots, R_n, \pi)$, where (i) T is a (linear) timeline; (ii) R_i ($i \in \mathcal{A}$) is an agent's accessibility relation over T, and (iii) $\pi : T \mapsto \varphi$ is a map associating a set $\pi(p)$ of time points in T with each propositional variable of *CTLK*.

The truth conditions for CTLK's *well-formed formulas* are then defined by the following satisfiability relation.

Definition 36 (Satisfiability of Temporal Formulas). Let $M = \langle T, R_i, \pi \rangle$ be a temporal model for *CTLK*. The satisfiability relation $\models$ is uniquely defined as follows:

   (i) $(M, t) \models p$ iff $t \in \pi(p)$;
   (ii) $(M, t) \models \neg \alpha$ iff $(M, t) \not\models \alpha$;
   (iii) $(M, t) \models \alpha \wedge \beta$ iff $(M, t) \models \alpha$ and $(M, t) \models \beta$;
   (iv) $(M, t) \models \alpha \vee \beta$ iff $(M, t) \models \alpha$ or $(M, t) \models \beta$;
   (v) $(M, t) \models \alpha \to \beta$ iff $(M, t) \not\models \alpha$ or $(M, t) \models \beta$;
   (vi) $(M, t) \models \Box \alpha$ iff for all $u \in T$, if $R(t, u)$ then $(M, u) \models \alpha$;
   (vii) $(M, t) \models \Diamond \alpha$ iff there exists a u such that $R(t, u)$ and $(M, u) \models \alpha$;
   (viii) $(M, t) \models \bigcirc \alpha$ iff $(M, t+1) \models \alpha$;
   (ix) $(M, t) \models K_i \alpha$ iff for all $u \in T$, if $R_i(t, u)$, then $(M, u) \models \alpha$.

Since every clause is labelled by a time point t ranging from 1 to n, if $\bigcirc A$ holds at time point n our timeline will have $n+1$ time points; otherwise, it will contain n time points. Some results provided by [44, 88, 198, 199] for temporal extensions of logic programming apply directly to CTLK. The following definitions are needed to express the computation of CTLK in neural networks.

Definition 37 (Temporal Clause). A clause of the form $t : \bigcirc L_1, \ldots, \bigcirc L_o \to \bigcirc L_{o+1}$ is called a CTLK temporal clause, which holds at time point t, where L_j ($1 \le j \le o+1$) is either a literal, a modal literal, or of the form $K_i L_j$ ($i \in \mathcal{A}$).

Definition 38 (Temporal Immediate-Consequence Operator $\bigcirc T_\mathbf{P}$). Let $\mathcal{P} = \{\mathcal{P}_1, \ldots, \mathcal{P}_k\}$ be a CTLK temporal-logic program (i.e. a finite set of CTLK temporal clauses). The mapping $\bigcirc T_{\mathcal{P}_i} : 2^{B_\mathcal{P}} \to 2^{B_\mathcal{P}}$ at time point t_i ($1 \le i \le k$) is defined as follows: $\bigcirc T_{\mathcal{P}_i}(I) = \{L \in B_\mathcal{P} \mid$ either (i) or (ii) or (iii) below holds$\}$. (i) There exists a clause $t_{i-1} : L_1, \ldots, L_m \to \bigcirc L$ in $\mathcal{P}_{i-1}$, and $\{L_1, \ldots, L_m\}$ is satisfied by an interpretation J for $\mathcal{P}_{i-1}$;[1] (ii) L is qualified by $\bigcirc$, there exists a clause $t_{i+1} : L_1, \ldots, L_m \to L$ in $\mathcal{P}_{i+1}$, and $\{L_1, \ldots, L_m\}$ is satisfied by an interpretation J for $\mathcal{P}_{i+1}$; (iii) $L \in MT_{\mathcal{P}_i}(I)$.

A *global* temporal immediate-consequence operator can be defined as $\bigcirc T_\mathcal{P}$ $(I_1, \ldots, I_k) = \bigcup_{j=1}^{k} \{\bigcirc T_{\mathcal{P}_j}\}$.

6.1.2 The CTLK Algorithm

In this section, we present an algorithm to translate temporal-logic programs into (two-dimensional) neural-network ensembles. We consider temporal clauses and make use of CML's Connectionist Modal Algorithm and CILP's Translation Algorithm. The Temporal Algorithm is concerned with how to represent the next-time connective $\bigcirc$ and the knowledge operator K, which may appear in clauses of the form $t_i : \bigcirc K_a L_1, \ldots, \bigcirc K_b L_o \to \bigcirc K_c L_{o+1}$, where $a, b, c, \ldots,$ are agents and $1 \le i \le n$. In such clauses, we extend a normal clause of the form $L_1, \ldots, L_o \to L_{o+1}$ to allow the quantification of each literal with a *knowledge* operator indexed by different agents $\{a, b, c, \ldots\}$ varying from 1 to m. We also label the clause with a time point t_i on our time scale, varying from 1 to n, and we allow the use of the next-time operator on the left-hand side of the knowledge operator.[2] For example, the clause $t_1 : K_j \alpha \wedge K_k \beta \to \bigcirc K_j \gamma$ states that if agent j knows α and agent k knows β at time t_1, then agent j knows γ at time t_2. The CTLK algorithm is presented below, where $\mathcal{N}_{k,t}$ denotes a CILP neural network for agent k at time t.

Let q denote the number of clauses occurring in $\mathcal{P}$. Let o_l denote the number of literals in the body of clause l. Let μ_l denote the number of clauses in $\mathcal{P}$ with the same consequent, for each clause l. Let $h(x) = 2/(1 + e^{-\beta x}) - 1$, where $\beta \in (0, 1)$.

As usual, let A_{min} be the minimum activation for a neuron to be considered 'active' (or *true*); $A_{min} \in (0, 1)$. Set $A_{min} > (MAX_\mathcal{P}(o_1, \ldots, o_q, \mu_1, \ldots, \mu_q) - 1)/(MAX_\mathcal{P}(o_1, \ldots, o_q, \mu_1, \ldots, \mu_q) + 1)$. Let W and $-W$ be the weights of connections associated with positive and negative literals, respectively. Set $W \ge (2/\beta) \cdot (\ln(1 + A_{min}) - \ln(1 - A_{min}))/(MAX_\mathcal{P}(o_1, \ldots, o_q, \mu_1, \ldots, \mu_q) \cdot (A_{min} - 1) + A_{min} + 1))$.

---

[1] Notice that this definition implements a *credulous* approach in which every agent is assumed to be truthful and, therefore, every agent believes not only what he or she knows about tomorrow, but also what he or she is told by other agents about tomorrow. A more *sceptical* approach could be implemented by restricting the derivation of $\bigcirc A$ to interpretations in $\mathcal{P}_i$ only.

[2] Recall that, according to Definition 36, if $\bigcirc A$ is true at time t, and t is the last time point n, the CTLK algorithm will create $n+1$ points, as described here.

Temporal Algorithm

For each time point t $(1 \leq t \leq n)$ in $\mathcal{P}$, and for each agent k $(1 \leq k \leq m)$ in $\mathcal{P}$, do:

1. For each clause l in $\mathcal{P}$ containing $\bigcirc K_k L_i$ in the body:

    (a) Create an output neuron $\bigcirc K_k L_i$ in $\mathcal{N}_{k,t}$ (if it does not exist yet).
    (b) Create an output neuron $K_k L_i$ in $\mathcal{N}_{k,t+1}$ (if it does not exist yet).
    (c) Define the thresholds of $\bigcirc K_k L_i$ and $K_k L_i$ as $\theta = (1 + A_{min}) \cdot (1 - \mu_l) \cdot W/2$.
    (d) Set $h(x)$ as the activation function of output neurons $\bigcirc K_k L_i$ and $K_k L_i$.
    (e) Add a hidden neuron $L^{\vee}$ to $\mathcal{N}_{k,t}$ and set the step function as the activation function of $L^{\vee}$.
    (f) Connect $K_k L_i$ in $\mathcal{N}_{k,t+1}$ to $L^{\vee}$ and set the connection weight to 1.
    (g) Set the threshold $\theta^{\vee}$ of $L^{\vee}$ such that $-m A_{min} < \theta^{\vee} < A_{min} - (m-1)$.[3]
    (h) Connect $L^{\vee}$ to $\bigcirc K_k L_i$ in $\mathcal{N}_{k,t}$ and set the connection weight to W^M such that $W^M > h^{-1}(A_{min}) + \mu_l W + \theta$.

2. For each clause in $\mathcal{P}$ containing $\bigcirc K_k L_i$ in the head:

    (a) Create an output neuron $\bigcirc K_k L_i$ in $\mathcal{N}_{k,t}$ (if it does not exist yet).
    (b) Create an output neuron $K_k L_i$ in $\mathcal{N}_{k,t+1}$ (if it does not exist yet).
    (c) Define the thresholds of $\bigcirc K_k L_i$ and $K_k L_i$ as $\theta = (1 + A_{min}) \cdot (1 - \mu_l) \cdot W/2$.
    (d) Set $h(x)$ as the activation function of $\bigcirc K_k L_i$ and $K_k L_i$.
    (e) Add a hidden neuron $L^{\bigcirc}$ to $\mathcal{N}_{k,t+1}$ and set the step function as the activation function of $L^{\bigcirc}$.
    (f) Connect $\bigcirc K_k L_i$ in $\mathcal{N}_{k,t}$ to $L^{\bigcirc}$ and set the connection weight to 1.
    (g) Set the threshold $\theta^{\bigcirc}$ of $L^{\bigcirc}$ such that $-1 < \theta^{\bigcirc} < A_{min}$.[4]
    (h) Connect $L^{\bigcirc}$ to $K_k L_i$ in $\mathcal{N}_{k,t+1}$ and set the connection weight to W^M such that $W^M > h^{-1}(A_{min}) + \mu_l W + \theta$.

3. Call CML's algorithm (Sect. 5.2.1).

Theorem 13 below shows that the network ensemble $\mathcal{N}$ obtained from the above Temporal Algorithm is equivalent to the original CTLK program $\mathcal{P}$ in the sense that $\mathcal{N}$ computes the *temporal immediate-consequence operator* $\bigcirc T_P$ of $\mathcal{P}$ (Definition 38). The theorem makes use of Theorems 8 (Chap. 4) and 12 (Chap. 5).

Theorem 13 (Correctness of CTLK). *For any* CTLK *program* $\mathcal{P}$, *there exists an ensemble of single-hidden-layer neural networks* $\mathcal{N}$ *such that* $\mathcal{N}$ *computes the temporal fixed-point operator* $\bigcirc T_{\mathcal{P}}$ *of* $\mathcal{P}$.

Proof. We need to show that $K_k L_i$ is active in $\mathcal{N}_{t+1}$ if and only if either (i) there exists a clause of $\mathcal{P}$ of the form $ML_1, \ldots, ML_o \rightarrow K_k L_i$ such that $ML_1, \ldots, ML_o$ are satisfied by an interpretation (input vector), or (ii) $\bigcirc K_k L_i$ is active in $\mathcal{N}_t$. Case (i) follows from Theorem 8. The proof of Case (ii) follows from Theorem 12, as the algorithm for $\bigcirc$ is a special case of the algorithm for $\Diamond$ in which a more careful selection of world (i.e. $t+1$) is made when applying the $\Diamond$ elimination rule. ∎

---

[3] A maximum number of m agents make use of $L^{\vee}$.
[4] A maximum number of one agent makes use of $L^{\bigcirc}$.

6.2 The Muddy Children Puzzle (Full Solution)

In this section, we describe the application of the CTLK system to the muddy children puzzle, a classic example of reasoning in multiagent environments (see Sect. 5.3 for a description). We also compare the CTLK solution with our previous (CML-based) solution, which uses snapshots of time instead of a time flow.

6.2.1 Temporal Knowledge Representation

The addition of a temporal variable to the muddy children puzzle allows one to reason about the knowledge acquired after each round. For example, assume as before that there are three muddy children playing in the garden. They all answer *no* when asked the first time if they know whether they are muddy or not. Moreover, as each muddy child can see the other children, they will reason as previously described, and answer *no* in the second round, reaching the correct conclusion at round three. This solution requires, at each round, that the CILP networks be expanded with the knowledge acquired from reasoning about what is seen and what is heard by each agent. This clearly requires each agent to reason about *time*. The snapshot solution should then be seen as representing the knowledge held by the agents at an arbitrary time t. The knowledge held by the agents at time $t+1$ would then be represented by another set of CILP networks appropriately connected to the original set of networks. Let us consider again the case in which $k=3$. There are alternative ways of modelling this, but one possible representation is as follows:

Temporal Rules for agent (child) 1:

$t_1 : \neg K_1 p_1 \wedge \neg K_2 p_2 \wedge \neg K_3 p_3 \rightarrow \bigcirc K_1 q_2$
$t_2 : \neg K_1 p_1 \wedge \neg K_2 p_2 \wedge \neg K_3 p_3 \rightarrow \bigcirc K_1 q_3$

Temporal Rules for agent (child) 2:

$t_1 : \neg K_1 p_1 \wedge \neg K_2 p_2 \wedge \neg K_3 p_3 \rightarrow \bigcirc K_2 q_2$
$t_2 : \neg K_1 p_1 \wedge \neg K_2 p_2 \wedge \neg K_3 p_3 \rightarrow \bigcirc K_2 q_3$

Temporal Rules for agent (child) 3:

$t_1 : \neg K_1 p_1 \wedge \neg K_2 p_2 \wedge \neg K_3 p_3 \rightarrow \bigcirc K_3 q_2$
$t_2 : \neg K_1 p_1 \wedge \neg K_2 p_2 \wedge \neg K_3 p_3 \rightarrow \bigcirc K_3 q_3$

In addition, the snapshot rules are still necessary here to assist each agent's reasoning at any particular time point. Finally, the interaction between the agents, as depicted in Fig. 5.5, is also necessary here to model the fact that each child will know that another child is muddy when they see each other, analogously to the $\Box$ modality. This can be represented as $t_i : p_1 \rightarrow K_2 p_1$ and $t_i : p_1 \rightarrow K_3 p_1$ for times $i = 1, 2, 3$, and analogously for p_2 and p_3. Together with $t_i : \neg p_2 \rightarrow K_1 \neg p_2$ and $t_i : \neg p_3 \rightarrow K_1 \neg p_3$, also for times $i = 1, 2, 3$, and analogously for K_2 and K_3, this completes the formalisation.

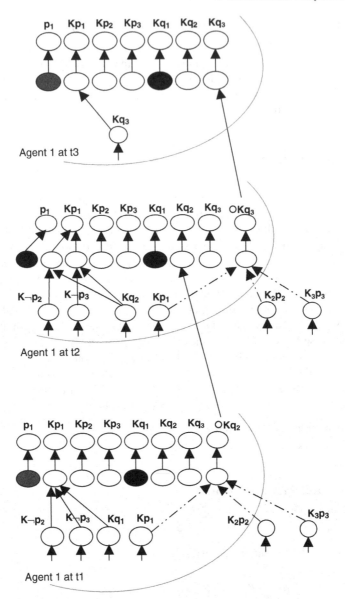

Fig. 6.3 The evolution in time of an agent's knowledge in the muddy children puzzle

The rules above, the temporal rules, and the snapshot rules for agent (child) 1 are described, following the Temporal Algorithm, in Fig. 6.3, where dotted lines indicate negative weights and solid lines indicate positive weights. The network of Fig. 6.3 provides a complete solution to the muddy children puzzle. It is worth noting that each network remains a simple single-hidden-layer neural network that can be trained with the use of standard backpropagation or some other off-the-shelf learning algorithm.

6.2.2 Learning in CTLK

The Temporal Algorithm introduced in this chapter allows one to perform theory and data learning in neural networks when the theory includes temporal knowledge.

In this section, we describe the use of the Temporal Algorithm and standard back-propagation to compare learning from data only and learning from theory and data with temporal background knowledge. Since we show that there is a relationship between temporal and epistemic logics and artificial-neural-network ensembles, we should also be able to learn epistemic and temporal knowledge in the ensemble (and, indeed, to perform knowledge extraction of revised temporal and epistemic rules after learning, but this is left as future work).

We trained two ensembles of CTLK neural networks to compute a solution to the muddy children puzzle. To one of them we added temporal and epistemic background knowledge in the form of a single rule, $t_1 : \neg K_1 p_1 \wedge \neg K_2 p_2 \wedge \neg K_3 p_3 \rightarrow \bigcirc K_1 q_2$, by applying the Temporal Algorithm. To the other, we did not add any rule. We then compared the average accuracies of the ensembles. We considered, in particular, the case in which agent 1 is to decide whether or not she is muddy at time t_2. Each training example expressed the knowledge held by agent 1 at t_2, according to the truth values of the atoms $K_1 \neg p_2$, $K_1 \neg p_3$, $K_1 q_1$, $K_1 q_2$, and $K_1 q_3$. As a result, we had 32 examples containing all possible combinations of truth values for input neurons $K_1 \neg p_2$, $K_1 \neg p_3$, $K_1 q_1$, $K_1 q_2$, and $K_1 q_3$, where an input value 1 indicates a truth value *true*, and an input -1 indicates a truth value *false*. For each example, we were concerned with whether or not agent 1 would know that she was muddy, that is, we were concerned with whether or not output neuron $K_1 p_1$ was active. For example, if the inputs ware *false* (input vector $[-1,-1,-1,-1,-1]$), then agent 1 should not know whether she was muddy ($K_1 p_1$ is *false*). If, however, $K_1 q_2$ was *true* and either $K_1 \neg p_2$ or $K_1 \neg p_3$ was *true*, then agent 1 should be able to recognise that she was indeed muddy ($K_1 p_1$ is *true*).

From the description of the muddy children puzzle, we know that at t_2, $K_1 q_2$ should be *true* (i.e. $K_1 q_2$ is a *fact*). This information can be derived from the temporal rule given as background knowledge above, but not from the training examples. Although the background knowledge can be changed by the training examples, it places a bias towards certain combinations (in this case, the examples in which $K_1 q_2$ is *true*), and this may produce better performance, typically when the background knowledge is correct. This effect has been observed, for instance, in [250] in experiments on DNA sequence analysis, in which background knowledge was expressed by *production rules*. The set of examples was noisy, and background knowledge counteracted the noise and reduced the chance of overfitting.

We evaluated the two CTLK ensembles using eightfold cross-validation, so that, at each time, four examples were left for testing. We used a learning rate $\eta = 0.2$, a term of momentum $\alpha = 0.1$, an activation function $h(x) = \tanh(x)$, and bipolar inputs in $\{-1, 1\}$. For each training task, the training set was presented to the network for 10 000 epochs. For both ensembles, the networks reached a training-set error smaller than 0.01 before 10 000 epochs had elapsed, i.e. the networks were trained successfully.

As for the networks' test set performance, the results corroborate the importance of exploiting any available background knowledge. For the first ensemble, in which the networks were trained with no background knowledge, an average test set accuracy of 81.25% was obtained. For the second ensemble, to which the temporal rule had been added, an average test set accuracy of 87.5% was obtained – a noticeable difference in performance, considering there was only a single rule in the background knowledge. In both cases, exactly the same training parameters were used.

The experiments above illustrate simply that the merging of temporal background knowledge and data learning may provide a system that is more effective than a purely connectionist system. The focus of this chapter has been on the reasoning capabilities of neural-symbolic systems. More extensive experiments to validate the system proposed here would be useful, and could be carried out in connection with knowledge extraction, and using applications containing continuous attributes.

6.3 Discussion

We have shown in Chap. 5 and the present chapter that temporal and modal logics provide neural-symbolic learning systems with the ability to make use of more expressive representation languages. In his seminal paper [253], Valiant argued for rich logic-based knowledge representation mechanisms in learning systems. The connectionist model proposed here addresses such a need, but still complies with important principles of connectionism such as massive parallelism and learning. A very important feature of our system is the temporal dimension, which can be combined with an epistemic dimension for knowledge/beliefs; this chapter has described how to integrate such dimensions into a neural-symbolic system. We have illustrated this by providing a full solution to the muddy children puzzle, where agents can reason about the evolution of knowledge in time. Further developments of the framework presented here, including an application in concurrent programming, can be found in [157].

Although a number of multimodal systems – for example systems combining knowledge and time [106, 123] and combining beliefs, desires, and intentions [219] – have been proposed for distributed knowledge representation and reasoning in multiagent systems, little attention has been paid to the integration of a learning component for knowledge acquisition. We seek to bridge this gap by allowing temporal knowledge representation to be integrated with a neural learning system. One could also think of the system presented here as a massively parallel distributed system where each ensemble (or set of ensembles) can be seen as a neural-symbolic processor. This would open up several interesting research avenues. For instance, one could investigate how to reason about protocols and actions in this neural-symbolic distributed system, or how to train the processors in order to learn how to preserve the security of such systems. The connectionist temporal and knowledge logic presented here allows the representation of a variety of properties, such as knowledge-based specifications, in the style of [87]. These specifications are frequently represented using temporal and modal logics, but without a learning feature, which comes naturally in CTLK.

Finally, since the models of the modal logic S4 can be used to model intuitionistic modal logic, we can propose a system that can combine reasoning about time with learning intuitionistic theories, as is shown in Chap. 7. This, per se, is an interesting result, as the proposed models can then be used to 'think' constructively, in the sense of Brouwer [106]. In summary, we believe that the connectionist temporal and epistemic computational model presented here opens up several interesting research avenues in the domain of neural-symbolic integration, allowing the distributed representation, computation, and learning of expressive knowledge representation formalisms.

Chapter 7
Connectionist Intuitionistic Reasoning

In this chapter, we present a computational model combining intuitionistic reasoning and neural networks. We make use of ensembles of neural networks to represent intuitionistic theories, and show that for each intuitionistic theory and intuitionistic modal theory, there exists a corresponding neural-network ensemble that computes a fixed-point semantics of the theory. This provides a massively parallel model for intuitionistic reasoning. As usual, the neural networks can be trained from examples to adapt to new situations using standard neural learning algorithms, thus providing a unifying foundation for intuitionistic reasoning, knowledge representation, and learning.

Intuitionistic logical systems have been advocated by many as providing adequate logical foundations for computation [5, 10, 55, 90, 150, 172, 206]. We argue, therefore, that intuitionism should also play an important part in neural computation. In this chapter, we follow the research path of Chaps. 5 and 6 to develop a neural-symbolic computational model for integrated reasoning about, representation of, and learning of intuitionistic knowledge. We concentrate on issues of reasoning and knowledge representation, which set the scene for connectionist intuitionistic learning, since effective knowledge representation precedes any learning algorithm. Nevertheless, we base the representation on standard, simple neural-network architectures, aiming at further developments in effective, experimental learning.

In order to compute intuitionistic knowledge in a connectionist framework, we set up ensembles of CILP networks (see Chap. 4) to compute a fixed-point semantics of intuitionistic programs (or intuitionistic modal programs). The networks are set up by a Connectionist Intuitionistic Algorithm or a Connectionist Intuitionistic Modal Algorithm, both introduced in this chapter. The proofs that the algorithms produce neural networks that compute the fixed-point semantics of their associated intuitionistic theories are then given. The networks can be trained from examples with the use of standard learning algorithms.

The chapter is organised as follows. In Sect. 7.1, we present the basic concepts of intuitionistic reasoning used throughout the chapter. In Sect. 7.2, we introduce the Connectionist Intuitionistic Algorithm, which translates intuitionistic theories into neural networks, and prove that these networks compute a fixed-point semantics

A.S. d'Avila Garcez et al., *Neural-Symbolic Cognitive Reasoning,* Cognitive Technologies,
© Springer-Verlag Berlin Heidelberg 2009

of the given intuitionistic theory (thus showing that the translation is correct). In Sect. 7.3, we introduce the Connectionist Intuitionistic Modal Algorithm, which translates intuitionistic modal theories into neural networks, and prove that these networks compute a fixed-point semantics of the given intuitionistic modal theory. Section 7.4 discusses directions for future work.

7.1 Intuitionistic Logic and Programs

Intuitionistic logic is considered by many authors to provide adequate logical foundations for computation [1, 10, 55, 90, 206, 236]. Intuitionistic logic was developed originally by Brouwer, and later by Heyting and Kolmogorov (see [258] for a historical account). In intuitionistic logic, a statement that there exists a proof of a proposition x is only made if there is a constructive method for the proof of x. One of the consequences of Brouwer's ideas is the rejection of the law of the excluded middle, namely $\alpha \vee \neg\alpha$, since one cannot always state that there is a proof of α or its negation, as accepted in classical logic and in (classical) mathematics. The development of these ideas and applications of them in mathematics have led to developments in *constructive* mathematics and have influenced several lines of research on logic and computing science [10, 172, 258].

An intuitionistic language $\mathcal{L}$ includes propositional letters (atoms) $p, q, r \ldots$, the connectives $\neg$, $\wedge$, and an intuitionistic implication $\Rightarrow$. Formulas are denoted by $\alpha, \beta, \gamma, \ldots$ We interpret this language using a Kripke-style semantics as in [28, 42, 106], which we define as follows.

Definition 39 (Kripke Models for Intuitionistic Propositional Logic). Let $\mathcal{L}$ be an intuitionistic language. A *model* for $\mathcal{L}$ is a tuple $\mathcal{M} = \langle \Omega, \mathcal{R}, v \rangle$ where Ω is a set of points, v is a mapping that assigns to each $\omega \in \Omega$ a subset of the atoms of $\mathcal{L}$, and $\mathcal{R}$ is a reflexive, transitive binary relation over Ω, such that:

1. $(\mathcal{M}, \omega) \models p$ iff $p \in v(\omega)$ (for atom p).
2. $(\mathcal{M}, \omega) \models \neg\alpha$ iff, for all ω' such that $\mathcal{R}(\omega, \omega')$, $(\mathcal{M}, \omega') \not\models \alpha$.
3. $(\mathcal{M}, \omega) \models \alpha \wedge \beta$ iff $(\mathcal{M}, \omega) \models \alpha$ and $(\mathcal{M}, \omega) \models \beta$.
4. $(\mathcal{M}, \omega) \models \alpha \Rightarrow \beta$ iff, for all ω' with $\mathcal{R}(\omega, \omega')$, we have $(\mathcal{M}, \omega') \models \beta$ whenever we have $(\mathcal{M}, \omega') \models \alpha$.

We now define *labelled intuitionistic programs* as sets of intuitionistic clauses where each clause is labelled by the point at which it holds, similarly to Gabbay's labelled deductive systems [42, 99].

Definition 40 (Labelled Intuitionistic Program). A labelled intuitionistic program is a finite set of clauses C of the form $\omega_i : A_1, \ldots, A_n \Rightarrow A_0$ (where ',' is an abbreviation for '$\wedge$', as usual), and a finite set of relations $\mathcal{R}$ between points ω_i ($1 \leq i \leq m$) in C, where the A_k ($0 \leq k \leq n$) are atoms and ω_i is a label representing a point at which the associated clause holds.

In what follows, we define a model-theoretic semantics for labelled intuitionistic programs. Throughout, we are concerned with propositional labelled intuitionistic programs, as defined above.

When computing the semantics of the program, we have to consider both the fixed point at a particular point where a clause holds and the fixed point of the program as a whole. When computing the fixed point at each point, we have to consider the consequences derived locally and the consequences derived from the interaction between points. Locally, fixed points are computed as in a fixed-point semantics for Horn clauses à la van Emden and Kowalski [163, 260]. When considering the interaction between points in a Kripke structure, one has to take into account the meaning of intuitionistic implication ⇒ in accordance with Definition 39. As for intuitionistic negation, we adopt the approach of [40, 116], as follows. We rename any negative literal ¬A as an atom A' not present originally in the language. This form of renaming, as used to represent *explicit negation*, [40] allows our definition of labelled intuitionistic programs above to consider atoms $A_0, A_1, \ldots, A_n$ only, with some of these atoms being negative literals renamed as above. For example, given $A_1, \ldots, A'_k, \ldots, A_n \Rightarrow A_0$, where A'_k is a renaming of ¬A_k, an interpretation that assigns *true* to A'_k represents that ¬A_k is *true*; it does not represent that A_k is *false*. The atom A'_k is called the *positive form* of the negative literal ¬A_k. Following Definition 39 (intuitionistic negation), A' will be true at a point ω_i if and only if A does not hold at every point ω_j such that $\mathcal{R}(\omega_i, \omega_j)$. Below, we define precisely the fixed-point semantics for labelled intuitionistic programs.

The renaming of negative literals described above allows us to make use of important results from distributed logic programming (reproduced below), and the fixed-point semantics of definite logic programs.[1] In order to define a fixed-point semantics for intuitionistic programs, we simply need to extend the definition of the consequence operator $T_\mathcal{P}$, which gives the semantics for definite programs [163], to cater for intuitionistic implication, as follows.

Definition 41 (Local Consequence Operator). Let $\mathcal{P} = \{\mathcal{P}_1, \ldots, \mathcal{P}_k\}$ be a labelled intuitionistic program, where $\mathcal{P}_i$ is a set of clauses that hold at a point ω_i $(1 \leq i \leq k)$. Let $B_\mathcal{P}$ denote the set of atoms occurring in $\mathcal{P}$, called the *Herbrand base* of $\mathcal{P}$. Let I be a *Herbrand interpretation* for $\mathcal{P}_i$. The mapping $IT_{\mathcal{P}_i} : 2^{B_\mathcal{P}} \to 2^{B_\mathcal{P}}$ in ω_i is defined as follows: $IT_{\mathcal{P}_i}(I) = \{A_0, A'_0 \in B_\mathcal{P} \mid A_1, \ldots, A_n \Rightarrow A_0$ is a clause in a program $\mathcal{P}_j$ such that $\mathcal{R}(\omega_i, \omega_j)$ and $\{A_1, \ldots, A_n\} \subseteq I$ or, in the case of A'_0, for all ω_j such that $\mathcal{R}(\omega_i, \omega_j)$, $A_0 \notin IT_{\mathcal{P}_i}(J)\}$, where $IT_{\mathcal{P}_j}(J)$ is defined as $IT_{\mathcal{P}_i}(I)$ and J is a Herbrand interpretation for $\mathcal{P}_j$.

Definition 42 (Global Consequence Operator). Let $\mathcal{P} = \{\mathcal{P}_1, \ldots, \mathcal{P}_k\}$ be a labelled intuitionistic program. Let $B_\mathcal{P}$ be the Herbrand base of $\mathcal{P}$ and let I_i be a Herbrand interpretation for $\mathcal{P}_i$ $(1 \leq i \leq k)$. The mapping $IT_\mathcal{P} : 2^{B_\mathcal{P}} \to 2^{B_\mathcal{P}}$ is defined as $IT_\mathcal{P}(I_1, \ldots, I_k) = \bigcup_{l=1}^{k} \{IT_{\mathcal{P}_l}\}$.

---

[1] Recall that a *definite logic program* is a finite set of clauses of the form $A_1, \ldots, A_n \to A_0$, where each A_i, $0 \leq i \leq n$, is an atom.

Theorem 15 below, regarding the fixed-point semantics of definite distributed logic programs, will be useful.

Definition 43 (Distributed Program [217]). Definite distributed logic programs are tuples $< \mathcal{P}_1, \ldots, \mathcal{P}_n >$, where each $\mathcal{P}_i$ is a set of Horn clauses (forming the program associated with a point i). Each $\mathcal{P}_i$ is called a *component program* of the *composite program*.

Theorem 15 (Fixed-Point Model of Distributed Program [217]). *For each definite distributed logic program $\mathcal{P}$, the function $T_{\mathcal{P}}$ has a unique fixed point. The sequence of all $T_{\mathcal{P}}^m(I_1, \ldots, I_k), m \in \mathbb{N}$, converges to this fixed point $T_{\mathcal{P}}^{\omega}(I_1, \ldots, I_k)$, for each $I_i \subseteq 2^{B_{\mathcal{P}}}$.*

Clearly, there is a correspondence between distributed programs and labelled programs in the sense that each $\mathcal{P}_i$ corresponds to a set of clauses labelled ω_i. Since we use renaming to deal with intuitionistic negation, we can construct the semantics of labelled intuitionistic programs by considering the semantics of definite distributed logic programs. As a result, Theorem 16 below follows directly from Theorem 15.

Theorem 16 (Fixed-Point Model of Labelled Intuitionistic Program). *For each labelled intuitionistic program P, the function $IT_{\mathcal{P}}$ has a unique fixed point. The sequence of all $IT_{\mathcal{P}}^m(I_1, \ldots, I_k), m \in \mathbb{N}$, converges to this fixed point $IT_{\mathcal{P}}^{\omega}(I_1, \ldots, I_k)$, for each $I_i \subseteq 2^{B_{\mathcal{P}}}$.*

7.2 Connectionist Intuitionistic Reasoning

In this section, we introduce the connectionist model for intuitionistic reasoning. We do so by translating the intuitionistic semantics presented above into an ensemble of CILP neural networks.

Owing to the simplicity of each CILP network, learning can be carried out in each possible world (i.e. each network) straightforwardly with the use of standard neural learning algorithms. The main problem we have to tackle is that of how to set up the connections that establish the necessary communication between networks (e.g. between ω_1 and ω_2 in Fig. 7.1). This will depend on the logic under consideration. In the case of modal logic, we connect the networks according to the possible-world semantics for the $\Box$ and $\Diamond$ modalities formally defined as (natural-deduction) reasoning rules in [42, 99]. In the case of intuitionistic logic, the way we connect the networks is different. Let us start by giving a simple example of how intuitionistic logic can be represented in this framework.

Example 11. **(Connectionist Intuitionistic Implication)** Consider the intuitionistic program $\mathcal{P} = \{\omega_1 : A \Rightarrow B, \mathcal{R}(\omega_1, \omega_2)\}$. Let $B_{\mathcal{P}} = \{A, B, C\}$. Figure 7.1 shows a network ensemble that implements $\mathcal{P}$. According to the semantics of the above intuitionistic implication, $\omega_1 : A \Rightarrow B$ and $\mathcal{R}(\omega_1, \omega_2)$ imply $\omega_2 : A \Rightarrow B$. This can be implemented by copying the neural representation of $A \Rightarrow B$ from ω_1 to ω_2. In

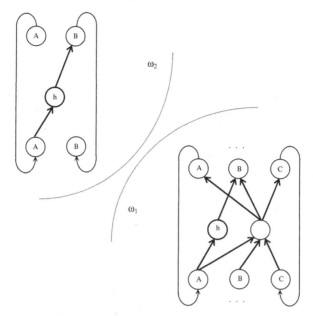

Fig. 7.1 Representing intuitionistic implication

Fig. 7.1, $A \Rightarrow B$ is implemented through the hidden neuron h such that output neuron B is active if input neuron A is active. We shall see exactly how this is done in Sect. 7.2.2.

Example 12. (**Connectionist Intuitionistic Negation**) In addition to intuitionistic implication, we need to implement the intuitionistic negation of Definition 39. Suppose $\mathcal{P} = \{\omega_1 : \neg A \Rightarrow B, \mathcal{R}(\omega_1, \omega_2), \mathcal{R}(\omega_1, \omega_3)\}$. We implement the implication as before. However, we must also make sure that $\neg A$ will be derived in ω_1 if A is not derived in ω_2 and ω_3. This can be implemented in the ensemble by connecting the occurrences of A in ω_2 and ω_3 to the neuron $\neg A$ in ω_1, as shown in Fig. 7.2, with the use of the hidden neuron n. The connections must be such that if A is not active in ω_2 and A is not active in ω_3, then $\neg A$ is active in ω_1. The activation of $\neg A$ in ω_1 should then trigger the activation of B in ω_1 (since $\neg A \Rightarrow B$) using the feedback connection from the output neuron $\neg A$ to the input neuron $\neg A$ in ω_1, and then also the connection from $\neg A$ to B (via the hidden neuron h) in ω_1. Note that, differently from the case of implication, the implementation of negation requires the use of negative weights (to account for the fact that the nonactivation of a neuron, for example A, needs to activate another neuron, in this case, $\neg A$). In Fig. 7.2, we have used dashed arrows to represent negative weights. Again, we shall see exactly how this is done in Sect. 7.2.2.

In what follows, we describe in detail how each network is built (Sect. 7.2.1), and then how the networks are connected to form an ensemble that represents labelled intuitionistic programs (Sect. 7.2.2).

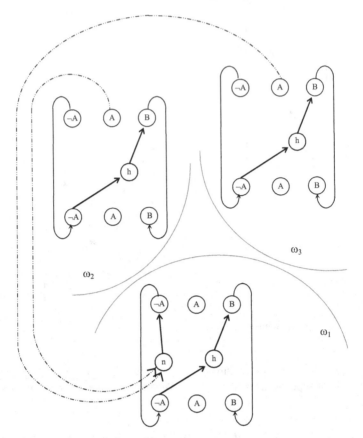

Fig. 7.2 Representing intuitionistic negation

7.2.1 Creating the Networks

To create the networks that are used to model each possible world, for example ω_1 in Fig. 7.1, we use the CILP system [66].

In this chapter, we do not need to use negation as failure. Instead, we use intuitionistic negation. To do so, we create a neuron (A) to represent positive literals, and another neuron $(\neg A)$ to represent negative literals. This is similar to the use of explicit negation in logic programming [116], where any negative literal $\neg A$ is renamed as a new positive literal A', not originally present in the language (see Sect. 2.5). As a result, we only need to worry about the part of CILP's Translation Algorithm that deals with definite programs (Chap. 4). In this case, the network will only contain positive weights W, since negative weights $-W$ are only used to implement negation as failure. CILP needs to exclude certain programs that might loop or have multiple stable states (as is well known from the semantics of negation as failure in logic programming). In this chapter, we do not need to worry about this problem, since we consider definite programs only. Then, to compensate for the lack of expressiveness of definite programs, we incorporate intuitionistic negation and modal reasoning into the model, aiming to strike a balance between expressiveness and tractability [264].

7.2.2 Connecting the Networks

Given a distributed (or labelled) definite program $\mathcal{P} = \langle \mathcal{P}_1, \dots, \mathcal{P}_n \rangle$, we apply the CILP translation algorithm n times to compute the neural counterpart of $\mathcal{P}$, resulting in an ensemble $\mathcal{N}_1, \dots, \mathcal{N}_n$ of CILP neural networks.

In the case of labelled intuitionistic programs, if $\mathcal{R}(\omega_i, \omega_j)$ and $\omega_i : A_1, \dots, A_k \Rightarrow A_0$, we need to add a clause of the form $A_1, \dots, A_k \Rightarrow A_0$ to $\mathcal{P}_i$ before we apply the Translation Algorithm. To do so, we say that $\{\omega_i : A_1, \dots, A_k \Rightarrow A_0, \mathcal{R}(\omega_i, \omega_j)\}$ can be written as $\{\omega_i : A_1, \dots, A_k \Rightarrow A_0, \omega_j : A_1, \dots, A_k \Rightarrow A_0\}$. In order to represent intuitionistic negation, once the network ensemble has been created, each network containing neurons labelled as $\neg A$ needs to be connected to each network containing neurons labelled as A (see Fig. 7.2). More precisely, whenever $\mathcal{R}(\omega_i, \omega_j)$, any output neuron A in $\mathcal{N}_j$ needs to be connected to the output neuron $\neg A$ in $\mathcal{N}_i$ through a new hidden neuron created in $\mathcal{N}_i$ such that if A is active in $\mathcal{N}_j$, then $\neg A$ is not active in $\mathcal{N}_i$. The algorithm below is responsible for implementing this. In the algorithm, we use an atom A' to represent $\neg A$, following the Gelfond and Lifschitz renaming of negative literals [116], as explained above.

Let $\mathcal{P} = \{\mathcal{P}_1, \dots, \mathcal{P}_n\}$ be a labelled intuitionistic program. As in the case of individual CILP networks, we start by calculating $MAX_{\mathcal{P}}(\overrightarrow{k}, \overrightarrow{\mu}, n)$ of $\mathcal{P}$ and A_{min} such that $A_{min} > (MAX_{\mathcal{P}}(\overrightarrow{k}, \overrightarrow{\mu}, n) - 1)/(MAX_{\mathcal{P}}(\overrightarrow{k}, \overrightarrow{\mu}, n) + 1)$, which now also considers the number n of networks (points) in the ensemble.

Connectionist Intuitionistic Algorithm

1. For each clause c_l of the form $A_1, \dots, A_k \Rightarrow A_0$ in $\mathcal{P}_i$ ($1 \le i \le n$) such that $\mathcal{R}(\omega_i, \omega_j) \in \mathcal{P}$, do:

   (a) add a clause $A_1, \dots, A_k \Rightarrow A_0$ to $\mathcal{P}_j$ ($1 \le j \le n$).

2. For each program $\mathcal{P}_i$ ($1 \le i \le n$) in $\mathcal{P}$, do:

   (a) Call CILP's Translation Algorithm.

3. For each atom of the form A' in a clause c_l of $\mathcal{P}_i$, do:

   (a) Add a hidden neuron $N_{A'}$ to $\mathcal{N}_i$.
   (b) Set the step function $s(x)$ as the activation function of $N_{A'}$.[2]

---

[2] Any hidden neuron created to encode negation should use the activation function $s(x) = y$, where $y = 1$ if $x > 0$, and $y = 0$ otherwise; $s(x)$ is known as the standard nonlinear activation function (also called the step function). This is so because these particular hidden neurons encode (metalevel)

(c) Set the threshold $\theta_{A'}$ of $N_{A'}$ such that $n - (1 + A_{min}) < \theta_{A'} < nA_{min}$.
(d) For each network $\mathcal{N}_j$ corresponding to the program $\mathcal{P}_j$ $(1 \leq j \leq n)$ in $\mathcal{P}$ such that $\mathcal{R}(\omega_i, \omega_j) \in \mathcal{P}$, do:
   i. Connect the output neuron A of $\mathcal{N}_j$ to the hidden neuron $N_{A'}$ of $\mathcal{N}_i$ and set the connection weight to -1.
   ii. Connect the hidden neuron $N_{A'}$ of $\mathcal{N}_i$ to the output neuron A' of $\mathcal{N}_i$ and set the connection weight to W^I such that $W^I > h^{-1}(A_{min}) + \mu_{A'}.W + \theta_{A'}$, where $\mu_{A'}$, W, and $\theta_{A'}$ are obtained from CILP's Translation Algorithm.[3]

Theorem 17 below shows that the translation from intuitionistic programs to CILP ensembles is correct. A corollary then guarantees that the ensemble converges to the least fixed point of the program.

Theorem 17 (Correctness of the Connectionist Intuitionistic Algorithm). *For each labelled intuitionistic program P, there exists an ensemble of neural networks $\mathcal{N}$ such that $\mathcal{N}$ computes the fixed-point operator $IT_{\mathcal{P}}$ of $\mathcal{P}$.*

Proof. We need to show that A' is active in $\mathcal{N}_i$ if and only if (i) there exists a clause of $\mathcal{P}_i$ of the form $A_1, \ldots, A_k \Rightarrow A'$ such that $A_1, \ldots, A_k$ are satisfied by an interpretation (input vector of $\mathcal{N}_i$) $\mathbf{i}$, or (ii) for all $\mathcal{P}_j \in \mathcal{P}$ such that $\mathcal{R}(\omega_i, \omega_j)$, there exists a clause of $\mathcal{P}_j$ of the form $A_1, \ldots, A_k \Rightarrow A$ such that A is not satisfied by an interpretation (input vector of $\mathcal{N}_j$) $\mathbf{j}$. Case (i) follows directly from Theorem 8. Case (ii) (if A is not active in any network $\mathcal{N}_j$ $(0 \leq j \leq n)$ to which $\mathcal{N}_i$ is related, A' is active in $\mathcal{N}_i$) is dealt with as follows. From the *Connectionist Intuitionistic Algorithm*, $N_{A'}$ is a nonlinear hidden neuron in $\mathcal{N}_i$. If A is not active ($A < -A_{min}$) in $\mathcal{N}_j$, the minimum input potential of $N_{A'}$ is $nA_{min} - \theta_{A'}$. Since $\theta_{A'} < nA_{min}$ (*Connectionist Intuitionistic Algorithm*, step 3c), the minimum input potential of $N_{A'}$ is greater than *zero* and, therefore, $N_{A'}$ presents an activation 1. As a result, the minimum activation of A' in $\mathcal{N}_i$ is $h(W^I - \mu_{A'}.W - \theta_{A'})$. Since $W^I > h^{-1}(A_{min}) + \mu_{A'}.W + \theta_{A'}$, we have $h(W^I - \mu_{A'}.W - \theta_{A'}) > A_{min}$ and, therefore, A' is active ($A' > A_{min}$). If A is active in some network $\mathcal{N}_j$ $(0 \leq j \leq n)$ to which $\mathcal{N}_i$ is related and, for all clauses of the form $A_1, \ldots, A_k \Rightarrow A'$ in $\mathcal{P}_i$, $A_1, \ldots, A_k$ are not satisfied by $\mathbf{i}$ (input vector of $\mathcal{N}_i$), then we need to show that A' is not active in $\mathcal{N}_i$. In the worst case, A is not active in $n-1$ networks with activation -1, and active in a single network with activation A_{min}. In this case, the input potential of $N_{A'}$ is $n - 1 - A_{min} - \theta_{A'}$ (recall that the weights to $N_{A'}$ are all set to -1). Since $\theta_{A'} > n - (1 + A_{min})$ (*Connectionist Intuitionistic Algorithm*, step 3c), the maximum input potential of $N_{A'}$ is *zero* and, since $s(x)$ is the activation function of $N_{A'}$, $N_{A'}$ presents an activation 0. From Theorem 8, if $A_1, \ldots, A_k$ are not satisfied by $\mathbf{i}$, then A' is not active. Finally, since the activation of $N_{A'}$ is *zero*, A' cannot be activated by $N_{A'}$, so A' is not active. ∎

---

knowledge about negation, while the other hidden neurons encode (object-level) knowledge about the problem. The former are not expected to be trained from examples and, as a result, the use of the step function simplifies the Connectionist Intuitionistic Algorithm. The latter are trained using backpropagation, and therefore require a differentiable, semilinear activation function instead.

[3] Recall that $\mu_{A'}$ is the number of connections to output neuron A'.

Corollary 18 (Connectionist Intuitionistic Fixed-Point Computation). *Let $\mathcal{P}$ be a labelled intuitionistic program. There exists an ensemble of recurrent neural networks $\mathcal{N}^r$ such that, starting from an arbitrary initial input, $\mathcal{N}^r$ converges to a stable state and yields the unique fixed point $(IT_{\mathcal{P}}^{\varnothing}(\mathbf{i}))$ of $IT_{\mathcal{P}}$.*

Proof. By Theorem 17, $\mathcal{N}$ computes $IT_{\mathcal{P}}$. Being recurrently connected, $\mathcal{N}^r$ computes the upward powers $(IT_{\mathcal{P}}^m(I))$ of $IT_{\mathcal{P}}$. Finally, by Theorem 16, $\mathcal{N}^r$ converges to the unique fixed point $(IT_{\mathcal{P}}^{\varnothing}(I))$ of $IT_{\mathcal{P}}$. ∎

The following example illustrates the computation of intuitionistic theories using neural-network ensembles.

Example 13. (**Connectionist Intuitionistic Fixed-Point Computation**) Consider again the ensemble of Fig. 7.2. For any initial set of input vectors (interpretations $\mathbf{i}$, $\mathbf{j}$, ...) to networks $\mathcal{N}_1$, $\mathcal{N}_2$, $\mathcal{N}_3$ (corresponding to points $\omega_1, \omega_2, \omega_3$), the output neuron A will not be activated in $\mathcal{N}_2$ or $\mathcal{N}_3$. As a result, the output neuron A' will eventually be activated (and remain activated) in $\mathcal{N}_1$. After that, a single step through $\mathcal{N}_1$'s recursive connection will activate the output neuron B. As a result, A' and B will belong to the stable state of $\mathcal{N}_1$ and, therefore, to the fixed point of $\mathcal{P}_1$.

7.3 Connectionist Intuitionistic Modal Reasoning

Intuitionistic modal logic allows the combination of the strengths of the model theory of modal logic and the proof theory of intuitionistic logic. This has led to a number of applications in computer science, including program analysis, formal specification and verification of computer systems, functional programming, type theory, and program refinement [5, 55, 203].

In what follows, we extend the language of labelled intuitionistic programs to allow the use of the *necessity* ($\Box$) and *possibility* ($\Diamond$) modal operators, as defined below.

Definition 44 (Labelled Intuitionistic Modal Program). A *modal atom* is of the form MA, where $M \in \{\Box, \Diamond\}$ and A is an atom. A labelled intuitionistic modal program is a finite set of clauses C of the form $\omega_i : MA_1, \ldots, MA_n \Rightarrow MA_0$, where the MA_k ($0 \leq k \leq n$) are modal atoms and ω_i is a label representing a point at which the associated clause holds, and a finite set of (accessibility) relations R between points ω_i ($1 \leq i \leq m$) in C.

The fixed-point operator for intuitionistic modal programs can now be defined as follows.

Definition 45 (Intuitionistic Modal Consequence Operator). Let $\mathcal{P} = \{\mathcal{P}_1,\ldots,\mathcal{P}_k\}$ be an intuitionistic modal program, where $\mathcal{P}_i$ is a set of modal intuitionistic clauses that hold at points ω_i ($1 \leq i \leq k$). Let $B_{\mathcal{P}}$ be the Herbrand base of $\mathcal{P}$ and let I be a Herbrand interpretation for $\mathcal{P}_i$. The mapping $I_M T_{\mathcal{P}_i} : 2^{B_{\mathcal{P}}} \to 2^{B_{\mathcal{P}}}$ in ω_i is defined as follows: $I_M T_{\mathcal{P}_i}(I) = \{MA_0, MA_0' \in B_{\mathcal{P}} \mid$ either (i), (ii), (iii), (iv), or (v) holds$\}$, where:

   (i) $MA_1,\ldots,MA_n \Rightarrow MA_0$ is a clause in $\mathcal{P}_i$ and $\{MA_1,\ldots,MA_n\} \subseteq I$ or, in the case of MA_0', for all ω_j such that $\mathcal{R}(\omega_i,\omega_j)$, $A_0 \notin I_M T_{\mathcal{P}_j}(J)$, where $I_M T_{\mathcal{P}_j}(J)$ is defined as $I_M T_{\mathcal{P}_i}(I)$ and J is a Herbrand interpretation for program $\mathcal{P}_j$;[4]

  (ii) MA_0 is of the form $\omega_i : A_0$, ω_i is a particular possible world uniquely associated with A_0, and there exists a world ω_k such that $\mathcal{R}(\omega_k,\omega_i)$, and $\omega_k : MA_1,\ldots,MA_n \to \Diamond A_0$ is a clause in $\mathcal{P}_k$, and $\{MA_1,\ldots,MA_n\} \subseteq K$, where K is a Herbrand interpretation for $\mathcal{P}_k$;

 (iii) MA_0 is of the form $\Diamond A_0$ and there exists a world ω_j such that $\mathcal{R}(\omega_i,\omega_j)$, and $\omega_j : MA_1,\ldots,MA_n \to A_0$ is a clause in $\mathcal{P}_j$, and $\{MA_1,\ldots,MA_n\} \subseteq J$, where J is a Herbrand interpretation for $\mathcal{P}_j$;

 (iv) MA_0 is of the form $\Box A_0$ and, for each world ω_j such that $\mathcal{R}(\omega_i,\omega_j)$, $\omega_j : MA_1,\ldots,MA_n \to A_0$ is a clause in $\mathcal{P}_j$, and $\{MA_1,\ldots,MA_n\} \subseteq J$, where J is a Herbrand interpretation for $\mathcal{P}_j$;

  (v) MA_0 is of the form $\omega_i : A_0$ and there exists a world ω_k such that $\mathcal{R}(\omega_k,\omega_i)$, and $\omega_k : MA_1,\ldots,MA_n \to \Box A_0$ is a clause in $\mathcal{P}_k$, and $\{MA_1,\ldots,MA_n\} \subseteq K$, where K is a Herbrand interpretation for $\mathcal{P}_k$.

As before, the *intuitionistic modal global consequence operator* $I_M T_{\mathcal{P}} : 2^{B_{\mathcal{P}}} \to 2^{B_{\mathcal{P}}}$ is defined as $I_M T_{\mathcal{P}}(I_1,\ldots,I_k) = \bigcup_{l=1}^{k}\{I_M T_{\mathcal{P}_l}\}$.

We rename each modal atom MA_i in $\mathcal{P}$ as a new atom A_j not in the language. This allows us to associate an intuitionistic program with every intuitionistic modal program, so that both programs have the same models. Hence, Theorem 19 below follows directly from Theorem 16.

Theorem 19 (Fixed-Point Model of Labelled Intuitionistic Modal Programs). *For each labelled intuitionistic modal program $\mathcal{P}$, the function $I_M T_{\mathcal{P}}$ has a unique fixed point. The sequence of all $I_M T_{\mathcal{P}}^m(I_1,\ldots,I_k), m \in \mathbb{N}$, converges to this fixed point $I_M T_{\mathcal{P}}^{\overline{\omega}}(I_1,\ldots,I_k)$, for each $I_i \subseteq 2^{B_{\mathcal{P}}}$.*

Labelled intuitionistic modal programs may be translated into neural-network ensembles by extending the above Connectionist Intuitionistic Algorithm to cater for the representation of the modal operators $\Box$ and $\Diamond$. The representation of $\Box$ and $\Diamond$ emulates the semantics of the operators. Recall that in the case of $\Box$, if $\Box\alpha$ holds

---

[4] Note that item (i) simply generalises the definition of the fixed-point operator for intuitionistic programs (Definition 41).

in a world (network) ω_i, appropriate network connections must be set up so that α holds in every world (network) ω_j to which ω_i is connected (according to the relation $\mathcal{R}(\omega_i, \omega_j)$). In the case of $\Diamond$, if $\Diamond\alpha$ holds in a world (network) ω_i, network connections must be set up so that α holds in an arbitrary world (network) ω_j to which ω_i is connected, reflecting the semantics of the modality $\Diamond$.

We are now in a position to introduce the *Connectionist Intuitionistic Modal Algorithm*. Let $\mathcal{P} = \{\mathcal{P}_1, \ldots, \mathcal{P}_n\}$ be a labelled intuitionistic modal program with clauses of the form $\omega_i : MA_1, \ldots, MA_k \rightarrow MA_0$, where each A_j is an atom and $M \in \{\Box, \Diamond\}$, $1 \leq i \leq n$, $0 \leq j \leq k$.

As in the case of intuitionistic programs, we start by calculating $MAX_{\mathcal{P}}(\overrightarrow{k}, \overrightarrow{\mu}, n)$ of $\mathcal{P}$ and A_{min} such that $A_{min} > (MAX_{\mathcal{P}}(\overrightarrow{k}, \overrightarrow{\mu}, n) - 1)/(MAX_{\mathcal{P}}(\overrightarrow{k}, \overrightarrow{\mu}, n) + 1)$. Let $W^M \in \mathbb{R}$ be such that $W^M > h^{-1}(A_{min}) + \mu_l W + \theta_A$, where μ_l, W, and θ_A are obtained from CILP's Translation Algorithm.

Connectionist Intuitionistic Modal Algorithm

1. For each $\mathcal{P}_i$ in $\mathcal{P}$, do:

    (a) Rename each modal atom MA_j as a new atom not occurring in $\mathcal{P}$ of the form $A_j^{\Box}$ if $M = \Box$, or $A_j^{\Diamond}$ if $M = \Diamond$.[5]
    (b) Call the Connectionist Intuitionistic Algorithm;

2. For each output neuron $A_j^{\Diamond}$ in network $\mathcal{N}_i$, do:

    (a) Add a hidden neuron A_j^M and an output neuron A_j to an arbitrary network $\mathcal{N}_z$ such that $R(\omega_i, \omega_z)$.
    (b) Set the step function $s(x)$ as the activation function of A_j^M, and set the semi-linear function $h(x)$ as the activation function of A_j.
    (c) Connect $A_j^{\Diamond}$ in $\mathcal{N}_i$ to A_j^M and set the connection weight to 1.
    (d) Set the threshold θ^M of A_j^M such that $-1 < \theta^M < A_{min}$.
    (e) Set the threshold θ_{A_j} of A_j in $\mathcal{N}_z$ such that $\theta_{A_j} = ((1 + A_{min}) \cdot (1 - \mu_l)/2)W$.
    (f) Connect A_j^M to A_j in $\mathcal{N}_z$ and set the connection weight to W^M.

3. For each output neuron $A_j^{\Box}$ in network $\mathcal{N}_i$, do:

    (a) Add a hidden neuron A_j^M to each $\mathcal{N}_u$ ($1 \leq u \leq n$) such that $R(\omega_i, \omega_u)$, and add an output neuron A_j to $\mathcal{N}_u$ if $A_j \notin \mathcal{N}_u$.
    (b) Set the step function $s(x)$ as the activation function of A_j^M, and set the semi-linear function $h(x)$ as the activation function of A_j.
    (c) Connect $A_j^{\Box}$ in $\mathcal{N}_i$ to A_j^M and set the connection weight to 1.
    (d) Set the threshold θ^M of A_j^M such that $-1 < \theta^M < A_{min}$.
    (e) Set the threshold θ_{A_j} of A_j in each $\mathcal{N}_u$ such that $\theta_{A_j} = ((1 + A_{min}) \cdot (1 - \mu_l)/2)W$.
    (f) Connect A_j^M to A_j in $\mathcal{N}_u$ and set the connection weight to W^M.

---

[5] This allows us to treat each MA_j as an atom and to apply the Connectionist Intuitionistic Algorithm directly to $\mathcal{P}_i$ by labelling neurons as $\Box A_j$, $\Diamond A_j$, or simply A_j.

4. For each output neuron A_j in network $\mathcal{N}_u$ such that $\mathcal{R}(\omega_i, \omega_u)$, do:

    (a) Add a hidden neuron $A_j^\vee$ to $\mathcal{N}_i$.

    (b) Set the step function $s(x)$ as the activation function of $A_j^\vee$.

    (c) For each output neuron $A_j^\Diamond$ in $\mathcal{N}_i$, do:

        i. Connect A_j in $\mathcal{N}_u$ to $A_j^\vee$ and set the connection weight to 1.

        ii. Set the threshold $\theta^\vee$ of $A_j^\vee$ such that $-nA_{min} < \theta^\vee < A_{min} - (n-1)$.

        iii. Connect $A_j^\vee$ to $A_j^\Diamond$ in $\mathcal{N}_i$ and set the connection weight to W^M.

5. For each output neuron A_j in network $\mathcal{N}_u$ such that $\mathcal{R}(\omega_i, \omega_u)$, do:

    (a) Add a hidden neuron $A_j^\wedge$ to $\mathcal{N}_i$.

    (b) Set the step function $s(x)$ as the activation function of $A_j^\wedge$.

    (c) For each output neuron $A_j^\Box$ in $\mathcal{N}_i$, do:

        i. Connect A_j in $\mathcal{N}_u$ to $A_j^\wedge$ and set the connection weight to 1.

        ii. Set the threshold $\theta^\wedge$ of $A_j^\wedge$ such that $n - (1 + A_{min}) < \theta^\wedge < nA_{min}$.

        iii. Connect $A_j^\wedge$ to $A_j^\Box$ in $\mathcal{N}_i$ and set the connection weight to W^M.

Let us now illustrate the use of the Connectionist Intuitionistic Modal Algorithm with the following example.

Example 14. Let $\mathcal{P} = \{\omega_1 : A \Rightarrow B, \ \omega_1 : \Box A, \ \omega_2 : \Diamond C, \ \mathcal{R}(\omega_1, \omega_2), \ \mathcal{R}(\omega_1, \omega_3)\}$. We apply the Connectionist Intuitionistic Modal Algorithm, which creates three neural networks $\mathcal{N}_1$, $\mathcal{N}_2$, and $\mathcal{N}_3$ to represent the points ω_1, ω_2, and ω_3, respectively (Fig. 7.3). Then, hidden neurons labelled M, $\wedge$, and n are created to interconnect networks in the ensemble. Taking $\mathcal{N}_1$, the output neuron $\Box A$ needs to be connected to output neurons A in $\mathcal{N}_2$ and $\mathcal{N}_3$ (Connectionist Intuitionistic Modal Algorithm, step 3). This is done using hidden neurons labelled M. Dually, output neurons A in $\mathcal{N}_2$ and $\mathcal{N}_3$ need to be connected to the output neuron $\Box A$ in $\mathcal{N}_1$ using the hidden neuron $\wedge$ (Connectionist Intuitionistic Modal Algorithm, step 5). Since $\omega_1 : A \Rightarrow B, \mathcal{R}(\omega_1, \omega_2)$, and $\mathcal{R}(\omega_1, \omega_3)$, $A \Rightarrow B$ is copied to $\mathcal{N}_2$ and $\mathcal{N}_3$ (Connectionist Intuitionistic Algorithm, step 1a). Intuitionistic negation is implemented using neurons labelled n, as illustrated in $\mathcal{N}_1$ for C' (Connectionist Intuitionistic Algorithm, step 3). Note that the neuron $\Diamond C$ in $\mathcal{N}_2$ would need to be connected to a network $\mathcal{N}_j$ if there was a relation $\mathcal{R}(\omega_2, \omega_j)$ for some ω_j (Connectionist Intuitionistic Modal Algorithm, step 2a). The computation of $\mathcal{P}$ in the ensemble leads to the following result: $\Box A$ is computed in $\mathcal{N}_1$ and $\Diamond C$ is computed in $\mathcal{N}_2$. From $\Box A$ in $\mathcal{N}_1$, A is computed in $\mathcal{N}_2$ and $\mathcal{N}_3$. From A and $A \Rightarrow B$ in $\mathcal{N}_2$ and $\mathcal{N}_3$, B is computed in $\mathcal{N}_2$ and $\mathcal{N}_3$, respectively. Since C does not hold in both $\mathcal{N}_2$ and $\mathcal{N}_3$, C' is computed in $\mathcal{N}_1$. Note that the addition of $\mathcal{R}(\omega_1, \omega_1)$ to $\mathcal{P}$, for example, for reflexivity, would allow one to derive A from $\Box A$ in $\mathcal{N}_1$ (Connectionist Intuitionistic Modal Algorithm, step 3). In summary, the logical consequences computed by the network are $\omega_1 : \{\neg C\}$, $\omega_2 : \{A, B\}$, and $\omega_3 : \{A, B\}$.

Finally, let us show that the ensemble of neural networks $\mathcal{N}$ obtained from the above Connectionist Intuitionistic Modal Algorithm is equivalent to the original intuitionistic modal program $\mathcal{P}$, in the sense that $\mathcal{N}$ computes the *intuitionistic modal consequence operator* $I_M T_P$ of P (Definition 45). The proof of the Connectionist Intuitionistic Modal Algorithm follows that of the Connectionist Intuitionistic Algorithm (Theorem 17), and makes use of the correctness results of CML [75].

Theorem 20 (Correctness of Connectionist Intuitionistic Modal Algorithm).
For any intuitionistic modal program P, there exists an ensemble of neural networks $\mathcal{N}$ such that $\mathcal{N}$ computes the intuitionistic modal fixed-point operator $I_M T_P$ of P.

Proof. We know from Theorem 8 that *CILP's Translation Algorithm* is correct. We know from Theorem 12 that the addition of modalities to *CILP* is correct. We also know from Theorem 17 that the addition of intuitionistic negation to *CILP* is correct. The only case we need to consider now is when modalities and negation are to be represented together in the same network (e.g. in network ω_1 of Fig. 7.3). Consider an output neuron A_0 with a neuron M and a neuron n among its predecessors in

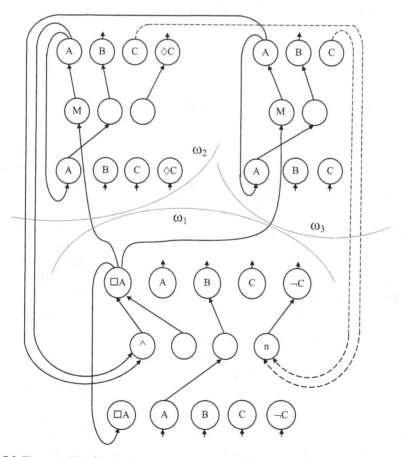

Fig. 7.3 The ensemble of networks representing an intuitionistic modal program

a network's hidden layer. There are four cases to consider. (*i*) Both M and n are not activated: since the activation function of M and n is the step function, their activations are *zero*. As a result, Theorem 8 applies. (*ii*) Only M is activated: *CML* guarantees that A_0 is activated with minimum input potential $W^M + \varsigma$, where $\varsigma \in \mathbb{R}$. (*iii*) Only n is activated: Theorem 17 guarantees that A_0 is activated with minimum input potential $W^I + \varsigma$. (*iv*) Both M and n are activated: the input potential of A_0 is at least $W^M + W^I + \varsigma$. Since $W^M > 0$ and $W^I > 0$, and since the activation function of A_0 ($h(x)$) is monotonically increasing, A_0 is activated when both M and n are activated. ∎

Corollary 21 (Connectionist Intuitionistic Modal Fixed-Point Computation).
Let $\mathcal{P}$ be a labelled intuitionistic modal program. There exists an ensemble of recurrent neural networks $\mathcal{N}^r$ such that, starting from an arbitrary initial input, $\mathcal{N}^r$ converges to a stable state and yields the unique fixed point $(I_M T_{\mathcal{P}}^{\varnothing}(I))$ of $I_M T_{\mathcal{P}}$.

Proof. By Theorem 20, $\mathcal{N}$ computes $I_M T_{\mathcal{P}}$. Being recurrently connected, $\mathcal{N}^r$ computes the upward powers of $I_M T_{\mathcal{P}} (I_M T_{\mathcal{P}}^m(I))$. Finally, by Theorem 19, $\mathcal{N}^r$ converges to the unique fixed point of $I_M T_{\mathcal{P}} (I_M T_{\mathcal{P}}^{\varnothing}(I))$. ∎

7.4 Discussion

In this chapter, we have presented a model of computation that integrates neural networks and intuitionistic reasoning. We have defined a class of labelled intuitionistic (modal) programs, and then presented algorithms to translate the intuitionistic theories into ensembles of neural networks, and showed that these ensembles compute a fixed-point semantics of the corresponding theories. As a result, each ensemble can be seen as a massively parallel model for the computation of intuitionistic (modal) logic. In addition, since each network can be trained efficiently using a neural learning algorithm, for example backpropagation [224], one can adapt the network ensemble by training possible-world representations from examples. Work along these lines has been done in [70, 73, 74], where learning experiments in possible worlds were investigated. As future work, we shall consider learning experiments based on the intuitionistic model introduced in this chapter. In Chap. 8, we shall illustrate the application of the intuitionistic model in a typical test bed for distributed knowledge representation [143]. This will also serve to compare the intuitionistic approach with negation as failure.

Extensions of the work presented in this chapter include the study of how to represent properties of other nonclassical logics (such as branching-time temporal logics [103, 167], and relevance and linear logics [1]), as well as logical formalisms for representing probabilities and reasoning under uncertainty [121]. In addition, as the Curry–Howard isomorphism (see e.g. [1]) establishes a relationship between intuitionism and typed λ−calculus (i.e. typed functional programs), it would be interesting to exploit this relationship with respect to the connectionist model presented here, so that one could present such concepts in a connectionist computational setting.

Chapter 8
Applications of Connectionist Nonclassical Reasoning

This chapter presents some benchmark distributed-knowledge-representation applications of connectionist modal and intuitionistic reasoning. It shows how CML can be used for distributed knowledge representation and reasoning, illustrating the capabilities of the proposed connectionist model. It also compares the CML representation of a distributed knowledge representation problem with the representation of the same problem in connectionist intuitionistic logic (CIL), the type of reasoning presented in Chap. 7. We begin with a simple card game, as described in [87].

8.1 A Simple Card Game

Suppose we have a deck consisting of three cards labelled A, B, and C, and two agents, 1 and 2. Each agent gets one of these cards, and a third card is left face down. A possible situation (world) is then characterised by describing the cards held by each agent. For instance, in the world (A, B), agent 1 holds card A and agent 2 holds card B; card C is face down. There are six possible situations: $(A, B), (A, C), (B, A), (B, C), (C, A), (C, B)$. Notice that in a situation such as (A, B), agent 1 thinks that two situations are possible, namely (A, B) and (A, C). Agent 1 knows that he has card A, but he considers it possible that agent 2 could hold either card B or card C. In the same situation, agent 2 considers two possibilities, (A, B) and (C, B). In general, in a world (x, y), agent 1 considers (x, y) and (x, z), to be possible, and agent 2 considers (x, y) and (z, y) to be possible, where z is different from both x and y.

We can now turn to the CML framework to represent the knowledge in a situation such as this. In our formalisation, a modality $\mathbf{K}_j$ that represents the knowledge of an agent j is used analogously to a modality $\Box$. In addition, we use p_i to denote that proposition p is *true* for agent i. For example, $\mathbf{K}_j p_i$ means that agent j knows that p is *true* for agent i. We omit the subscript j of $\mathbf{K}$ whenever it is clear from the context.

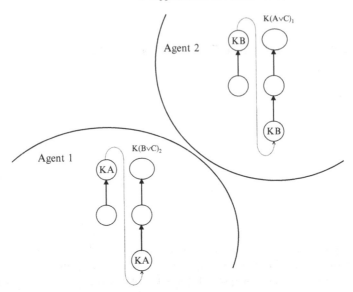

Fig. 8.1 Representation of a possible world in the card game

In the case of the card game, we can represent the situation in which agent 1 holds card A (and knows it) by the neuron labelled KA in Fig. 8.1. Moreover, as agent 1 knows he is holding card A, then he concludes that agent 2 holds either card B or C. As for agent 2, he holds card B (and knows it) and, as a result, he knows that agent 1 holds either A or C, as also represented in Fig. 8.1.

So far, we have not been representing formulas such as $A \vee B$ as neurons, but only literals. The neurons denoting such disjunctive information in Fig. 8.1 should actually be seen as shorthand for the following, more accurate representation: for agent 1, there is a possible world in which B is true for agent 2, and another posssible world in which C is true; for agent 2, there is a possible world in which A is true and another in which C is true for agent 1.

8.2 The Wise Men Puzzle

We now apply the framework of CML to the *wise men puzzle*. Below, we follow the description of the puzzle as given in [143].

A king wishes to test his wise men. There are three wise men (who are all perceptive, truthfull, and intelligent, and this is common knowledge in the group). The king arranges them in a circle so that they can see and hear each other. It is common knowledge among them that the king has with him three red hats and two white hats, and five hats in total. The king puts a hat on each of the wise men in such a way that they are not able to see their own hats, and then asks each one, sequentially, whether he knows the colour of the hat on his head. As there are only two white hats, at least one of them is wearing a red hat. The first wise man says he does not know the colour of his hat; the second wise man says he does not know either. Then the third wise man is able to say that he knows the colour of the hat on his head. Why does this happen? How can the third wise man answer the question? To solve the puzzle, let us enumerate the seven possibilities which exist: RRR, RRW, RWR, RWW, WRR, WRW, WWR. For instance, RWR refers to the situation in which the first, second, and third wise men are wearing red, white, and red hats, respectively. Note that WWW is immediately ruled out as there are only two white hats. The reasoning of the wise men goes as follows.

When the second and the third man hear the first answering *no*, they rule out the possibility of the true situation being RWW, since if this were the case, the first man would have answered *yes* when he saw that the others were both wearing white hats, and knew there were only two white hats. Since he said *no*, RWW is ruled out.

When the third man hears the second man answering *no*, he rules out the possibility of the situation being WRW as, if that were the case, the second wise man would have answered *yes*. In addition, the third wise man rules out the possibility RRW when he hears the second wise man's answer, for if the second wise man had seen the first man wearing red and the third man wearing white, he would have known the situation was RRW, and that he was wearing a red hat. But he did not conclude that, and then the third man concludes that the situation cannot be RRW.

After hearing the first and second wise men answering *no*, the third man has thus ruled out the following possibilities: RWW, WRW, RRW. This leaves him with RRR, RWR, WRR, and WWR as possible situations. In all of these, the third man is wearing a red hat, allowing him to conclude that he must be wearing a red hat.

The above example illustrates well how the wise men learn from hearing the others answer the original question. However, what makes them come to the correct conclusion is that they have *common knowledge* of the situation, each one of them being truthful, perceptive, and intelligent. Recall that common knowledge about a fact ϕ means that everyone in a group simultaneously knows ϕ, everyone knows that everyone knows ϕ, and so on.

8.2.1 A Formalisation of the Wise Men Puzzle

In the wise men puzzle, we have to represent the fact that it is common knowledge in the group that there are three red hats and two white ones. The king puts the hats on their heads and then asks, sequentially, whether they *know* the colour of the hat they are wearing. As discussed above, if the first two men say *no*, the third wise man will be able to come to the right conclusion (i.e. he is wearing a red hat). In what follows, p_i represents that wise man i wears a red hat and $\neg p_i$ represents that wise man i does not wear a red hat (i.e. he is wearing a white hat). Let the following set Γ of formulas correspond to the common knowledge in the initial situation; $C(\varphi)$ denotes that formula φ is common knowledge among the agents:

$$\{C(p_1 \lor p_2 \lor p_3),$$
$$C(p_1 \to K_2 p_1), \quad C(\neg p_1 \to K_2 \neg p_1),$$

$$C(p_1 \rightarrow K_3 p_1), \quad C(\neg p_1 \rightarrow K_3 \neg p_1),$$
$$C(p_2 \rightarrow K_1 p_2), \quad C(\neg p_2 \rightarrow K_1 \neg p_2),$$
$$C(p_2 \rightarrow K_3 p_2), \quad C(\neg p_2 \rightarrow K_3 \neg p_2),$$
$$C(p_3 \rightarrow K_1 p_3), \quad C(\neg p_3 \rightarrow K_1 \neg p_3),$$
$$C(p_3 \rightarrow K_2 p_3), \quad C(\neg p_3 \rightarrow K_3 \neg p_3)\}.$$

Next, we have that the first wise man says he does not know the colour of his hat. This can be represented by the following formula:

$$C(\neg K_1 p_1 \wedge \neg K_1 \neg p_1),$$

i.e. it is common knowledge that wise man 1 does not know if his hat is red and does not know if his hat is white.

Now we can conclude that at least one of the others must be wearing a red hat, which can be formalised by a lemma, proved in [143]:

Lemma 22. [143] *From the set of formulas in* Γ *and* $C(\neg K_1 p_1 \wedge \neg K_1 \neg p_1)$, $C(p_2 \vee p_3)$ *can be derived.*

Moreover, since it is common knowledge that either p_2 or p_3 is true, $p_2 \vee p_3$ remains true over time, and this can be used to prove the following lemma.

Lemma 23. [143] *If the set of formulas in* Γ, *and* $C(p_2 \vee p_3)$, *and* $C(\neg K_2 p_2 \wedge \neg K_2 \neg p_2)$ *are all valid, then* $K_3 p_3$ *can be derived.*

Notice that these two lemmas state that given some negative information with respect to knowledge about a situation, positive knowledge has to be derived so that the solution can eventually be reached. This means that, at each round, more knowledge is acquired, allowing an intelligent agent to infer the conclusion from his or her knowledge base. The task at hand in our neural-symbolic system is to represent the reasoning process of this problem and then construct the ensembles that correspond to the reasoning rules.

8.2.2 Representing the Wise Men Puzzle Using CML

Turning to the framework of connectionist modal logic (CML), one can represent the above reasoning process by ensembles of neural networks. CML also allows the representation of the reasoning of each individual wise man in individual networks, and the above deductions. For instance, Fig. 8.2 represents that it is common knowledge that either agent 1, agent 2, or agent 3 is wearing a red hat (for simplicity, we refer to wise men numbers 1, 2, and 3 as agents 1, 2, and 3, respectively). Agent 1 knows that agents 2 and 3 are wearing red and white hats, respectively, but he is not able to state the colour of his own hat. Similarly, agent 2 knows the colours of the other agents' hats, but cannot state, in his turn, what the colour of his own hat is. However, after hearing the others saying *no*, agent 3 will be able to say *yes*. Notice that Fig. 8.2 represents a *snapshot* of the situation, as we have not introduced a time variable to deal with knowledge evolution.

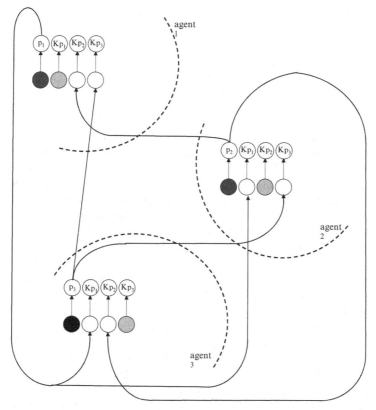

Fig. 8.2 Knowledge in the wise men puzzle: each agent knows the colours of the other agents' hats

Furthermore, agent 3 may deduce that he is wearing a red hat if he happens to know that agents 1 and 2 do not know whether they themselves are wearing a red hat. This is the case because, as discussed in Sect. 8.2.1, if agents 1 and 2 do not know that they are wearing a red hat, then they must be seeing at least one red hat. And that must be agent 3's hat. This can be formalised as an extended modal program, as follows (where r_i^j is used to denote rule r_i for agent j):

$$r_1^1 : K_1 \neg p_2 \wedge K_1 \neg p_3 \rightarrow K_1 p_1$$
$$r_1^2 : K_2 \neg p_1 \wedge K_2 \neg p_3 \rightarrow K_2 p_2$$
$$r_1^3 : K_3 \neg p_1 \wedge K_3 \neg p_2 \rightarrow K_3 p_3$$

$$r_2^1 : K_1 p_2 \rightarrow \neg K_1 p_1$$
$$r_3^1 : K_1 p_3 \rightarrow \neg K_1 p_1$$

$$r_2^2 : K_2 p_1 \rightarrow \neg K_2 p_2$$
$$r_3^2 : K_2 p_3 \rightarrow \neg K_2 p_2$$

$$r_2^3 : \neg K_1 p_1 \wedge \neg K_2 p_2 \rightarrow K_3 p_3,$$

together with the rules obtained from Γ stating that each agent knows the colours of the other agents' hats[1] (as depicted in Fig. 8.2):

$$r_4^2 : p_1 \rightarrow K_2 p_1 \quad r_3^3 : p_1 \rightarrow K_3 p_1$$
$$r_4^1 : p_2 \rightarrow K_1 p_2 \quad r_4^3 : p_2 \rightarrow K_3 p_2$$
$$r_5^1 : p_3 \rightarrow K_1 p_3 \quad r_5^2 : p_3 \rightarrow K_2 p_3.$$

Figure 8.3 contains an implementation of the rules $r_2^1, \ldots, r_5^1$, $r_2^2, \ldots, r_5^2$, and $r_2^3, \ldots, r_4^3$, for agents 1, 2, and 3, respectively. Whenever agent 3 is wearing a red hat, output neuron p_3 is clamped in the active state in the network for agent 3 to denote that p_3 is a fact. The activation of p_3 triggers the activation of $K p_3$ in the network for agent 1, and this triggers the activation of $\neg K p_1$ in the same network. Similarly, p_3 triggers the activation of $K p_3$, and $K p_3$ triggers the activation of $\neg K p_2$ in the network for agent 2. Finally, the activation of $\neg K p_1$ in network 1 and of $\neg K p_2$ in network 2 produces the activation of $K p_3$ in network 3, indicating that agent 3 knows that he is wearing a red hat.

A set of weights for the ensemble shown in Fig. 8.3 complying with this reasoning process is given in Table 8.1. This set of weights was calculated by use of the CILP Translation Algorithm (Chap. 4) and the CML Connectionist Model Algorithm (Chap. 5) for $\mathcal{P} = \{r_2^1, r_3^1, r_4^1, r_5^1, r_2^2, r_3^2, r_4^2, r_5^2, r_2^3, r_3^3, r_4^3, \mathcal{R}(1,2), \mathcal{R}(2,3), \mathcal{R}(1,3)\}$. In this calculation, we first apply the Translation Algorithm, which creates three neural networks to represent agents 1, 2, and 3. Then, we apply the Connectionist Modal Algorithm. Hidden neurons labelled $h_1, h_2, \ldots, h_{11}$ are created (one for each rule) using the Connectionist Modal Algorithm. The remaining neurons are all created by use of the Translation Algorithm. In Table 8.1, we have used (X^i, Y^j) to denote the weight from neuron X in network i to neuron Y in network j, and (X^i) to denote the threshold of neuron X in network i. The calculations are as follows. From Equation 4.1, $A_{min} > (MAX_{\mathcal{P}}(2,2) - 1)/(MAX_{\mathcal{P}}(2,2) + 1)$. Let $A_{min} = 0.6$. From Equation 4.2, taking $\beta = 1$, $W \geq 2(\ln(1.6) - \ln(0.4))/(2(-0.4) + 1.6) = 1.1552$. Let $W = 2$. Thus, all feedforward connections created by the Translation algorithm will receive a weight 2. Recall that all feedback connections also created by the Translation Algorithm will receive a weight 1. For simplicity, feedback connections are not listed in Table 8.1.

---

[1] Notice the difference between $K_1 p_1$ being false and $\neg K_1 p_1$ being true. When $K_1 p_1$ is false (neuron $K_1 p_1$ is not active), nothing can be said about whether agent 1 knows the colour of his hat. When $\neg K_1 p_1$ is true (neuron $\neg K_1 p_1$ is active), agent 1 has had to reason in order to reach such a conclusion. The difference between K and $\neg K$ is a subject to which we shall return later. From a practical perspective, the fact that $\neg K_1 p_1$ is true means that some propagation of activation must have occurred in the neural network, leading to the activation of neuron $\neg K_1 p_1$. This allows us to write $\neg K_1 p_1 \wedge \neg K_2 p_2 \rightarrow K_3 p_3$ and use this rule in a valid neural implemetation of the wise men puzzle. Strictly speaking, however, the rule for the wise men according to the formalisation of the puzzle should be $K_3 \neg K_1 p_1 \wedge K_3 \neg K_2 p_2 \rightarrow K_3 p_3$. This rule could also have been implemented in the neural network, but with the use of a larger number of neurons and connections.

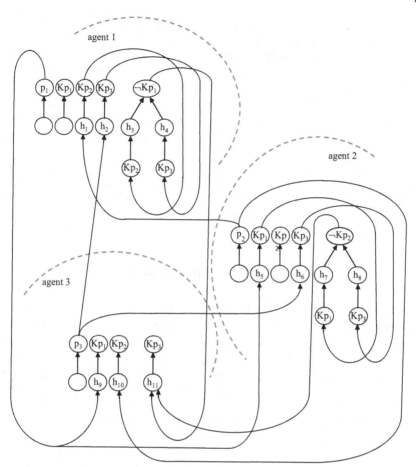

Fig. 8.3 Wise men puzzle: implementing all the rules

Table 8.1 A valid set of weights for the network for the wise men puzzle

$(h_1, Kp_2^1) = 4$	$(h_1) = 0.5$	$(h_5, Kp_1^2) = 4$	$(h_5) = 0.5$
$(h_2, Kp_3^1) = 4$	$(h_2) = 0.5$	$(h_6, Kp_3^2) = 4$	$(h_6) = 0.5$
$(Kp_2^1, h_3) = 2$	$(h_3) = 0$	$(Kp_1^2, h_7) = 2$	$(h_7) = 0$
$(h_3, \neg Kp_1^1) = 2$	$(h_4) = 0$	$(h_7, \neg Kp_2^2) = 2$	$(h_8) = 0$
$(Kp_3^1, h_4) = 2$	$(Kp_2^1) = 1.6$	$(Kp_3^2, h_8) = 2$	$(Kp_1^2) = 1.6$
$(h_4, \neg Kp_1^1) = 2$	$(Kp_3^1) = 1.6$	$(h_8, \neg Kp_2^2) = 2$	$(Kp_3^2) = 1.6$
	$(\neg Kp_1^1) = 0$		$(\neg Kp_2^2) = 0$
	$(h_9) = 0.5$	$(p_1, h_9) = 1$	
	$(h_{10}) = 0.5$	$(p_1, h_5) = 1$	
$(h_9, Kp_1^3) = 4$	$(h_{11}) = 1.6$	$(p_2, h_1) = 1$	
$(h_{10}, Kp_2^3) = 4$	$(Kp_1^3) = 1.6$	$(p_2, h_{10}) = 1$	
$(h_{11}, Kp_3^3) = 4$	$(Kp_2^3) = 1.6$	$(p_3, h_2) = 1$	$(\neg Kp_1^1, h_{11}) = 1$
	$(Kp_3^3) = 1.6$	$(p_3, h_6) = 1$	$(\neg Kp_2^2, h_{11}) = 1$

The next step is to calculate the thresholds of the hidden neurons h_3, h_4, h_7, h_8 according to Equation 4.3, and the thresholds of the output neurons according to Equation 4.4. For example, $(h_3) = 2((1+0.6) \cdot (1-1))/2 = 0$, $(\neg K p_1^1) = 2((1+0.6) \cdot (1-1))/2 = 0$, and $(K p_2^1) = 2((1+0.6) \cdot (1-0))/2 = 1.6$. Finally, weights and thresholds for the neurons interconnecting networks in the ensemble need to be calculated using the Connectionist Modal Algorithm. Connections between networks, for example (p_3, h_2), receive weight 1, the thresholds θ^M of neurons $h_1, h_2, h_5, h_6, h_9, h_{10}$ must satisfy $-1 < \theta^M < A_{min}$ (we take $\theta^M = 0.5$), and the threshold θ of neuron h_{11} must satisfy $n - (1 + A_{min}) < \theta < n A_{min}$ (we take $\theta = 1.6$).[2] Finally, the weights $W > h^{-1}(0.6) + 2\mu_L + \theta_L$ from $h_1, h_2, h_5, h_6, h_9, h_{10}$, and h_{11} to the output must be calculated.[3] For example, for the output neuron $K p_1^3$, $\mu = 0$ and $\theta = 1.6$, and thus $W > 2.986$. Although it is not necessary, we choose $W = 4$ to unity all of the seven remaining weights (see Table 8.1).

8.3 Applications of Connectionist Intuitionism

Since its origins, intuitionistic logic has been used as a logical foundation of constructive mathematics and, more recently, in several areas of computation. For instance, Artëmov has developed a semantics for Gödel's logic of proofs based on intuitionism [10]. Moreover, an intuitionistic temporal logic has been successfully used to characterise timing analysis in combinatorial circuits [180], and intuitionistic logic has been shown to be relevant to spatial reasoning, with possible applications in geographical information systems. Bennett's propositional intuitionistic approach [23] provides for tractable yet expressive reasoning about topological and spatial relations, in contrast to some more involved (first-order) reasoning frameworks. Intuitionistic modal logic has also been used to characterise notions of knowledge in philosophical logic, and more recently in artificial intelligence [206, 236].

In this section, we apply the model of connectionist intuitionistic logic to the wise men puzzle so that it can be compared with the CML solution to the problem given above. Our aim is also to ground the theoretical work presented in Chap. 7 in a practical example, showing that the type of neural-network architecture advocated there may well be required in a connectionist setting to represent even a simple situation in the case of distributed commonsense reasoning. Although simple, the wise men puzzle has been used extensively to model reasoning about knowledge in distributed, multiagent environments [87, 121]. This and other puzzles have been shown to be suitable not only because of their simplicity, but also because of their generality, as they represent typical situations occurring in practice in distributed, multiagent environments.

---

[2] Recall that $n = 3$ in this example.

[3] Recall that $W = 2$ in this example; $h^{-1}(A_{min}) = -(1/\beta)\ln((1-A_{min})/(1+A_{min}))$.

Recall from Sect. 8.2 that, since there are only two white hats, at least one of the wise men is wearing a red hat. The first wise man says he does not know the colour of his hat; the second wise man says he does not know either. Then the third wise man, if he sees two white hats, should be able to conclude that he knows the colour of the hat on his head. If not, it becomes common knowledge that there must exist at most a single white hat on their heads (because, if there were two, a wise man would have said in the previous round that he knew he was wearing a red hat). A wise man who can see such a white hat should then be able to conclude that he is wearing a red hat. Again, if they all fail to reach such a conclusion, then it becomes common knowledge that they all must be wearing red hats.

This puzzle illustrates a situation where intuitionistic implication and intuitionistic negation occur. Knowledge evolves over time, with the current knowledge persisting in time. For example, in the first round it is known that there are at most two white hats. Then, if the wise men get to the second round, it becomes known that there is at most one white hat on their heads. This new knowledge subsumes the previous knowledge, which in turn persists. This means that if $A \Rightarrow B$ is *true* at a point t_1, then $A \Rightarrow B$ will be *true* at a point t_2 that is related to t_1 (intuitionistic implication). Now, in any situation in which a wise man knows that his hat is red (and therefore not white), this knowledge – constructed with the use of sound reasoning processes – cannot be refuted. In other words, if $\neg A$ is *true* at point t_1 then A cannot be *true* at a point t_2 that is related to t_1 (intuitionistic negation).

To model the puzzle, we do the following. Let p_i denote the fact that wise man i wears a red hat, $i \in \{1,2,3\}$. As before, we use RRR to denote $p_1 \wedge p_2 \wedge p_3$, RRW to denote $p_1 \wedge p_2 \wedge \neg p_3$, and so on. If the second and third men hear the first answering *no*, they rule out the RWW option. If the third man then hears the second man answering *no*, he rules out WRW and RRW. The reasoning process continues until one of the wise men is capable of concluding whether or not he is wearing a red hat. This reasoning process is intuitionistic. Given some limited information with respect to knowledge about a situation, further knowledge has to be derived so that the solution can be reached eventually.

8.3.1 Representing the Wise Men Puzzle Using CIL

We can model the wise men puzzle by constructing the relative knowledge of each wise man along a sequence of time points. This allows us to explicitly represent the relativistic notion of knowledge, which is a fundamental principle of intuitionistic reasoning. As before, we refer to wise men 1, 2, and 3 as agents 1, 2, and 3, respectively. We model the relative knowledge of each agent at points t_1, t_2, t_3 in a Kripke structure, each point being associated with a discrete time point. The resulting model is a two-dimensional network ensemble (agents × time), containing three networks in each dimension. In addition to p_i – denoting the fact that wise man i

wears a red hat – in order to model each agent's individual knowledge, we need to use a modality K_j, $j \in \{1,2,3\}$, which represents the relative notion of knowledge at each point. Thus, $K_j p_i$ denotes the fact that agent j knows that agent i wears a red hat.

The fact that each agent knows the colours of the other agents' hats is implemented as before, as illustrated in Fig. 8.2. For example, if wise man 3 wears a red hat (neuron p_3 is active), then wise man 1 knows that wise man 3 wears a red hat (neuron Kp_3 is active for wise man 1). However, this is an example of the intuitionistic implication $t_1 : p_3 \Rightarrow K_1 p_3$, which clearly persists at points t_2 and t_3. In other words, the structure of Fig. 8.2 repeats itself twice, as it should be valid for each point in the Kripke structure (t_1, t_2, t_3), given that $\mathcal{R}(t_1, t_2)$ and $\mathcal{R}(t_2, t_3)$. This creates the two-dimensional network ensemble mentioned above. Note that, according to the Connectionist Intuitionistic Modal Algorithm (Sect. 7.3), connections linking different networks in the ensemble receive a weight 1.

We now need to model the reasoning process of each wise man. For this example, let us consider the case RWR (i.e. we make neurons p_1 and p_3 active). For agent 1, we have the rule $t_1 : K_1 \neg p_2 \wedge K_1 \neg p_3 \Rightarrow K_1 p_1$, which states that agent 1 can deduce that he is wearing a red hat if he knows that the other agents are both wearing white hats. Analogous rules exist for agents 2 and 3. As before, the implication is intuitionistic, so that it persists at t_2 and t_3, as depicted in Fig. 8.4 for wise man 1. In addition, according to the interpretation of intuitionistic negation, we may only conclude that agent 1 knows $\neg p_2$ if, in every world that agent 1 envisages, p_2 is not derived. This is illustrated by the use of dotted lines in Fig. 8.4.[4] In the case of RWR, the network ensemble will never derive p_2 (as one should expect), and thus it will derive $K_1 \neg p_2$ and $K_3 \neg p_2$. Note that, according to the Connectionist Intuitionistic Algorithm (Sect. 7.2), connections linking different networks receive a weight -1, as depicted in Fig. 8.4.

Finally, to complete the formalisation of the problem, we know that, at t_1, it is common knowledge that there exist at most two white hats. As the reasoning process takes us into t_2 (in the case of RWR), it becomes common knowledge that there exists at most one white hat on their heads. As a result, the following rules hold at t_2 (and at t_3): $K_1 \neg p_2 \Rightarrow K_1 p_1$ and $K_1 \neg p_3 \Rightarrow K_1 p_1$. Analogous rules exist for agents 2 and 3. If the reasoning process were to take us into t_3 (the only case here would be RRR), then it would be common knowledge that there exist no white hats on their heads. This can be modelled by the rule $t_3 : K_1 p_2 \wedge K_1 p_3 \Rightarrow K_1 p_1$. Again, analogous rules exist for agents 2 and 3 at t_3.

It is interesting to note that the connectionist intuitionistic approach to solving the wise men puzzle produces a neater model than does our previous, CML-based approach (contrast Figs. 8.3 and 8.4). In CML, an agent's lack of knowledge needed to be modelled, requiring the use of a different type of negation. In CIL, the use of intuitionistic negation seems to facilitate the modelling of a full solution to the puzzle.

---

[4] Recall that the accessibility relation is reflexive and transitive, so that the intuitionistic algorithm also connects, for example, $K_1 p_2$ in t_3 to $K_1 \neg p_2$ in t_1, and $K_1 p_2$ in t_i to $K_1 \neg p_2$ in t_i, $i \in \{1,2,3\}$. For simplicity, we have omitted such connections.

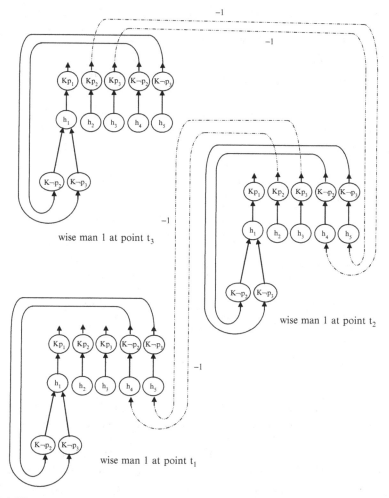

Fig. 8.4 Wise men puzzle: intuitionistic negation and implication

A set of weights for the networks in the ensemble of Fig. 8.4 is given in Table 8.2. In this table, we have used (X,Y) to denote the weight from neuron X to neuron Y, and θX to denote the threshold of neuron X in a particular neural network. First, we calculate $A_{min} > ((MAX_{\mathcal{P}}(\overrightarrow{k},\overrightarrow{\mu}) - 1)/(MAX_{\mathcal{P}}(\overrightarrow{k},\overrightarrow{\mu}) + 1))$, i.e. $A_{min} > (MAX_{\mathcal{P}}(2,2) - 1)/(MAX_{\mathcal{P}}(2,2) + 1)$. We take $A_{min} = 0.6$. Then, taking $\beta = 1$, we calculate $W \geq (2/\beta) \cdot (\ln(1 + A_{min}) - \ln(1 - A_{min}))/(MAX_{\mathcal{P}}(\overrightarrow{k},\overrightarrow{\mu}) \cdot (A_{min} - 1) + A_{min} + 1))$, i.e. $W \geq 2(\ln(1.6) - \ln(0.4))/(2(-0.4) + 1.6) = 1.1552$. Let $W = 2.0$. Thus, all feedforward connections that are created by CILP's Translation Algorithm will receive a weight 2. In addition, recall that all feedback connections that are created by the Translation Algorithm receive a weight 1. The next step is to calculate the thresholds of the hidden and output neurons. The threshold of h_1 is given by the

Table 8.2 A valid set of weights for the intuitionistic network for the wise men puzzle

Wise man 1 at t_1	Wise man 1 at t_2	Wise man 1 at t_3
$\theta h_1 = 1.6$	$\theta h_1 = 1.6$	$\theta h_1 = 1.6$
$\theta h_2 = 0.0$	$\theta h_2 = 0.0$	$\theta h_2 = 0.0$
$\theta h_3 = 0.0$	$\theta h_3 = 0.0$	$\theta h_3 = 0.0$
$\theta h_4 = 1.5$	$\theta h_4 = 1.5$	$\theta h_4 = 1.5$
$\theta h_5 = 1.5$	$\theta h_5 = 1.5$	$\theta h_5 = 1.5$
$(K\neg p_2, h_1) = 2.0$	$(K\neg p_2, h_1) = 2.0$	$(K\neg p_2, h_1) = 2.0$
$(K\neg p_3, h_1) = 2.0$	$(K\neg p_3, h_1) = 2.0$	$(K\neg p_3, h_1) = 2.0$
$(h_1, Kp_1) = 2.0$	$(h_1, Kp_1) = 2.0$	$(h_1, Kp_1) = 2.0$
$(h_2, Kp_2) = 4.0$	$(h_2, Kp_2) = 4.0$	$(h_2, Kp_2) = 4.0$
$(h_3, Kp_3) = 4.0$	$(h_3, Kp_3) = 4.0$	$(h_3, Kp_3) = 4.0$
$(h_4, K\neg p_2) = 2.0$	$(h_4, K\neg p_2) = 2.0$	$(h_4, K\neg p_2) = 2.0$
$(h_5, K\neg p_3) = 2.0$	$(h_5, K\neg p_3) = 2.0$	$(h_5, K\neg p_3) = 2.0$
$(K\neg p_2, K\neg p_2) = 1.0$	$(K\neg p_2, K\neg p_2) = 1.0$	$(K\neg p_2, K\neg p_2) = 1.0$
$(K\neg p_3, K\neg p_3) = 1.0$	$(K\neg p_3, K\neg p_3) = 1.0$	$(K\neg p_3, K\neg p_3) = 1.0$
$\theta Kp_1 = 0.0$	$\theta Kp_1 = 0.0$	$\theta Kp_1 = 0.0$
$\theta Kp_2 = 0.0$	$\theta Kp_2 = 0.0$	$\theta Kp_2 = 0.0$
$\theta Kp_3 = 0.0$	$\theta Kp_3 = 0.0$	$\theta Kp_3 = 0.0$
$\theta K\neg p_2 = 0.0$	$\theta K\neg p_2 = 0.0$	$\theta K\neg p_2 = 0.0$
$\theta K\neg p_3 = 0.0$	$\theta K\neg p_3 = 0.0$	$\theta K\neg p_3 = 0.0$

Translation Algorithm: $\theta_l = ((1 + A_{min}) \cdot (k_l - 1)/2)W$, i.e. $\theta h_1 = 1.6$. The thresholds of h_2 and h_3 are given by the Connectionist Intuitionistic Modal Algorithm: $-1 < \theta^M < A_{min}$. We let $\theta h_2, \theta h_3$ equal zero.[5] The thresholds of h_4 and h_5 are given by the Connectionist Intuitionistic Modal Algorithm: $n - (1 + A_{min}) < \theta_{A'} < nA_{min}$, i.e. $1.4 < \theta_{A'} < 1.8$. We let $\theta h_4, \theta h_5$ equal 1.5. The threshold of any output neuron is given by the Translation Algorithm: $\theta_{A_0} = ((1 + A_{min}) \cdot (1 - \mu_l)/2)W$. Since $\mu_l = 1$, these are all zero. Finally, we consider the feedforward connections that are created by the Connectionist Intuitionistic Modal Algorithm. These are (h_2, Kp_2) and (h_3, Kp_3) for each network. According to the algorithm, these weights should be greater than $h^{-1}(A_{min}) + \mu_l W + \theta_A = 2.986$.[6] We set these to 4.0.

8.4 Discussion

In this chapter we have illustrated the use of connectionist modal logic and connectionist intuitionistic logic in distributed knowledge representation and reasoning. The ability of these models to represent and learn richer logic-based distributed

---

[5] Note that the information coming from agents 2 and 3 is gathered by agent 1 via hidden neurons h_2 and h_3.

[6] Note that $h^{-1}(A_{min}) = -(1/\beta)\ln((1 - A_{min})/(1 + A_{min}))$.

knowledge representation mechanisms achieves a long-term aim of learning languages and models. By means of a formalisation which allows the representation of modal operators, we have proposed a solution to problems in which agents can reason about their knowledge in a situation and learn from their experience.

It is interesting also to relate the results in this chapter to the examples in Chaps. 5 and 6. In Chap. 6, we saw that the provision of a Temporal Algorithm can provide the Connectionist Modal Algorithm of Chap. 5 with explicit capabilities for reasoning about time. In the case of the muddy children puzzle considered in Chaps. 5 and 6, a full solution to the problem would require metalevel knowledge about the problem domain to define the number s of relevant time points. The formalisation of the full solution to the puzzle would then require the addition of a modality to deal with the notion of *next time* in a linear time flow. Graphically, this can be seen as a chain of size s of recurrent networks (as opposed to simply the unfolded version of a recurrent network). At each time point, a recurrent network is still responsible for carrying out the computations for each agent at that point (thus implementing the concept of *short-term memory*). Once the networks are stable, the computations can be carried forward to the next time point in the chain; this is responsible for implementing the concept of *long-term memory*. The definition of the number of points s necessary to solve a given problem clearly depends on the problem domain (i.e. on the number of time points that are needed for reasoning about the problem). For example, in the case of the muddy children puzzle, we know that it suffices to have s equal to the number of children that are muddy, and if we do not know this number, to have s equal to the number of children playing. The definition of s in a different domain might not be as straightforward, possibly requiring a fine-tuning of the value of s similar to that performed on the usual learning parameters of a network. Essentially, this produces a network ensemble of varying size, or a varying network architecture with *memory on demand*. This is an interesting avenue for further research.

As an exercise, the reader is invited to design a connectionist temporal logic (CTLK) solution to the wise men puzzle. Although a full solution to the muddy children puzzle does require a temporal dimension, it seems that this is not needed in the case of the wise men puzzle. Nevertheless, in the same way that the intuitionistic design of the problem seems neater than the exclusively modal design, the CTKL design might offer the most appropriate solution to the problem (i.e. a better design than the intuitionistic version).

Chapter 9
Fibring Neural Networks

As we have seen in Chaps. 4 to 7, neural networks can deal with a number of reasoning mechanisms. In many applications these need to be combined (fibred) into
a system capable of dealing with the different dimensions of a reasoning agent. In
this chapter, we introduce a methodology for combining neural-network architectures based on the idea of fibring logical systems [101]. Fibring allows one to combine different logical systems in a principled way. Fibred neural networks may be
composed not only of interconnected neurons but also of other networks, forming a
recursive architecture. A fibring function then defines how this recursive architecture
behaves by defining how the networks in the ensemble relate to each other, typically
by allowing the activation of neurons in one network (A) to influence the change of
weights in another network (B). Intuitively, this can be seen as training network B
at the same time as network A is running. Although both networks are simple, standard networks, we can show that, in addition to being universal approximators like
standard feedforward networks, fibred neural networks can approximate any polynomial function to any desired degree of accuracy, thus being more expressive than
standard feedforward networks.

9.1 The Idea of Fibring

To explain the basic idea of fibring two systems, we begin with some examples.

Example 15. (**Language**) Suppose we see a sentence in English with a few German
words in it, say, 'John expressed grosse Respekt for Mary's actions', and we want
to understant its meaning. The natural thing is to start parsing the sentence using an
English parser, and when we get to the phrase 'grosse Respekt' we know that it is
supposed to be an object noun phrase. Since we do not know its meaning, we regard
it as 'atomic'. To find its meaning, we send the expression to a German/English
translation machine. This machine understands German phrases and sends back an

English equivalent. The functionals (or fibring functions, as we call them) involved here are the following:

- $f_{E,G}(x)$ is a fibring function that sends a German phrase x from an English text to a German/English translation machine.
- $f_{G,E}(x)$ is a fibring function that sends back an equivalent English value of x.

The following example deals with the fibring of networks.

Example 16. (**Networks**) Let S be a network, such as a neural or Bayesian network, or just a graph with nodes and some connections between the nodes. Let a and b be two nodes in S. Suppose we replace the node a by an entire network T_a. We denote the new network thus obtained by $S(a/T_a)$. T_a may be a network of the same type or an entirely different network of a completely new type. How do we handle this new network? Figure 9.2 describes the situation, where we start with $S = (c \Rightarrow a \Rightarrow b)$ and where T_a is as in Fig. 9.1

The '$\Rightarrow$' in Fig 9.2 indicates a relationship between nodes of network S, and '$\rightarrow$' indicates a relationship between nodes of network T_a. The network S expects a node a with suitable properties. Instead, we gave it a network T_a. So, again, we need two fibring functions: $f_{n,b}$ takes the first network's kind of input and transforms it into something the second network can understand and do something with, and $f_{b,n}$ takes the second network's output and transforms it into something the first network can understand. The combined effect of these two functions is to make T_a look like a node in S. So, we are actually replacing a by $[f_{n,b}, T_a, f_{b,n}]$.

The general fibring problem may be outlined as follows. Given a system S_1 and a system S_2, we take an atomic unit $a \in S_1$ and substitute for it a part of S_2. This creates a new system $S_{1,2}$. We need two fibring functions $f_{1,2}$ and $f_{2,1}$ to handle $S_{1,2}$. When the system S_1 calls upon what used to be node a, it sees a part X_a of system S_2. $f_{1,2}$ feeds a translation of the environment of a into X_a and obtains a

Fig. 9.1 A simple network

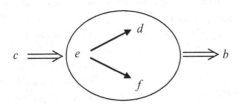

Fig. 9.2 Fibring two networks

result, possibly by embedding X_a in an S_2 environment provided by $f_{1,2}$. Then $f_{2,1}$ takes the result and transforms it into something system S_1 can understand. Thus, the entire operation of $f_{1,2}$ and then $f_{2,1}$ works as a component of system S_1. We have thus defined what a system of the form $S_{1,2}$ can do.

Similarly, we can define $S_{2,1}$ and, inductively, $S_{1,2,1}, S_{2,1,2}, ..., S_{x_1,x_2,x_3,...,x_n}$, with $x_i \neq x_{i+1}, i = 1,...,n-1$. The same fibring functions $f_{1,2}$ and $f_{2,1}$ will be used throughout. Note that an essential part of the fibring process is the notion of substitution. This has to be defined specially for each case. So, the fibring process requires $Sub_{1,2}$ and $Sub_{2,1}$ as well as $f_{1,2}$ and $f_{2,1}$.

Example 17. (**Modal and Fuzzy Logic**) Our next example is one of fibring modal logic into many-valued logic. Consider the expression $q \Rightarrow \Diamond b$. Here, $\Rightarrow$ is a fuzzy implication. It can compute a fuzzy value $x \Rightarrow y$ out of any two fuzzy values x and y; for example, $x \Rightarrow y = min(1, 1 - x + y)$. Let v be an assignment of values to the atoms of the fuzzy logic. We have $v(q \Rightarrow \Diamond b) = (v(q) \Rightarrow v(\Diamond b))$. We cannot evaluate the right-hand expression, because $v(\Diamond b)$ is not known; v gives values to atoms but not to a modal expression. We need a fibred modal model $\mathcal{M} = (S, a, h)$ in which $\Diamond b$ can be evaluated. A value $y = h(\Diamond b)$ can be extracted from the model $\mathcal{M}$, and a function $F_{modal, fuzzy}$ will transmit $F_{modal, fuzzy}(y)$ back to v. The final answer will be $v(q \Rightarrow \Diamond b) = v(q) \Rightarrow F_{modal, fuzzy}(y)$.

We now turn to the idea of self-fibring. This is a special case of fibring, where we embed the system as a basic unit into itself. So, if the system S contains the basic unit $a \in S$, then we form the new system $S^1 = S(a/S)$, where we substitute S itself for a. This actually brings the metalevel (S itself) into the object level (a in S). A good example is the logic of the conditional.

Example 18. (**Conditionals**) Consider a nonmonotonic consequence relation $|\sim$ defined on the language of classical logic. This language contains only the classical connectives $\neg, \wedge, \vee, \rightarrow$. We write $A |\sim_S B$ to indicate that B is a nonmonotonic consequence of A in one of the many well-known nonmonotonic systems, say S. Clearly, $|\sim_S$ is a metalevel relation. Consider $A |\sim_S (B |\sim_S C)$. This expression has no meaning. It is obtained by taking the object-level atom a in $A |\sim_S a$ and substituting $(B |\sim_S C)$ for it. The fibring methodology can give meaning to this expression and its iterations in a natural way, and if we follow the process through we obtain well-known systems of conditional logic, $|\sim$ being the conditional at the object level.

9.2 Fibring Neural Networks

Fibring can be used to combine several different systems, such as logical systems of space and time, neural networks and Bayesian networks [63, 70, 270], and declarative and procedural programming languages, the main challenge being how these systems may be put to work together in a coordinated manner to solve a particular

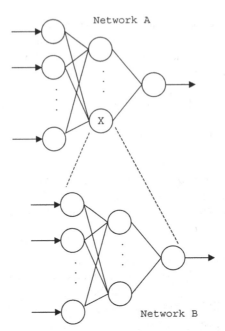

Fig. 9.3 Fibring neural networks

problem.[1] To this end, we know that a fundamental aspect of symbolic computation
is the ability to implement recursion. As a result, to make neural networks behave
like logic, we need to add recursion to them by allowing networks to be composed
not only of interconnected neurons but also of other networks. Figure 9.3 exemplifies how a network (*B*) can be embedded recursively into another network (*A*). Of
course, the idea of fibring is not only to organise networks as a number of subnetworks (*A*, *B*, etc). In Fig. 9.3, for example, the hidden neuron *X* of network *A* is
expected to be a neural network (network *B*) in its own right. The input, weights,
and output of network *B* may depend on the activation state of neuron *X*, according
to a fibring function. One such function might multiply the weights of network *B* by
the input potential of neuron *X*.

Most of the work on how to implement recursion in neural networks has concen-
trated on the use of recurrent autoassociative networks and symmetric networks to
represent formal grammars [85, 208, 238, 239, 248]. In general, the networks learn
how to simulate a number of recursive rules by similarity to a set of examples, and
the question of how such rules are represented in the network is treated as secondary.
In this chapter, we give a different treatment of the subject, looking at it from a perspective of neural-symbolic fibring. The idea is to be able to represent and learn
expressive symbolic rules, such as rules containing embedded implications of the

---

[1] For example, a robot's motion control system may require a logic of space, a logic of time, and a
neural-network-based system for visual pattern recognition.

form $(a \rightarrow b) \rightarrow c$, where $(a \rightarrow b)$ would be encoded into network B, and then $X \rightarrow c$, with $X = (a \rightarrow b)$, would be encoded into network A so that the fibred network represents $(a \rightarrow b) \rightarrow c$.

In what follows, we introduce and define fibred neural networks (fNNs) and show that, in addition to being universal approximators,[2] fNNs can approximate any polynomial function in an unbounded domain, thus being more expressive than standard feedforward networks. Briefly, this can be shown by noting that fibred neural networks compute the function $f(x) = x^2$ exactly for any given input x in $\mathbb{R}$, as opposed to feedforward networks, which are restricted to compact (i.e. closed and bounded) domains [52, 140]. Intuitively, fibring neural networks can be seen as running and training neural networks at the same time. In Fig. 9.3, for example, at the same time as we run network A, we perform learning in network B because we allow the weights of B to change according to the fibring function. In other words, object-level network running and metalevel network training occur simultaneously in the same system, and this is responsible for the added expressiveness of the system.

9.3 Examples of the Fibring of Networks

As mentioned above, the main idea behind fibring neural networks is to allow single neurons to behave like entire embedded networks according to a fibring function φ. This function qualifies the function computed by the embedded network so that the embedded network's output depends on φ. For example, consider network A and its embedded network (network B) in Fig. 9.3. Let $\mathbf{W}_A$ and $\mathbf{W}_B$ be the sets of weights of network A and network B, respectively. Let $f_{\mathbf{W}_A}(\mathbf{i}_A)$ be the function computed by network A, and $g_{\mathbf{W}_B}(\mathbf{i}_B)$ the function computed by network B, where $\mathbf{i}_A$ and $\mathbf{i}_B$ are input vectors for networks A and B, respectively. If network B is embedded into neuron X of network A with a fibring function φ, the function computed by network B becomes $g_{\mathbf{W}'_B}(\mathbf{i}_B)$, where $\mathbf{W}'_B = \varphi(\mathbf{W}_B)$, and then the output of neuron X becomes the output of network B, as the following example illustrates.

Consider the two simple networks (C and D) shown in Fig. 9.4. Let us assume, without loss of generality, that the input and output neurons have the identity as their activation function, while the hidden neurons have $h(x) = \tanh(x)$ as their activation function. We use bipolar inputs $i_j \in \{-1, 1\}$, $W_{jk} \in \mathbb{R}$, and outputs $o_k \in (-1, 1)$. The output of network C is $o_C = W_{3C}.h(W_{1C}.i_{1C} + W_{2C}.i_{2C})$, and the output of network D is $o_D = W_{3D}.h(W_{1D}.i_{1D} + W_{2D}.i_{2D})$. Now, let network D be embedded into network C as shown in Fig. 9.4. This indicates that the input potential of neuron Y will influence D according to the fibring function φ. Let us refer to the input potential of Y as $\mathbf{I}(Y)$.[3] In addition, this indicates that the output of D (o_D) will influence C (in this example,

---

[2] Universal approximators, such as feedforward neural networks, can approximate any (Borel) measurable function *in a compact domain* to any desired degree of accuracy.

[3] Note that, in this particular example, $\mathbf{I}(Y) = o_C$ owing to the use of the identity as the activation function in the output layer.

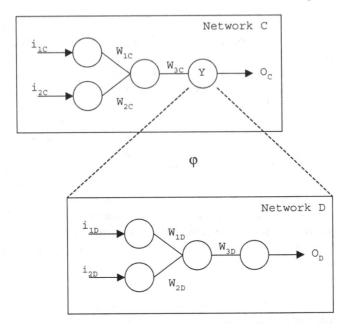

Fig. 9.4 Fibring two simple networks

only the output of C). Suppose $\varphi(\mathbf{W}_D) = \mathbf{I}(Y) \cdot \mathbf{W}_D$, where $\mathbf{W}_D = [W_{1D}, W_{2D}, W_{3D}]$, i.e. φ multiplies the weights of D by the input potential of Y. Let us use $\overline{o}_C$ and $\overline{o}_D$ to denote the outputs of networks C and D, respectively, after they are fibred. $\overline{o}_D$ is obtained by applying φ to $\mathbf{W}_D$ and calculating the output of such a network, as follows: $\overline{o}_D = (\mathbf{I}(Y).W_{3D}) \cdot h((\mathbf{I}(Y) \cdot W_{1D}) \cdot i_{1D} + (\mathbf{I}(Y) \cdot W_{2D}) \cdot i_{2D})$. $\overline{o}_C$ is obtaining by taking $\overline{o}_D$ as the output of neuron Y. In this example, $\overline{o}_C = \overline{o}_D$. Notice how network D is being trained (as φ changes its weights) at the same time as network C is running.

Clearly, fibred networks can be trained from examples in the same way that standard feedforward networks are (for example, with the use of backpropagation [224]). Networks C and D in Fig. 9.4, for example, could have been trained separately before being fibred. Network C could have been trained, for example, with a robot's visual system, while network D could have been trained with its planning system. For simplicity, we assume for now that, once defined, the fibring function itself should remain unchanged. Future extensions of the fibring of neural networks could, however, consider the task of learning the fibring functions as well.

Not that, in addition to using different fibring functions, networks can be fibred in a number of different ways as far as their architectures are concerned. The networks of Fig. 9.4, for example, could have been fibred by embedding network D into an input neuron of network C (say, the one with input i_{1C}). In this case, the outputs $\overline{o}_D$ and $\overline{o}_C$ would have been $\overline{o}_D = \varphi(W_{3D}) \cdot h(\varphi(W_{1D}) \cdot i_{1D} + \varphi(W_{2D}) \cdot i_{2D})$, where φ is a function of $\mathbf{W}_D$ (say, $\varphi(\mathbf{W}_D) = i_{1C} \cdot \mathbf{W}_D$), and then $\overline{o}_C = W_{3C} \cdot h(W_{1C} \cdot \overline{o}_D + W_{2C} \cdot i_{2C})$.

Let us now consider an even simpler example, which nevertheless illustrates the power of the fibring of networks. Consider two networks A and B, both with a single input neuron (i_A and i_B, respectively), a single hidden neuron, and a single output neuron (o_A and o_B, respectively). Let all the weights in both networks have a value 1, and let the identity ($f(x) = x$) be the activation function of all the neurons (including the hidden neurons). As a result, we simply have $o_A = f(W_{2A} \cdot f(W_{1A} \cdot f(i_A))) = i_A$ and $o_B = f(W_{2B} \cdot f(W_{1B} \cdot f(i_B))) = i_B$, where W_{1A} and W_{2A} are the weights of network A, and W_{1B} and W_{2B} are the weights of network B. Now, assume we embed network B into the input neuron of network A. We obtain $\bar{o}_B = f(\varphi(W_{2B}) \cdot f(\varphi(W_{1B}) \cdot f(i_B)))$, and then $\bar{o}_A = f(W_{2A} \cdot f(W_{1A} \cdot \bar{o}_B))$. Since $f(x) = x$, we have $\bar{o}_B = \varphi(W_{2B}) \cdot \varphi(W_{1B}) \cdot i_B$ and $\bar{o}_A = W_{2A} \cdot W_{1A} \cdot \bar{o}_B$. Now, let our fibring function be $\varphi(\mathbf{W}_A, \mathbf{i}_A, \mathbf{W}_B) = i_A \cdot \mathbf{W}_B$, where $\mathbf{W}_B = [W_{1B}, W_{2B}]$. Since W_{1A}, W_{2A}, W_{1B}, and W_{2B} are all equal to 1, we obtain $\bar{o}_B = i_A \cdot i_A \cdot i_B$ and $\bar{o}_A = \bar{o}_B$. This means that if we fix $i_B = 1$, the output of network A (fibred with network B) will be the square of its input. As a result, if the sequence $n, 1/n, n+1, 1/(n+1), n+2, 1/(n+2), \ldots$ for $n \in \mathbb{R}$, is given as input to A (fibred with B), the corresponding output sequence will be $n^2, 1, (n+1)^2, 1, (n+2)^2, 1, \ldots$ Note that the input n changes the weights of B from 1 to n, the input $1/n$ changes the weights of B back to 1, the input $n+1$ changes the weights of B from 1 to $n+1$, the input $1/(n+1)$ changes the weights of B back to 1, and so on.[4] The interest in this sequence lies in the fact that, for alternating inputs, the square of the input is computed exactly by the network for any input in $\mathbb{R}$. This illustrates an important feature of fibred neural networks, namely their ability to approximate functions in an unbounded domain [126, 128]. This results from the recursive characteristic of fibred networks as indicated by the fibring function, and will be discussed in more detail in the following section. Note that, in practice, the fibring function φ is defined depending on the problem domain.

9.4 Definition of Fibred Networks

We shall now define fibred neural networks (fNNs) precisely. Then, we shall define the dynamics of fNNs, and show that fNNs can approximate unbounded functions. For the sake of simplicity, we restrict the definition of fibred networks to feedforward networks with a single output neuron. We also concentrate on networks with linear input and linear output activation functions, and either a linear or a sigmoid hidden-layer activation function. We believe, however, that the principles of fibring can be applied to any artificial-neural-network model.[5] Below, we allow not only two networks, but also any number of embedded networks to be nested into a fibred network. We also allow an unlimited number of hidden layers per network.

---

[4] Since the fibring function changes the weights of the embedded network, we use $1/n$, $1/(n+1)$, $1/(n+2), \ldots$ to *reset* the weights back to 1 during the computation of the sequence.

[5] It would be particularly interesting to consider fibring recurrent networks (i.e. networks with feedback connections).

Definition 46 (Fibring Function). Let A and B be two neural networks. A function $\varphi_n : \mathbf{I} \to \mathbf{W}$ is called a fibring function from A to B if $\mathbf{I}$ is the input potential of a neuron n in A and $\mathbf{W}$ is the set of weights of B.

Definition 47 (Fibred Neural Network). Let A and B be two neural networks. We say that B is embedded into A if φ_n is a fibring function from A to B, and the output of neuron n in A is given by the output of network B. The resulting network, composed of networks A and B, is said to be a fibred neural network.

Note that many networks can be embedded into a single network, and that networks can be nested so that network B is embedded into network A, network C is embedded into network B, and so on. The resulting fibred network can be constructed by applying Definition 47 recursively; for example, we first embed C into B and then embed the resulting network into A.

Example 19. Consider three identical network architectures (A, B, and C), each containing a single linear input neuron, a single linear hidden neuron, and a single linear output neuron, as depicted in Fig. 9.5. Let us denote the weight from the input

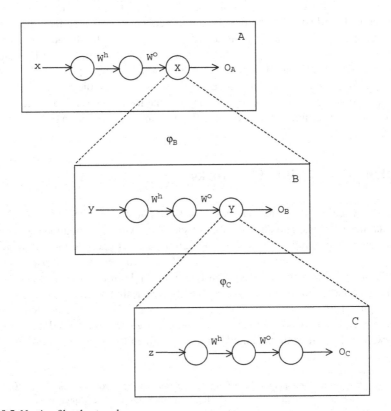

Fig. 9.5 Nesting fibred networks

neuron to the hidden neuron of network N, $N \in \{A,B,C\}$, by W_N^h, and the weight from the hidden neuron to the output neuron of N by W_N^o. Assume we embed network C into the output neuron (Y) of network B, and embed the resulting network into the output neuron (X) of network A (according to Definition 47). Let φ_B denote the fibring function from A to B, and φ_C denote the fibring function from B to C. As usual, we define $\varphi_B = I(X) \cdot \mathbf{W}_B$ and $\varphi_C = I(Y) \cdot \mathbf{W}_C$, where $I(X)$ is the input potential of neuron X, $I(Y)$ is the input potential of neuron Y, $\mathbf{W}_B$ denotes the weight vector $[W_B^h, W_B^o]$ of B, and $\mathbf{W}_C$ denotes the weight vector $[W_C^h, W_C^o]$ of C. Initially, let $W_A^h = \sqrt{a}$, where $a \in \mathbb{R}^+$, and $W_A^o = W_B^h = W_B^o = W_C^h = W_C^o = 1$. As a result, given an input x to A, we have $I(X) = x\sqrt{a}$. Then, φ_B is used to update the weights of network B to $W_B^h = x\sqrt{a}$ and $W_B^o = x\sqrt{a}$. If we had only networks A and B fibred, the input $y = 1$, for example, would then produce an output $o_B = ax^2$ for network B, and the same $(o_A = ax^2)$ for network A. Since network C is also embedded into the system, however, given an input y to network B, the fibring function φ_C is used to update the weights of network C, using $I(Y)$ as a parameter. Thus, if $y = 1$, we have $I(Y) = ax^2$, and the weights of network C are changed to $W_C^h = ax^2$ and $W_C^o = ax^2$. Finally, if $z = 1$, the output of network C (and then that of networks B and A as well) is a^2x^4. This illustrates the computation of polynomials in fNNs. The computation of odd-degree polynomials and of negative coefficients can be achieved by adding more hidden layers to the networks, as we shall see later.

9.5 Dynamics of Fibred Networks

Example 19 also illustrates the dynamics of fibred networks. Let us now define such a dynamics precisely.

Definition 48 (Nested fNNs). Let $N_1, N_2, \ldots, N_n$ be neural networks. $N_1, N_2, \ldots, N_n$ form a nested fibred network if N_i is embedded into a neuron of N_{i-1} with a fibring function φ_i for any $2 \leq i \leq n$. We say that $j - 1$ $(1 \leq j \leq n)$ is the level of network N_j.

Definition 49 (Dynamics of FNNs). Let $N_1, N_2, \ldots, N_n$ be a nested fibred network. Let φ_i be the fibring function from N_{i-1} to N_i for $2 \leq i \leq n$. Let $\mathbf{i}_j$ denote an input vector to network N_j, let $\mathbf{W}_j$ denote the current weight vector of N_j, *let* $\mathbf{I}_n(\mathbf{i}_j)$ denote the input potential of the neuron n_j of N_j into which N_{j+1} is embedded given input vector $\mathbf{i}_j$, *let* $\mathbf{O}_{n_j}$ denote the output of neuron n_j, and let $f_{\mathbf{W}_j}(\mathbf{i}_j)$ denote the function computed by network N_j given $\mathbf{W}_j$ and $\mathbf{i}_j$, as in the standard way for feedforward networks. The output o_j of network N_j $(1 \leq j \leq n-1)$ is defined recursively in terms of the output o_{j+1} of network N_{j+1} as follows:

$$\mathbf{W}_{j+1} := \varphi_{j+1}(\mathbf{I}(\mathbf{i}_j), \mathbf{W}_{j+1}), 1 \leq j \leq n-1,$$

$$o_n = f_{\mathbf{W}_n}(\mathbf{i}_n),$$

$$o_j = f_{\mathbf{W}_j}(\mathbf{i}_j, \mathbf{O}_{n_j} := o_{j+1}),$$

where $f_{\mathbf{W}_j}(\mathbf{i}_j, \mathbf{O}_{n_j} := o_{j+1})$ denotes the function computed by N_j when the output of its neuron n_j is substituted by the output of network N_{j+1}.

9.6 Expressiveness of Fibred Networks

Now that fNNs have been defined, we proceed to show that, in addition to being universal approximators, fNNs can approximate any polynomial function, and thus are more expressive than standard feedforward neural networks.

Proposition 24. *Fibred neural networks can approximate any (Borel) measurable function in a compact domain to any desired degree of accuracy (i.e. fNNs are universal approximators).*

Proof. This follows directly from the proof that single-hidden-layer feedforward neural networks are universal approximators [140], together with the observation that level-zero fibred networks are a generalisation of single-hidden-layer feedforward networks.   ∎

Proposition 25. *Fibred neural networks can approximate any polynomial function to any desired degree of accuracy.*[6]

Proof. Consider the level-zero network N in Fig. 9.6. Let $n+1$ ($n \in \mathbb{N}$) be the number of input neurons of N, $0 \leq i \leq n$, $a_i \in \mathbb{R}$. Now, embed $n-1$ networks into the input neurons of N, all at level 1, as indicated in Fig. 9.6 for networks A, B, and C, such that network A is embedded into neuron A of network N, network B is embedded into neuron B of N, and network C is embedded into neuron C of N. Each of the $n-1$ embedded networks is used to represent one of $x^2, x^3, \ldots, x^n$. In Fig. 9.6, A represents x^2, B represents x^3, and C represents x^n. In the ensemble, all networks, including N, contain linear neurons. A network N_j that represents x^j ($2 \leq j \leq n$) contains two input neurons (to allow the representation of $a_j \in \mathbb{R}$), $j-1$ hidden layers, each layer containing a single hidden neuron (let us number these $h_1, h_2, \ldots, h_{j-1}$), and a single output neuron. In addition, let $a_j/2$ be the weight from each input neuron to h_1, and let 1 be the weight of any other connection in N_j. We need to show that N_j computes $a_j x^j$. From Definition 49, given an input x to N and $\varphi_j = x \cdot \mathbf{W}_j$, the weights of N_j are multiplied by x. Then, given an input $(1,1)$ to N_j, neuron h_1 will produce an output $a_j x$, neuron h_2 will produce an output $a_j x^2$, and so on. Neuron h_{j-1} will produce an output $a_j x^{j-1}$, and the output neuron will produce $a_j x^j$. Finally, by Definition 47, the neuron in N into which N_j is embedded will present an activation $a_j x^j$, and the output of N will be $\sum_j a_j x^j$. The addition of $a_1 x$ and a_0 is straightforward (see network N in Fig. 9.6), completing the proof that fNNs compute $\sum_i a_i x^i$.   ∎

---

[6] Recall that, differently from functions in a compact domain, polynomial functions are not bounded functions.

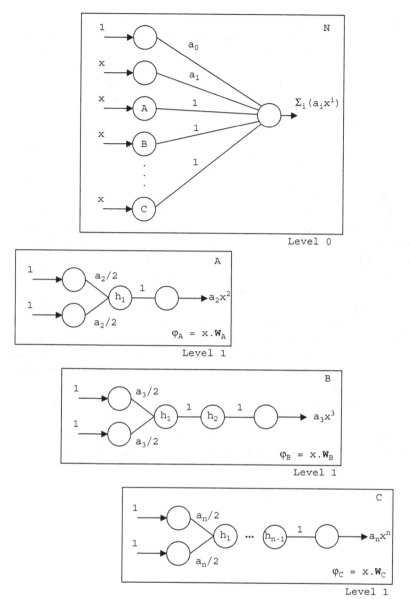

Fig. 9.6 Computing polynomials in fibred networks

9.7 Discussion

This chapter has introduced a neural-network architecture named 'fibred neural networks' (fNNs), which combines a number of standard feedforward neural networks (which can be trained using backpropagation) by means of a fibring function.

We have shown that, in addition to being universal approximators, fNNs can approximate any polynomial function, therefore being more expressive than standard feedforward neural networks. Pi–sigma networks [233, 272] are also more expressive than standard networks, and can be seen as a special type of fNN where only multiplication is allowed to be used in the fibring function. In fact, it was sufficient to use only multiplication for the purpose of proving Proposition 25. In practice, however, other functions might be more useful.

The question of which logics can be represented in fNNs is an interesting open question. In particular, fibring may be of interest for the representation of variables and for reasoning with function symbols in connectionist first-order logic systems, as is discussed in some detail in Chap. 10. Another interesting line of work to pursue would be on the fibring of recurrent neural networks. Recurrent networks already possess a limited ability to compute unbounded functions [126]. A comparison of the computational capabilities of these two architectures would be highly desirable.

Ultimately, our goal is to strike a balance between the reasoning and learning capabilities of connectionist systems. There are generally two courses of action: (i) to take simple network structures that support effective learning (e.g. [269]) and show that they can represent languages more expressive than propositional logic (this is our approach), or (ii) to take (more complex) connectionist systems capable of representing expressive languages (typically first-order logic [137]) and have efficient learning algorithms developed for those. This is necessary in practice because many interesting real-world applications require languages more expressive than propositional logic; there are examples in failure diagnosis, engineering, and bioinformatics. Bioinformatics, for example, requires an ability to reason about relations as used in first-order logic [6] and to learn from structured data. For neural-symbolic integration to be successful on this front, for example to compete with inductive logic programming [189], it needs to offer such more expressive languages. We shall address the problem of performing relational learning in neural-symbolic systems in Chap. 10.

Chapter 10
Relational Learning in Neural Networks

Neural networks have been very successful as robust, massively parallel learning systems [125]. On the other hand, they have been severely criticised as being essentially propositional. In [176], John McCarthy argued that neural networks use unary predicates only, and that the concepts they compute are ground instances of these predicates. Thus, he claimed, neural networks could not produce concept descriptions, only discriminations.

Since then, there has been a considerable amount of work on representing first-order logic in artificial neural networks [2, 3, 13, 17, 114, 133, 137, 204, 205, 229, 230] (see [138] for a collection of papers on the representation of first-order logic). Generally speaking, the community has focused on the following three issues:

(i) showing the equivalence of neural networks with Turing machines and super-Turing computation (i.e. the computation of nonTuring-computable functions) [234];

(ii) computing (or approximating the computation of) first-order logic using neural networks (using theorem proving [152] and semantics [229, 259]);

(iii) tackling first-order applications (notably language processing [239] and relational databases [252]), though this has mainly been done through propositionalisation [223].

Using networks derived from the CILP system, languages more powerful than classical propositional logic were considered in Chaps. 5 to 7 and [20, 120, 136], but the networks were kept simple in an attempt to benefit from efficient inductive learning. In [20], for example, the LINUS inductive logic programming (ILP) system [159, 160] was used to translate first-order concepts into a propositional attribute-value language, and then CILP was applied. The idea was to induce relational concepts with neural networks using LINUS as the front end.[1] Some

---

[1] In fact, our interest in LINUS originated from the fact that it provides a translation from first-order, nonrecursive logic programs to the form of attribute-value propositions, and vice versa, the idea being that any efficient machine learning method could be used in the process of hypothesis generation between these translations. In [20], we simply chose to use CILP neural networks as such a method.

A.S. d'Avila Garcez et al., *Neural-Symbolic Cognitive Reasoning*, Cognitive Technologies, 127
© Springer-Verlag Berlin Heidelberg 2009

first-order inductive learning tasks, taken from the literature on symbolic machine learning, were learned successfully, thus indicating that such simple neural networks can indeed induce relations.

One may argue, however, that the combination of CILP and LINUS is not different from the CILP experiments using ground programs [66], because the learning process itself is essentially propositional. The following statement is as true today as it was in 1999:

'Despite the progress in knowledge-based neurocomputing (KBN), many open problems remain. KBN can not yet harness the full power of predicate logic representations frequently used in AI. Although good progress has been made to represent symbolic structures in KBN, the dynamic variable binding problem remains to be solved. Further questions to address include the development of new integration strategies and more diverse types of knowledge representations, e.g., procedural knowledge, methods to exchange knowledge, and reasoning capabilities' [51].

This is a vast area for further research. In this chapter, we argue that the focus of the research should be on relational learning [84]. In particular, instead of solving the connectionist variable-binding problem, we are concerned about answering the following question: are neural networks capable of generalising rules of the form $Q(Y,Z) \to P(X,Y)$ from instances such as $Q(b,c) \to P(a,b)$ and $Q(d,e) \to P(c,d)$? Standard neural networks lack two concepts that are fundamental in symbolic artificial intelligence, namely variables and relations. Are neural networks effective precisely because they do not use such concepts as a matter of course? In what follows, we try to answer this question negatively (although it may well be the case that neural networks are more effective when they use propositionalisation).

We introduce a standard representation for variables and relations that preserves the simplicity of neural networks, and in doing this we seek to also maintain effective, robust learning capabilities. This approach has advantages over previous work in that it seeks to strike a more natural balance between two clearly important concepts in symbolic AI and standard connectionist systems (instead of imposing symbolism onto connectionism, which leads frequently to rather inefficient systems). In a nutshell, we see variable binding as a learning task, and we use temporal synchonisation between networks in an ensemble to learn and reason about relations. A network may represent a concept $Q(Y,Z)$ and another network may represent a concept $P(X,Y)$. Then, if the training examples associated with Q and P are synchronised, a relation between these two concepts/networks needs to be learned, for example $Q(Y,Z) \to P(X,Y)$. We use the key idea of *metalevel networks* relating networks Q and P to implement this, as detailed in what follows.

10.1 An Example

Let us start by considering an example traditionally used in ILP [189] to illustrate relational learning in neural networks. Consider the variables X, Y, Z and the relations (predicates) *father*, *mother*, and *grandparent*. Our goal is to learn a description of *grandparent* from examples of the *father, mother,* and *grandparent* relations such as *father(charles, william)*, *mother(elisabeth, charles)*, and *grandparent(elisabeth, william)*. To help in the ILP search for the goal description, some background knowledge may be available; for example, the concept of *parent* may be useful (*parent(X, Y)* iff mother(X, Y) or father(X, Y)). Given a set of examples *e* and background knowledge *bk*, the ILP learning problem can be expressed as 'find a hypothesis *h* such that $bk \cup h \vdash e$'. The bulk of the work is then on how to search the hypothesis space (in this example, the space of possible descriptions of *grandparent* in terms of *mother* and *father*). The idea of inverse resolution is typically used [189]. For example, given *grandparent(elisabeth, william)* and *mother(elisabeth, charles)*, one can induce *grandparent(X, Y) if mother(X, Z)* with substitutions $X/elisabeth$, $Y/william$, and $Z/charles$, and given this and *father(charles, william)*, one can induce *grandparent(X, Y) if mother(X, Z)* and *father(Z, Y)*. Sometimes, negative examples can also be used to help reduce the hypothesis space, mainly by checking for consistency between the negative examples and the induced rules; *father(philip, william)* would be a negative example.

As can be seen, ILP is very appealing from the point of view of the rich descriptions it can generate with the use of variables and relations. ILP is richer than for example, probabilistic relational models (PRMs) [93], which are in turn more efficient than ILP. And ILP is more comprehensible than neural networks or support vector machines [232], which are in turn more robust than ILP or PRMs. Most of the criticism of ILP concerns the lack of efficacy of its methods and algorithms. The response of the ILP community has been mainly to try to create more efficient algorithms, and to obtain better accuracy in specific applications. Instead, we see learning as a long-term adaptation process, the product of experience, arising from the stimulation of neurons in the brain that results from varied cognitive stimulation. The modelling of learning therefore should, in our view, account for the necessary parallelism, robustness, and fault tolerance associated with this process. Contrast, for example, the ILP approach with Doumas and Hummel's comparison-based relational learning [82], which, despite the use of propositionalisation, is well founded on the above aspects of human cognition.

In most real-life domains, one cannot state that $P(X)$ is *true* from a single observation of, say, $P(a)$, even if all there is available is $P(a)$. In our view, a system that does this – we may call it *hasty generalisation* (some may call it a form of overfitting) – is bound to achieve poor generalisation at a later stage because there is very little support/evidence for the target predicate in the set of examples.[2] Notice further that ILP does not in general tolerate noise. This is true for most ILP systems,

---

[2] Notice that when hasty generalisation takes place, the role of negative examples becomes crucial for trying to curb wrong conclusions, but in real-world applications negative examples are harder to come by. Consider, for example, a power plant case study where alarms in a power plant have to be associated with faults in the transmission lines and generators. Sensors in the system relate alarms and associated possible faults over time, and these form our set of training examples. Of course, there may be noise in the system because the sensors themselves may be faulty; the training system should be able to deal with this. Now, a useful negative example is not simply the complement of the set of examples; it is information about a component in the system which we are certain is not faulty and therefore did not cause the alarm. To obtain such a negative example (ruling out a

although probabilistic and kernel ILP try to address this problem [158]. Noise may occur in the form of a mistaken observation (an incorrect positive example in the data set), for example *mother(elisabeth, william)* in the above family relationship problem, or in the form of contradicting background knowledge rules, which are common, for example, in fault diagnosis domains. Noise intolerance is unrealistic in most applications. Neural networks have been shown to be particularly suitable for dealing with noise.

10.2 Variable Representation

Let us look at the above example of family relationships in the context of neural-symbolic integration. Our goal is to offer a neural-network framework for relational learning. We shall take inspiration from the framework of connectionist modal logic (CML) [79], since it can represent relations in the form of modal logic's accessibility relations. How could it be used to represent relations such as *mother(X, Y)*? The first question we need to answer, however, is how can we represent variables such as X and Y and, perhaps more importantly, what is an appropriate representation for the purpose of machine learning?

We know that variable grounding (propositionalisation) can be quite effective in many real-world applications, but it may lead to very large (or even infinite) networks, according to the size of the domain. As discussed above, in this chapter we want to consider alternatives to propositionalisation. With this in mind, it seems natural to treat each neuron as a variable so that the burden of instantiation is left to the network's inputs (which, in turn, can be any real number). The task of learning relationships between variables would then be analogous to that of learning rules in propositional logic, but in the space of reals. One could have a network *mother* whose task was to learn to relate variables/input neurons X and Y. This network's output neuron[3] should be *activated* whenever the values of X and Y are to be related.

As usual, we say that a neuron is activated whenever it presents an activation greater than $A_{min} \in \mathbb{R}^+$. We need to provide a mapping of variable instances to real numbers. One such mapping is simply to denote instances $a, b, c, \ldots$ by the naturals $1, 2, 3, \ldots$, respectively. Now, suppose that *mother(a, b)* and *mother(b, c)* are *true*. The network needs to learn that the inputs $(1, 2)$ and $(2, 3)$ should activate the output neuron *mother*. In practice, for learning purposes, we should associate each instance with an interval so that a is associated with an interval $1 \pm \varepsilon$, b with a interval $2 \pm \varepsilon$, and so on, where ε is a small real number. If, in addition, *mother(X, Y)* is *true*, then the output neuron should be activated whenever $X > A_{min}$ and $Y > A_{min}$. In this case, it is desirable that $A_{min} + 2\varepsilon < 1$ so that $A_{min} \in (0, 1)$ and there is no overlap with the

---

fault), an engineer would have to analyse the behaviour of the component in relation to its detailed specification, testing it extensively, possibly in the context of the entire system.

[3] When it is clear from the context, we use the term *mother* to refer to the output neuron as well as the network.

interval for a. In summary, if $P(X)$ holds, we activate output neuron P for any input $X > A_{min}$. If $P(a)$ holds, we activate P for $X = 1 \pm \varepsilon$. If $P(b)$ holds, we activate P for $X = 2 \pm \varepsilon$, and so on.

10.3 Relation Representation

So far, our networks represent predicates (or concepts), having variables as input neurons. The next step is to learn how to relate predicates by relating networks. In other words, we need to be able to represent relations between concepts as connections between networks. Relations are a metalevel notion. One can think of the learning of relations as being at a different level of abstraction from the learning of a concept. A parallel can be drawn here with the idea of different abstraction levels in a Kohonen map [112]. We see those different levels, however, as conceptual (or for organisational purposes only), and we believe that the structures in one level should be the same as those in the next. Hence, we may have a network that represents $P(X,Y)$, a network that represents $Q(Y,Z)$, and a network that represents the fact that, for example, $P(X,Y) \rightarrow Q(Y,Z)$. These can be organised into a network ensemble so that one can see such relationships, but it should also be possible to present the ensemble as a single, large massively parallel structure because the principles governing the entire model ought to be the same. With this in mind, if we consider that a single-hidden-layer network represents concept P, and that another single-hidden-layer network represents concept Q, a third single-hidden-layer (metalevel) network should be sufficient to represent a relation between P and Q. These are relations between the concepts P and Q, which are effectively encoded in the set of weights and the hidden layers of such networks. So, if Q is our *target predicate* (e.g. *grandparent* in the example above), a metanetwork maps the hidden layer of network P to the output of network Q through a number of hidden neurons of its own (only now at a different level of abstraction). If P were the target predicate for learning, then the metanetwork would take the hidden layer of Q as input and the output of P as output.

   Figure 10.1 illustrates the idea. The object-level networks represent $P(X,Y)$, $Q(Y,Z)$, and $R(X,Z)$. In addition, a metalevel network maps P and Q to R, our target predicate in this example. This network itself may have a number of hidden neurons (two in Fig. 10.1) through which relations such as $P(X,Y) \wedge Q(Y,Z) \rightarrow R(X,Z)$ can be learned. The learning process in the metanetwork can be the same as that in the object-level networks. This allows general relational knowledge to be represented in relatively simple, modular networks.

   It is worth noting that, given our definition of *fibring* in Chap. 9, the representation of function symbols should come naturally with this framework. If a neuron represents a variable X and this neuron is fibred into a network that computes a function f, then the neuron's output can be made to represent $f(X)$ through fibring. We know that neural networks can compute (and indeed learn to approximate) any n-ary Borel measurable function. So, it is not difficult to see that, with fibring,

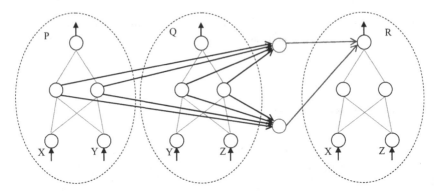

Fig. 10.1 Representation of relational knowledge

we can represent predicates containing function symbols such as $P(f(X), Y, g(Z))$. Notice how, for the purposes of learning, although it is quite general, this structure is very modular, with each function being computed by a separate network in the ensemble, which can itself be treated as a black box within the system and trained separately. It should not be very difficult to show that this set-up can account for n-ary functions and composite functions with the use of nested fibring [67, 101]. However, we leave this as future work for now.

10.4 Relational Learning

Let us continue to use the family relationship example to illustrate relational learning. Consider the target predicate *grandparent*, for which a description needs to be learned, given examples of the predicates *father* and *mother* (all binary predicates). Assume that the following training examples are available: *grandparent(elisabeth, william)*, *mother(elisabeth, charles)*, and *father(charles, william)*. Each example can be presented to each of the object-level networks separately for training, following some convention for a numerical representation for each instance, say, *elisabeth* = 1, *charles* = 2, and *william* = 3. In addition, we say that the metalevel network is to be trained whenever examples are presented simultaneously to the object-level networks. The idea is that if examples are presented to two or more networks at the same time, then a relation between the concepts associated with these networks can be learned. Imagine a child who, when faced with many examples of who is the mother or the father of whom, still does not seem to create a description of *grandparent*. Only when this child pays attention to the relevant examples together, visualising them at the same time either physically or mentally, will he or she manage to establish the appropriate relationship. When examples are presented to the object-level networks at the same time, relational learning among such networks can take place in the metalevel. When a child visualises *elisabeth*, *charles*, and *william* together as *mother, father*, and *grandchild*, he or she may induce a (hopefully more general) description of an attentional target concept. We are therefore proposing that the *timing* of one's experience with respect to the target concept be treated as a crucial aspect for relational learning. This idea of *temporal synchrony* is akin to the synchronisation used by Shastri and Ajjanagadde's SHRUTI system [229]. Notice, however, that we do not seek to impose synchronisation as a feature of the system. If neurons are labelled as *X*, the networks do not control the fact that identical input values should be presented to such neurons. Instead, given simultaneous examples *mother(elisabeth, charles)* and *father(charles, william)*, if *charles* is associated with *Y* in the network *mother*, then *charles* is expected to be associated with *Y* in the network *father*.

Consider Fig. 10.1 again. Whenever training examples are presented simultaneously to the object-level networks *P*, *Q*, and *R*, a learning step can be triggered in the metalevel network. The activation values of the hidden neurons of *P* and *Q* become the input vector, and the activation value of the output of *R* becomes the target output for the metalevel network. The algorithm below describes the idea more precisely for an ensemble in the general case. Notice how, for the family relationship problem, if we let network *P* denote the *mother* predicate, network *Q* denote the *father* predicate, and network *R* denote the *grandparent* predicate, a training example $<i_P, o_P>$ where $i_P = (1,2)$ and $o_P = 1$ will represent *mother(elisabeth, charles)*, a training example $<i_Q, o_Q>$ where $i_Q = (2,3)$ and $o_Q = 1$ will represent *father(charles, william)*, and a training example $<i_R, o_R>$ where $i_R = (1,3)$ and $o_R = 1$ will represent *grandparent(elisabeth, william)*. Let $Act_P^{h_1}(i_P)$ and $Act_P^{h_2}(i_P)$ denote the activation states of the hidden neurons of network *P* given an input vector i_P (given a current set of weights for *P*). Similarly, let $Act_Q^{h_1}(i_Q)$ and $Act_Q^{h_2}(i_Q)$ denote the activation states of the hidden neurons of network *Q* for an input vector i_Q (given a current set of weights for *Q*). Finally, let $Act_R(i_R)$ denote the activation state of the output neuron of network *R* for an input i_R and a set of weights for *R*. If i_P, i_Q, and i_R are presented at the same time to the networks, a new training example $<i, o>$ can be created, where $i = (Act_P^{h_1}(i_P), Act_P^{h_2}(i_P), Act_Q^{h_1}(i_Q), Act_Q^{h_2}(i_Q))$ and $o = Act_R(i_R)$. Since the target concept *grandparent* is represented by network *R*, a metalevel network from *P* and *Q* to *R* can be trained with the example $<i, o>$. This network, call it $R(P, Q)$, contains the hidden neurons of *P* and *Q* as input, and the output neuron of *R* as output. The number of hidden neurons in $R(P, Q)$ is a matter for the learning process, as are the numbers of hidden neurons in *P*, *Q*, and *R* themselves. For learning, $R(P, Q)$ can be treated just like *P*, *Q*, *R*. In the experiments described below, we used *backpropagation* [224].[4]

---

[4] A complete learning of the *grandparent* concept would require synchronisation of the relevant examples combining the necessary *father* and *mother* predicates. For instance, if examples *mother(elisabeth, ann)*, *mother(ann, zara)*, and *grandparent(elisabeth, zara)* were made available for learning synchronisation, a copy P' of the *mother* network would be needed, so that a metanetwork $R(P, P')$ could be trained. Alternatively, intermediate concepts such as *parent*, *grandmother*, and *grandfather* could be used. In any case, we place the burden of unification and clause copying on the set-up/synchronisation of the training examples, not on the network ensemble itself.

Relational Learning Algorithm

1. Let $\mathcal{N}_1, \mathcal{N}_2, \ldots, \mathcal{N}_n$ be single-hidden-layer neural networks in a network ensemble. Let $P_1, P_2, \ldots, P_n$ denote the concepts (predicates) represented by $\mathcal{N}_1, \mathcal{N}_2, \ldots, \mathcal{N}_n$, respectively.
2. Let P_n represent a target predicate for learning.
3. Let $h_1^j, \ldots, h_m^j$ denote the hidden neurons of network $\mathcal{N}_j$, $1 \leq j \leq n$.
4. Let $o_1^n, \ldots, o_m^n$ denote the output neurons of (target) network $\mathcal{N}_n$.
5. Let $Act_x(i)$ denote the activation state of neuron x given input vector i (and a current set of weights).
6. For each input vector i_n presented to $\mathcal{N}_n$ at a time point t, if input vectors $i_1, i_2, \ldots, i_{n-1}$ are presented to any of $\mathcal{N}_1, \mathcal{N}_2, \ldots, \mathcal{N}_{n-1}$ at the same time point t, then:

   (a) Create a single-hidden-layer neural network $\mathcal{N}_n(\mathcal{N}_1, \mathcal{N}_2, \ldots, \mathcal{N}_{n-1})$ with input neurons $h_1^1, h_2^1, \ldots, h_m^1, h_1^2, h_2^2, \ldots, h_m^2, \ldots, h_1^{n-1}, h_2^{n-1}, \ldots, h_m^{n-1}$, and output neurons $o_1^n, o_2^n, \ldots, o_m^n$ (if one does not exist yet).
   (b) Create a training example $<i, o>_t$ where $i = (Act_{h_1^1}(i_1), Act_{h_2^1}(i_1), \ldots, Act_{h_m^1}(i_1), Act_{h_1^2}(i_2), Act_{h_2^2}(i_2), \ldots, Act_{h_m^2}(i_2), \ldots, Act_{h_1^{n-1}}(i_{n-1}), Act_{h_2^{n-1}}(i_{n-1}), \ldots, Act_{h_m^{n-1}}(i_{n-1}))$ and $o = (Act_{o_1^n}(i_n), Act_{o_2^n}(i_n), \ldots, Act_{o_m^n}(i_n))$.

7. Train $\mathcal{N}_n(\mathcal{N}_1, \mathcal{N}_2, \ldots, \mathcal{N}_{n-1})$ with examples $<i, o>_t$; the network will contain relational knowledge about P_n with respect to $P_1, P_2, \ldots, P_{n-1}$.

10.5 Relational Reasoning

In the propositional case, we have seen that we can associate neurons with atoms, and neuronal activation with truth values, so that reasoning and learning can be combined (reasoning being associated with network computation and learning with network structure). When we associate neurons with variables, the question of variable binding springs to mind. From the point of view reasoning, the problem lies in how to associate different neurons labelled as the same variable with the same constant. In our setting, the answer to this is left to the learning process. Assume, for example, that $P(X) \rightarrow Q(X)$. Whenever output neuron P is activated, output neuron Q should be activated. This is done through the metanetwork. Recall that we use the parameter A_{min} to say that X is *true*. Therefore, if the hidden layer of P activates Q for $X > A_{min}$, we say that $P(X) \rightarrow Q(X)$. If $X = 1 \pm \varepsilon$, we say that $P(a) \rightarrow Q(a)$. If $X = 2 \pm \varepsilon$, we say that $P(b) \rightarrow Q(b)$, and so on. Using this mapping, we can set up a network quite easily to implement $P(X) \rightarrow Q(X)$ for all X. Now, assume that $P(X) \rightarrow Q(a)$. If, in addition, $P(X)$ is a *fact*, then output neuron P should be activated for any input value $X > A_{min}$. Output neuron Q, however, should be activated when P is activated and $X = 1 \pm \varepsilon$ only, denoting $Q(a)$. Finally, suppose that $P(a) \rightarrow Q(X)$. Output neuron P should be activated for input $X = 1 \pm \varepsilon$

(denoting a), and the hidden layer of P should activate output neuron Q through the metalevel network when the input to Q is $X > A_{min}$.

Most connectionist first-order logic systems require multiple copies of neurons for the various variable bindings. This is a difficult problem, and we do not claim to have solved it. However, as mentioned above, most such systems also have to deal with the added complexity of consistency control across the network. Instead, we avoid this problem by placing the burden of binding on the learning process. Take, for example, the program $\mathcal{P} = \{P(a); P(b); P(X) \rightarrow Q(X); Q(a) \wedge Q(b) \rightarrow R(Y)\}$. We need a network P for which the input a can be provided, and a network P' for which the input b can be provided simultaneously. Then, the hidden layers of P and P' need to be connected to the outputs of Q and Q', respectively, and, finally, the hidden layers of Q and Q' need to be connected to the output of R. The fact that Q and Q' should activate R for inputs a and b, respectively, is to be learned from the set of examples.

As another example, consider again the family relationship problem. With the neurons already labelled as X, Y, Z, we can afford to ignore variable binding, and either learn the relationships between the variables or learn the relationships between the constants. In order to learn the relationships between the variables, we simply treat relational learning as propositional and use A_{min} instead of instances $1, 2, 3$. It is up to the learning process to synchronise the relevant examples and assign appropriate input and output values to the neurons labelled as the same variables across the network ensemble. It is interesting to note, though, that different assignments of values to the constants may affect the learning performance in any particular application, so that alternative mappings other than the simple, uniform distribution used here should be considered (e.g. a bimodal or Gaussian distribution). The choice of distribution can be treated as data preprocessing, again as part of the learning process.

10.6 Experimental Results

In this section, we use Michalski's archetypal example of east–west trains [181] to illustrate the relational model.[5] In this example, the goal is to classify the eastbound and westbound trains, each train having a set of cars as shown in Fig. 10.2. In order to classify a train, certain features of the train, along with features of its cars, must be considered.

The data set contains the following attributes: for each train, (a) the number of cars (3 to 5), and (b) the number of different loads (1 to 4); and for each car, (c) the number of wheels (2 or 3), (d) the length (short or long), (e) the shape (closed-top rectangle, open-top rectangle, double open rectangle, ellipse, engine, hexagon, jagged top, open trap, sloped top, or U-shaped), (f) the number of loads (0 to 3), and (g) the shape of the load (circle, hexagon, rectangle, or triangle). Then, ten boolean variables describe whether any particular pair of types of load are on adjacent cars

---

[5] We are grateful to Rafael Borges for pointing out errors in a previous version of this chapter, and for helping us with the running of some of the experiments.

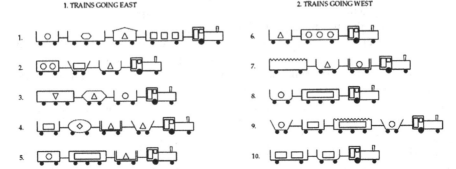

Fig. 10.2 Data set for east–west trains data

of the train (each car carries a single type of load): (h) there is a rectangle next to a rectangle (*false* or *true*), (i) a rectangle next to a triangle (*false* or *true*), (j) a rectangle next to a hexagon (*false* or *true*), (k) a rectangle next to a circle (*false* or *true*), (l) a triangle next to a triangle (*false* or *true*), (m) a triangle next to a hexagon (*false* or *true*), (n) a triangle next to a circle (*false* or *true*), (o) a hexagon next to a hexagon (*false* or *true*), (p) a hexagon next to a circle (*false* or *true*), and (q) a circle next to a circle (*false* or *true*). Finally, the class attribute may be either *east* or *west*. The number of cars in a train varies from 3 to 5. Therefore, attributes referring to properties of cars that do not exist are assigned the value *false*. As usual, -1 is used to denote *false* and 1 to denote *true* in the case of boolean variables. Further, we assign values $1, 2, 3, \ldots$ to any attributes that have multiple values, in the order which they are presented above. So, in the case, for example, of the shape of the load, 1 is used to denote *circle*, 2 to denote *hexagon*, 3 to denote *rectangle*, and so on. Of course, for the corresponding neurons, instead of the bipolar function, we use a linear activation function $h(x) = x$.

Let us compare two ways of performing neural modelling of the above example: one which is akin to propositionalisation, and another way, which is our relational learning model with metanetworks. In the former, a network containing 32 input neurons and one output neuron (denoting *east*) was used, which we call the *flat network* to contrast with the metanetwork approach. The 32 inputs encode: the number of cars in a train; the number of different loads in a train; the number of wheels, the length, and the shape of each car; the number of loads in each car; the shape of the load of each car; and the ten boolean variables described above. In the latter model, 11 networks were created, one for each concept, as follows: $num\_cars(t, nc)$, where the number of cars is $nc \in [3..5]$ in a train $t \in [1..10]$; $num\_loads(t, nl)$, where the number of loads is $nl \in [1..4]$ in a train t; $num\_wheels(t, c, w)$, where the number of wheels is $w \in \{2, 3\}$ in a car $c \in [1..4]$ of train t; $length(t, c, l)$, where the length is $l \in \{-1, 1\}^6$ for car c in train t; $shape(t, c, s)$, where the shape of a car is $s \in [1..10];^7$ $num\_car\_loads(t, c, ncl)$,

---

[6] Here, -1 denotes *short*, and 1 denotes *long*.

[7] As before, 1 denotes *closed-top rectangle*, 2 denotes *open-top rectangle*, and so on.

where the number of loads in a car is $ncl \in [0..3]$; $load\_shape(t,c,ls)$, where the shape of a car's load is $ls \in [1..4]$; $next\_crc(t,c,x)$, where car c has an adjacent car loaded with $circles$, $x \in \{-1,1\}$;[8] $next\_hex(t,c,x)$, where car c has an adjacent car loaded with $hexagons$; $next\_rec(t,c,x)$, where car c has an adjacent car loaded with $rectangles$; and $next\_tri(t,c,x)$, where car c has an adjacent car loaded with $triangles$. Each concept/predicate was represented by a network containing the predicate's arity as the number of inputs and a single output with a value in $\{-1,1\}$; for example, $length(t,c,l)$ had input neurons t, c, and l, and an output neuron $length = 1$ when l was the correct length for the car in question, or $length = -1$ otherwise. In addition, a metanetwork was used to map the hidden layers of the 11 networks to $east \in \{-1,1\}$.

We trained the flat network with backpropagation using a learning rate of 0.3, a term of momentum of 0.4, and nine hidden neurons. We performed leaving-one-out cross-validation on a set of 10 examples. Each training set was presented to the network for 10000 epochs. The test set results are shown in Table 10.1. If we use a threshold $A_{min} = 0.5$, then outputs in the interval $[0.5, 1)$ are associated with $east$, and outputs in the interval $(-1, -0.5]$ are associated with $west$. We can conclude that four out of the five eastbound trains and three out of the five westbound trains were classified correctly. Considering, however, the mean square error (mse) on the test set, the network shows a test set performance of 62% ($mse = 0.38$).

We then trained the 11 networks of the metanetwork by splitting the original 10 examples into 40 examples (10 trains × 4 cars). We trained each network for 30000 epochs[9] on all available examples.[10] Here we had to use a much smaller learning

Table 10.1 Test set results for flat network

Train	Output of flat network	Desired output	Class
1	0.84	1	east
2	0.97	1	east
3	−0.39	1	east
4	0.99	1	east
5	0.51	1	east
6	−0.59	−1	west
7	0.35	−1	west
8	−0.77	−1	west
9	0.84	−1	west
10	−0.99	−1	west

[8] Here, -1 denotes $false$ and 1 denotes $true$. If car c is next to $circles$, then $next\_crc$ is $true$ when $x = 1$ and $false$ when $x = -1$. Otherwise, $next\_crc$ is $true$ when $x = -1$ and $false$ when $x = 1$. Alternative ways of modelling the loads of adjacent cars are possible, for example $next\_crc(t,c)$ or $next\_to(t,c,ls)$.

[9] This took about 30 seconds on a mid-range personal computer.

[10] Notice that at this stage the examples did not contain any information as to whether a train was eastbound or westbound.

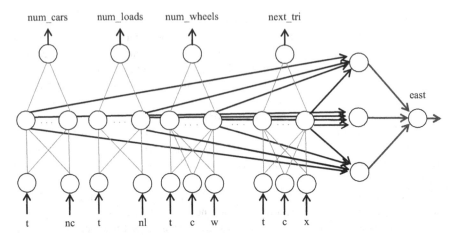

Fig. 10.3 Metalevel network for the east–west trains example

rate $\eta = 0.01$ and term of momentum $\mu = 0.01$, and a relatively large number (20) of hidden neurons. This was necessary so that the networks could learn the intricate relationships between the variables; learning from real-valued data clearly seems harder in this case than learning from binary data. Figure 10.3 shows the set-up of the network.

For the metanetwork, we performed leaving-one-out cross-validation (leaving out one train at a time); we left out four examples for testing at a time, and trained the metanetwork on the remaining 36 examples. Each set of 4 examples corresponded exactly to the possible cars in a particular train. In this way, we made sure that the metanetwork could not use information about a car in a train in order to classify another car in the same train. This is probably the most appropriate way of comparing the learning performance of the metanetwork with that of the flat network, for which leaving-one-out cross-validation was used on the set of 10 trains. We used a learning rate of 0.3 and a term of momentum of 0.4 to train the metanetwork for 10000 epochs, as was done for the flat network. We chose to use only three hidden neurons to connect the metanetwork's 220 input neurons (11 networks with 20 hidden neurons each) to an output neuron denoting *east*.

The metanetwork classified nine out of the 10 trains correctly. The number of cars correctly classified, again using $A_{min} = 0.5$, is shown in Table 10.2. Only train 5 was not classified correctly, with an average network output very close to zero in this case. Rather than a wrong classification of train 5 as westbound, this output indicates a high level of uncertainty. The metanetwork shows a test set performance of 92.5% ($mse = 0.075$).

The results are an indication of the potential of metalevel networks as a model for fault-tolerant, robust relational learning. The main differences between the two approaches are (i) they use different network architectures, and (ii) metanetworks can learn from structured examples. Because the examples were structured the metanetwork included the labels of the trains (variable t) and cars (variable c) as part of

Table 10.2 Test set results for the metanetwork

Train	Cars correctly classified	Average network output	Desired output	Class
1	4 out of 4	1.00	1	*east*
2	3 out of 3	0.99	1	*east*
3	3 out of 3	1.00	1	*east*
4	4 out of 4	1.00	1	*east*
5	1 out of 3	0.09	1	*east*
6	2 out of 2	−1.00	−1	*west*
7	3 out of 3	−0.98	−1	*west*
8	2 out of 2	−1.00	−1	*west*
9	4 out of 4	−1.00	−1	*west*
10	2 out of 2	−1.00	−1	*west*

the learning. Although this is common in ILP and other types of symbolic machine learning, it is normally not the case for connectionist learning. Neural-symbolic systems can promote learning from structured data, as the east–west trains example illustrates. However, a more detailed study of how the labels can influence learning performance is required (including how the labelling order may affect results).

Training the flat network to a training-set *mse* very close to zero was straightforward. Training the 11 networks associated with the predicates proved to be harder, with the *mse* on the training set remaining at about 10% after 30000 epochs. As mentioned, we attribute this to the real-valued examples used by such networks. Training the metanetwork, however, turned out to be straightforward, with the training-set *mse* reducing quickly to zero after as little as 5000 epochs. Recall that this metanetwork contained 220 input neurons. Even then, learning was very efficient, taking less than 10 seconds for each fold. Although one may argue that the metanetwork turned out to be more complex in structure (with 663 weighted connections) than the flat network (with 297 connections), the gain in generalisation and the modularity of the networks[11] offer the metanetwork approach a clear advantage over propositionalisation.

It may help to think of the relational approach as learning in two stages, at the object-level and metalevel. The two stages seem to add to the system's generalisation capability, reducing the chances of overfitting. Further investigations are required, however: in particular, comparative larger-scale experiments. Performance comparisons with ILP and PRMs with respect to accuracy and learning time in both noisy and uncertain domains are also needed.

There is a clear trade-off and a balance to be struck between expressiveness and performance in machine learning. The relational model proposed here tries to address this issue. It departs from the idea of learning as inverse resolution, but acknowledges the need for rich relational structures. It could be seen as an alternative to ILP, but it could equally and more generally be seen as a relational framework

---

[11] Notice that each network can be trained independently and then deployed in a particular relational-learning scenario.

encompassing connectionist learning and symbolic approaches, where the idea of modular, object-level, and metalevel learning is embraced.

In summary, this chapter's message is that networks can represent concepts and variables, and when examples are presented simultaneously to networks, relations between such concepts can be learned by a metanetwork, which has the same form as the original networks but is at a different level of abstraction. This structure prompts us to organise the problem in terms of concepts and relations, and to learn in stages from structured data, hopefully producing a better generalisation performance.

10.7 Discussion

Although symbolic descriptions of learning can be clear and unambiguous, first-order logic may not be the appropriate representation for learning and, as natural as it may seem, inverse resolution may equally well not be the most appropriate method for learning. Of course, logical descriptions are generally more convenient than interconnected neurons/graphs (some graphical representations may be easier to understand than logic, but this is not true in general in the case of neural networks). For example, despite the encouraging results obtained above on the east–west trains dataset, it is not easy to spot by inspecting the metanetwork that the classification problem can be described as $car(T, C) \land short(C) \land closed\_top(C) \rightarrow east(T)$. This motivates the research that is being done on knowledge extraction from neural networks. In this book, we have focused on representation and reasoning. However, (first-order) knowledge extraction is an important part of neural-symbolic integration.

In a previous book [66], a general knowledge extraction method was proposed. Others have also proposed extraction methods, and for each logic considered in this book, there is scope for further research on knowledge extraction. Most of the work so far on knowledge extraction has used production rules or interval rules, i.e. propositional logic. Clearly, rules containing relations, modalities, variables, etc. would improve the comprehensibility of the rule set, and possibly offer more effective extraction methods. Extraction is an integral part of neural-symbolic systems whenever these are required to provide descriptions as opposed to discriminations. This book opens up a number of avenues for research on knowledge extraction. We believe that the general extraction method proposed in [66] can be adapted to the various logics considered in this book. Since we have shown that connectionism can deal with such logics, there is no reason to believe that we should not be able to perform knowledge extraction based on such representations, and indeed benefit from it, particularly in terms of rule set comprehensibility.

Another interesting area for further research is goal-directed reasoning [107]. This form of reasoning may be advantageous from a computational standpoint. Goal-directed reasoning can be thought of as reversing the network in order to reason backwards from a goal, say $east(T)$, to subgoals, say $car(T, C)$ and $short(C)$, until facts are reached, for example $short(c_1)$. Unfortunately, the problem is more complicated than simply reverting the network, because the inverse relation is not one-to-one. This is similar to the problem of abductive reasoning, i.e. the problem of reasoning to the best explanation. In a nutshell, given $a \rightarrow b$, if b is observed as a matter of course, then a is a possible explanation as to why it is so. One can assume that a is *true* (i.e. abduce a) and reason hypothetically towards an explanation for b. If, in addition, $c \rightarrow b$, then c is an alternative explanation for b, also to be considered in this hypothetical reasoning process. We do not tackle abductive reasoning in this book, but we would like to point the interested reader to [58], where we have used CML and possible worlds to label such alternative hypotheses, thereby controlling the fact that the inverse relation is not one-to-one. However, a considerable amount of work is still needed in this area. Regarding, for example, the integration of learning and abductive (or goal-directed) reasoning, a key open question is how to control the reasoning process while still providing the system with the flexibility necessary for effective learning.

Chapter 11
Argumentation Frameworks as Neural Networks

Formal models of argumentation have been studied in several areas, notably in logic, philosophy, decision making, artificial intelligence, and law [25, 31, 39, 48, 83, 111, 153, 210, 212, 267]. In artificial intelligence, models of argumentation have been one of the approaches used in the representation of commonsense, nonmonotonic reasoning. They have been particularly successful in modelling chains of *defeasible arguments* so as to reach a conclusion [194, 209]. Although symbolic logic-based models have been the standard for the representation of argumentative reasoning [31, 108], such models are intrinsically related to artificial neural networks, as we shall show in this chapter.

We shall establish a relationship between neural networks and argumentation networks, combining reasoning and learning in the same argumentation framework. We do so by presenting a *neural argumentation algorithm*, similar to the CILP algorithm extended with metalevel priorities (Sect. 4.5), but capable of translating argumentation networks into standard neural networks. We show a correspondence between the two networks. The proposed algorithm works not only for acyclic argumentation networks, but also for circular networks. Then, as an application, we show how the proposed approach enables the accrual of arguments through learning and the parallel computation of arguments. Finally, we discuss how different argumentation models can be combined through the fibring of networks discussed in Chap. 9.

Although we show that the neural network computes the prevailing arguments in the argumentation network (and thus that the argumentation algorithm is sound), arguments will frequently attack one another in such a way that cycles are formed in the network. In such cases, a notion of the relative strength of arguments may be required to decide which arguments should prevail. Nevertheless, in some cases, circularities may lead to an infinite loop in the computation. To tackle this problem, we propose the use of a learning mechanism. Learning can be used to resolve circularities by an iterative change of the strengths of arguments as new information becomes available.[1] Learning and its relation to cumulative argumentation [210, 265] in neural networks will also be discussed.

---

[1] This is closely related to the situation where CILP loops (and the situation where Prolog loops) owing to cycles through negation. Hence, the solution to this problem that we propose in this chapter would also apply to CILP, relaxing the requirement for well-behaved programs.

A.S. d'Avila Garcez et al., *Neural-Symbolic Cognitive Reasoning,* Cognitive Technologies,   143
© Springer-Verlag Berlin Heidelberg 2009

11.1 Value-Based Argumentation Frameworks

We start by describing the notion of a value-based argumentation framework, following Bench-Capon's work [22]. In order to record the values associated with arguments, Bench-Capon extended Dung's argumentation framework [83] by adding to it a set of values and a function mapping arguments to values. A notion of relative strength of arguments may then be defined by use of an audience, which essentially creates an ordering on the set of values. As a result, if an argument A attacks an argument B and the value of B is preferred over the value of A, then it may be the case that A is accepted, but A is not able to defeat B. Therefore, a distinction between *attacks* and *defeats* – which are typically defined as successful attacks – is used [48, 209].

Definition 50. [83] An argumentation network has the form $\mathcal{A} = <\alpha, attack>$, where α is a set of arguments, and 'attack' $\subseteq \alpha^2$ is a relation indicating which arguments attack which other arguments.

Definition 51. [22] A value-based argumentation framework is a 5-tuple $VAF = <\alpha, attacks, V, val, P>$, where α is a finite set of arguments, 'attacks' is an irreflexive binary relation on α, V is a nonempty set of values, *val* is a function mapping elements in α to elements in V, and P is a set of possible audiences, where we may have as many audiences as there are orderings on V. For every $A \in \alpha$, $val(A) \in V$.

Bench-Capon also uses the notion of *colouring* in order to define the preferences of audiences. For example, consider an audience *red* (which prefers red over blue) and an audience *blue* (which prefers blue over red), and the following value-based argumentation: A (coloured red) attacks B (coloured blue), which attacks C (coloured blue). As a result, $\{A, C\}$ are the prevailing arguments for the audience *red*; however, for the audience *blue*, the prevailing arguments are $\{A, B\}$. It is also important to note that Bench-Capon defines the notions of *objective* and *subjective* acceptability of arguments. The first relates to arguments that are acceptable no matter what the choice of preferred values for every audience is, whereas the second relates to arguments that are acceptable to only some audiences. Arguments which are neither objectively nor subjectively acceptable are called *indefensible*. Following Bench-Capon and the extension to argumentation networks given in [18], we model the strength of arguments by defining a function v from *attack* to $\{0, 1\}$, which gives the relative strength of an argument. Given $\alpha_i, \alpha_j \in \alpha$, if $v(\alpha_i, \alpha_j) = 1$, then α_i is said to be stronger than α_j. Otherwise, α_i is said to be weaker than α_j.

Let us consider briefly the relationship between argumentation frameworks and neural networks. As usual, we can think of a neural network as a graph. If we represent an argument as a neuron, then a connection from neuron i to neuron j can be used to indicate that argument i either attacks or supports argument j. The weight of the connection can be seen as corresponding to the strength of the attack or support. Any real number can be assigned to the weight of a connection in a neural network, and thus we shall associate negative weights with attacks, and positive weights with supporting arguments,[2] as detailed later on.

In order to compute the prevailing arguments in a neural network, one needs to take into consideration the relative strength of the attacks as given, for example, by an audience. Since the strengths of the different arguments are represented by the weights of the network, and since learning is the process of progressively changing the weights, it seems natural to use neural learning algorithms to change the network as new information becomes available. We shall investigate this in more detail in Sect. 11.3.

In the case of argumentation networks, it is sufficient to consider definite logic programs (i.e. programs without $\sim$). In this case, the neural network will contain only positive weights (W). We shall then extend such a positive network to represent attacks by using negative weights from the network's hidden layer to its output layer, as explained in detail in what follows.

11.2 Argumentation Neural Networks

In what follows, we introduce an algorithm that translates value-based argumentation networks into neural networks. But first, let us see how the translation works in a typical example of argumentation, namely, the *moral-debate* example [22].

Hal, a diabetic, loses his insulin in an accident through no fault of his own. Before collapsing into a coma, he rushes to the house of Carla, another diabetic. She is not at home, but Hal breaks into her house and uses some of her insulin. Was Hal justified? Does Carla have a right to compensation? The following are some of the arguments in this example:

A: Hal is justified, he was trying to save his life.
B: It is wrong to infringe the property rights of another.
C: Hal will compensate Carla.
D: Hal is endangering Carla's life.
E: Carla has abundant insulin.
F: If Hal is too poor to compensate Carla, he should be allowed to take the insulin as no one should die because they are poor.

Arguments and counter-arguments can be arranged in an argumentation network, as in Fig. 11.1, where an arrow from argument X to argument Y indicates that X attacks Y. For example, the fact that it is wrong to infringe Carla's property rights (B) attacks Hal's justification (A).

---

[2] Generally speaking, an argument i supports an argument j if the coordination of i and j reduces the likelihood of j being defeated. There are several different ways in which an argument may support another. For example, argument i may support argument j by attacking an argument k that attacks j, or argument i may support j directly, for example by strengthening the value of j [266]. In this chapter, we use the terms *attack* and *support* in a loose way, since it will be sufficient to define precisely just the notion of *defeat*.

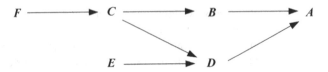

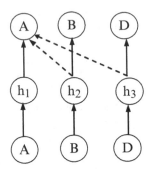

Fig. 11.1 The argumentation network for the moral debate

Fig. 11.2 A neural network for arguments A, B, D

In the argumentation network of Fig. 11.1, some aspects may change as the debate progresses and actions are taken, with the strength of an argument in attacking another changing over time. We see this as a learning process that can be implemented using a neural network in which the weights encode the strength of the arguments. The neural network for the set of arguments $\{A, B, D\}$ is depicted in Fig. 11.2. The network is single-hidden-layer, with inputs (A, B, D), outputs (A, B, D), and a hidden layer (h_1, h_2, h_3). Solid arrows represent positive weights and dotted arrows represent negative weights. Arguments are supported by positive weights and attacked by negative weights. Argument A (input neuron A), for example, supports itself (output neuron A) with the use of hidden neuron h_1. Similarly, argument B supports itself (via h_2), and so does argument D (via h_3). From the argumentation network, B attacks A, and D attacks A; these attacks are implemented in the neural network by negative weights (see the dotted lines in Fig. 11.2) with the use of h_2 and h_3, respectively.

The network of Fig. 11.2 is a standard feedforward neural network that can be trained with the use of a standard learning algorithm. Learning should change the initial weights of the network (or the initial beliefs in the strength of arguments and counter-arguments), according to examples (input and output patterns) of the relationship between the arguments A, B, and D. This will become clearer in Sect. 11.3, where we shall give examples of learning in relation to argumentation.

In Fig. 11.2, generally speaking, if the absolute value of the weight from neuron h_1 to output neuron A (i.e. the strength of A) is greater than the sum of the absolute values of the weights from neurons h_2 and h_3 to A (i.e. the strength of the attacks on A), then one should be able to say that argument A prevails (in which case output neuron A should be *active* in the neural network). Let us implement this form of reasoning using CILP neural networks.

The Neural Argumentation Algorithm introduced below takes a value-based argumentation framework as input and produces a CILP neural network as output. This network uses a semilinear activation function $h(x) = 2/(1+e^{-x}) - 1$ and inputs in $\{-1, 1\}$, where 1 represents *true* and -1 represents *false*. As usual, $0 < A_{min} < 1$ indicates the minimum activation for a neuron to be considered active. The algorithm then defines the set of weights of the neural network as a function of A_{min} such that the neural network computes the prevailing arguments according to the argumentation framework. The values of the weights derive from the proof of Theorem 26, which shows that the neural network indeed executes a sound computation of the argumentation framework.

Neural Argumentation Algorithm

1. Given a value-based argumentation framework $\mathcal{A}$ with arguments $\alpha_1, \alpha_2, \ldots, \alpha_n$, let:
   $$\mathcal{P} = \{r_1 : \alpha_1 \to \alpha_1, r_2 : \alpha_2 \to \alpha_2, \ldots, r_n : \alpha_n \to \alpha_n\}.$$
2. Number each atom of $\mathcal{P}$ from 1 to n and create the input and output layers of a neural network $\mathcal{N}$ such that the i-th neuron represents the i-th atom of $\mathcal{P}$.
3. Given $0 < A_{min} < 1$, calculate $W \geq (1/A_{min}) \cdot (\ln(1+A_{min}) - \ln(1-A_{min}))$.
4. For each rule r_l of $\mathcal{P}$ $(1 \leq l \leq n)$, do:

   (a) Add a neuron N_l to the hidden layer of $\mathcal{N}$.
   (b) Connect neuron α_l in the input layer of $\mathcal{N}$ to hidden neuron N_l and set the connection weight to W.
   (c) Connect hidden neuron N_l to neuron α_l in the output layer of $\mathcal{N}$ and set the connection weight to W.

5. For each $(\alpha_i, \alpha_j) \in attack,$[3] do:

   (a) Connect hidden neuron N_i to output neuron α_j.
   (b) If $v(\alpha_i, \alpha_j) = 0$, then set the connection weight to
       $W' > h^{-1}(A_{min}) - WA_{min}.$
   (c) If $v(\alpha_i, \alpha_j) = 1$, then set the connection weight to
       $W' < (h^{-1}(-A_{min}) - W)/A_{min}.$

6. Set the threshold of each neuron in $\mathcal{N}$ to zero.
7. Set $g(x) = x$ as the activation function of the neurons in the input layer of $\mathcal{N}$.
8. Set $h(x) = 2/(1+e^{-x}) - 1$ as the activation function of the neurons in the hidden and output layers of $\mathcal{N}$.

Note that, differently from the general CILP translation algorithm, in which rules may have any number of literals in the antecedent [66], here there is always a single

---

[3] Recall that if $v(\alpha_i, \alpha_j) = 1$, then α_i should defeat α_j, and if $v(\alpha_i, \alpha_j) = 0$, then α_i should not defeat α_j. The notion of defeat will be defined precisely in later sections.

literal α_i in the antecedent of each rule r_i. This allows us to use a threshold of zero in the algorithm above. Note also that $W > 0$ and $W' < 0$. This fits well with the idea of arguments having strengths (W), and of attacks also having strengths (W'). In practice, the values of W and W' could be defined, for example, by an audience using some form of voting system [22].

The notion of an argument that *supports* another seems natural in argumentation neural networks. If argument α_i supports argument α_j, this may be implemented easily in the neural network by the addition of a rule of the form $\alpha_i \rightarrow \alpha_j$ to the program $\mathcal{P}$.[4] We need to make sure that the neural network *computes* the prevailing arguments of the argumentation framework. For example, if argument α_i attacks an argument α_j, and α_i is stronger than α_j, then neuron α_i should be able to deactivate neuron α_j. Conversely, if α_i is weaker than α_j, and no other argument attacks α_j, then neuron α_i should not be allowed to deactivate neuron α_j. The following definition captures this.

Definition 52 ($\mathcal{N}$ computes $\mathcal{A}$). Let $(\alpha_i, \alpha_j) \in$ attacks. Let $A_\alpha(t)$ denote the activation state of neuron α at time t. We say that a neural network $\mathcal{N}$ computes an argumentation framework $\mathcal{A}$ if (*i*) whenever $v(\alpha_i, \alpha_j) = 1$, if $A_{\alpha_i}(t) > A_{min}$ and $A_{\alpha_j}(t) > A_{min}$, then $A_{\alpha_j}(t+1) < -A_{min}$,[5] and (*ii*) whenever $v(\alpha_i, \alpha_j) = 0$, if $A_{\alpha_i}(t) > A_{min}$ and $A_{\alpha_j}(t) > A_{min}$ and for every $\alpha_k \; {}_{(k \neq i,j)}$ such that $(\alpha_k, \alpha_j) \in$ attacks, $A_{\alpha_k}(t) < -A_{min}$, then $A_{\alpha_j}(t+1) > A_{min}$.

We now show that the translation from argumentation frameworks to neural networks is correct.

Theorem 26 (Correctness of Argumentation Algorithm). *For each argumentation network $\mathcal{A}$, there exists a feedforward neural network $\mathcal{N}$ with exactly one hidden layer and semilinear neurons, such that $\mathcal{N}$ computes $\mathcal{A}$.*

Proof. First, we need to show that the neural network computes $\mathcal{P}$. When $r_i : \alpha_i \rightarrow \alpha_i \in \mathcal{P}$, we need to show that (a) if $A_{\alpha_i} > A_{min}$ in the input layer, then $A_{\alpha_i} > A_{min}$ in the output layer. We also need to show that (b) if $A_{\alpha_i} < -A_{min}$ in the input layer, then $A_{\alpha_i} < -A_{min}$ in the output layer. (a) In the worst case, the input potential of hidden neuron N_i is $W \cdot A_{min}$, and the output of N_i is $h(W \cdot A_{min})$. We want $h(W \cdot A_{min}) > A_{min}$. Then, again in the worst case, the input potential of output neuron α_i will be $W \cdot A_{min}$, and we want $h(W \cdot A_{min}) > A_{min}$. As a result, $W > h^{-1}(A_{min})/A_{min}$ needs to be verified, which gives $W > (1/A_{min}) \cdot (\ln(1 + A_{min}) - \ln(1 - A_{min}))$, as in the algorithm. The proof of (b) is analogous to the proof of (a). Now, we need to show that the addition of negative weights to the neural network implements attacks in the argumentation framework. When $v(\alpha_i, \alpha_j) = 1$, we want to ensure that the

---

[4] In this way, an accumulation of arguments $(\alpha_1, \ldots, \alpha_n)$, where none of them is individually stronger than the argument they attack (α_{n+1}), might produce an input potential $n \cdot W'$ that overcomes the strength W of α_{n+1}. This is naturally the way that neural networks work, and it relates to the accrual of arguments. We shall discuss this in more detail in the next section.

[5] Recall that we use $-A_{min}$ for mathematical convenience, so that neuron α is said to be not active if $A_\alpha(t) < -A_{min}$, and active if $A_\alpha(t) > A_{min}$.

activation of output neuron α_j is smaller than $-A_{min}$ whenever both of the hidden neurons N_i and N_j are active. In the worst-case scenario, N_i has activation A_{min} while N_j has activation 1. We have $h(W + A_{min}W') < -A_{min}$. Thus, we need $W' < (h^{-1}(-A_{min}) - W)/A_{min}$; this is satisfied by the Neural Argumentation Algorithm. Similarly, when $v(\alpha_i, \alpha_j) = 0$, we want to ensure that the activation of output neuron α_j is larger than A_{min} whenever both of the hidden neurons N_i and N_j are active. In the worst-case scenario, N_i now has activation 1 while N_j has activation A_{min}. We have $h(A_{min}W + W') > A_{min}$. Thus, we need $W' > h^{-1}(A_{min}) - WA_{min}$. Again, this is satisfied by the Neural Argumentation Algorithm. This completes the proof. ∎

11.3 Argument Computation and Learning

In this section, we consider the computation and learning of arguments in neural networks. We start by giving an example. We then consider the case in which arguments attack each other so as to form a cycle in the argumentation network. This may result in an infinite computation in the neural network. To tackle this problem, we propose the use of learning as a way of breaking the circularity. Learning can be seen as a way of implementing the accrual of arguments. We conclude the section by discussing this issue. There is interesting further research on each of these topics. In this section, our purpose is to introduce a range of issues for argumentation neural networks, but we are far from exhausting the subject.

Once we have translated argumentation networks into neural networks, our next step is to run the neural network to find out which arguments prevail. As usual, to run the network, we connect output neurons to their corresponding input neurons using weights $W_r = 1$ so that, for example, the activation of output neuron A is fed into input neuron A at the next round in time. This implements chains such as A attacks B, B attacks C, C attacks D, and so on, by propagating activation around the network. The following example illustrates this computation in the case of the moral-debate example described above (see Fig. 11.3).

Example 20. (**Neural Network for Moral Debate**) We apply the Neural Argumentation Algorithm to the argumentation network of Fig. 11.1, and obtain the neural network of Fig. 11.3. From the algorithm, we know that we should have $A_{min} > 0$ and $W > 0$. Let us take $A_{min} = 0.5$ and $W = 5$ (recall that W is the weight of the solid arrows in the network). Following [108], let us consider the problem by grouping arguments according to the aspects of *life*, *property*, and *facts*; arguments A, D, and F are related to the right to life, arguments B and C are related to property rights, and argument E is a fact. We may argue whether property is stronger than life, but facts are always the strongest. If property is stronger than life then $v(B,A) = 1$, $v(D,A) = 1$, $v(C,B) = 1$, $v(C,D) = 1$, $v(E,D) = 1$, and $v(F,C) = 0$. From the Neural Argumentation Algorithm, when $v(\alpha_i, \alpha_j) = 0$ we must have $W' > -1.4$, and when $v(\alpha_i, \alpha_j) = 1$ we must have $W' < -12.2$. The actual value of each attack may depend on an audience. Nevertheless, provided that the above conditions on W' are satisfied, the network will compute the expected prevailing arguments according to

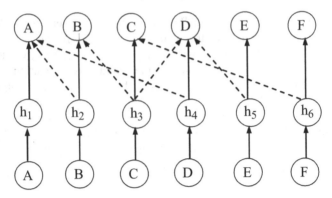

Fig. 11.3 The moral-debate example as a neural network

Theorem 26, as follows: F does not defeat C, C defeats B, E defeats D, and, as a result, we obtain $\{A,C,E\}$ as the acceptable set of arguments. Now, if *life* is considered stronger than *property*, then $v(F,C) = 1$. As a result, F defeats C and, since C is defeated, it cannot defeat B, which in turn cannot defeat A (because life is stronger than property). Thus, the network converges to the state $\{A,B,E,F\}$ of acceptable arguments.[6] This shows that two different lines of value-based argumentation will provide the same answer to the question of whether Hal was justified (A), but two different answers to the question of whether Carla has the right to compensation (C).

11.3.1 Circular Argumentation

Arguments may frequently attack one another in such a way that cycles are formed. In such cases, the relative strength of the arguments will decide which of them should prevail, if any. In [18], as part of a study of the dynamics of argumentation networks [39], Barringer, Gabbay, and Woods discussed how to handle loops during the computation of arguments. They differentiated between *syntactic* and *semantic* loops, in that the former occur as cycles in the argumentation network (e.g. when argument A attacks argument B and vice versa), whereas the latter also depend on the strength of the arguments involved in the loop.

In this way, if A is considerably stronger than B or vice versa, no semantic loop will exist, despite the fact that there is a (syntactic) loop in the network; the relative strength of the arguments resolves the loop. Even if A and B both have similar strengths, one possible interpretation is that neither argument should prevail. This would also resolve the loop and, as we shall see in what follows, the dynamics

---

[6] The complete set of argument values in this case is $v(B,A) = 0$, $v(D,A) = 1$, $v(C,B) = 1$, $v(C,D) = 0$, $v(E,D) = 1$, and $v(F,C) = 1$. The constraints on W' are calculated in the same way as before.

of argumentation neural networks follows this interpretation. Still, there are situations in which the network oscillates between stable states, which indicates the existence of alternative, conflicting sets of arguments. This problem may be resolved by changing the strength of certain arguments. Such a change may either be due to the fact that new information has become available, or may come from an investigation of the oscillating behaviour of the argumentation network itself, as exemplified below.

Example 21. (**Argument Computation**) Take the case in which an argument A attacks an argument B, and B attacks an argument C, which in turn attacks A in a cycle, as shown in Fig. 11.4. In order to implement this in a neural network, we need three hidden neurons (h_1, h_2, h_3), and positive weights to explicitly represent the fact that A supports itself (*via* h_1), B supports itself (*via* h_2), and so does C (*via* h_3). In addition, we need negative weights from h_1 to B, from h_2 to C, and from h_3 to A, to implement attacks (see Fig. 11.5). If the value of argument A (i.e. the weight from h_1 to A) is stronger than the value of argument C (the weight from h_3 to C, which is expected to be the same in absolute terms as the weight from h_3 to A), C cannot attack and defeat A. As a result, A is active and succeeds in attacking B (since we assume that the weights from h_1 and h_2 to B have the same absolute value). Since B is not active, C will be active, and a stable state $\{A,C\}$ will be reached. In Bench-Capon's model [22], this is precisely the case in which the colour *blue* is assigned to A and B, and the colour *red* is assigned to C, with *blue* being stronger than *red*. Note that the order in which we reason does not affect the final result (the stable state reached). For example, if we had started with B successfully attacking C, C would not have been able to defeat A, but then A would successfully defeat B, which would, this time round, not be able to successfully defeat C, which in turn would be active in the final stable state $\{A,C\}$.

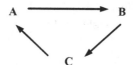

Fig. 11.4 Circular arguments

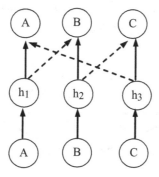

Fig. 11.5 A neural network for circular argumentation

In Example 21, a *syntactic loop* exists in that the attacks in the argumentation network form a loop in Fig. 11.4. However, there is no *semantic loop*, as the computation of the arguments converges to a stable state, as exemplified above. Even if the strengths of the arguments were all the same, the neural network of Fig. 11.5 would converge to an empty set, as follows. Assume that solid arrows have weight W, and dotted arrows have weight $-W$ in the network of Fig. 11.5. Let $(A, B, C) = [1, 1, 1]$ denote the network's input vector. Thus, $h(W)$ will be the activation state of each hidden neuron, where h is the activation function of such neurons. Then, $W \cdot h(W) - W \cdot h(W) = 0$ will be the input potential of each output neuron, and thus $h(0) = 0$ (recall that $\theta = 0$) will be the activation state of each output neuron A, B, and C. Now, given an input vector $(A, B, C) = [0, 0, 0]$, the activation state of each hidden neuron will be zero, and then the activation state of each output neuron will be zero. As a result, the network converges to a stable state $\{ \}$ in which no argument prevails. This stable state is reached after a single computation step from $[1, 1, 1]$ to $[0, 0, 0]$.

According to Definition 52, an argument prevails if its associated neuron has an activation in the interval $(A_{min}, 1]$ with $A_{min} > 0$. Dually, whenever an argument is defeated, its associated neuron should have an activation in the interval $[-1, -A_{min})$. In the case of circular-argumentation networks, however, there is a third possibility, when arguments cancel each other and the neurons' activations lie in the interval $[-A_{min}, A_{min}]$, typically converging to zero, as illustrated above. In this case, we know that arguments do not prevail, and it might be useful in some situations to make a distinction between a clear defeat and a failure to prevail. We shall return to this issue when we consider argument learning. First, we need to study the more involved situation where the network oscillates between states.

Unfortunately, not all argumentation neural networks are as well behaved as the ones considered so far. Take the case in which an argument A attacks two arguments B and C, B and C in turn both attack an argument D, and D attacks A in a cycle, as depicted in Fig. 11.6. Assume that all the attacks have the same strength. Figure 11.7 shows the neural network for the argumentation network of Fig. 11.6. Assume, as before, that the solid arrows have weight W, and the dotted arrows have weight $-W$. Given an input $(A, B, C, D) = [1, 1, 1, 1]$, it is clear from Fig. 11.7 that the values of output neurons A, B, and C will be zero, as the weights W and $-W$ cancel each other out. The input potential of output neuron D, however, will be $-W \cdot h(W)$, and so the value of output neuron D will be $O_D = h(-W \cdot h(W))$. The next time round, the input potential of output neuron A will be $-W \cdot h(O_D \cdot W)$, and A will have a

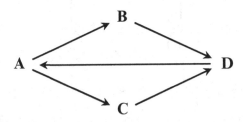

Fig. 11.6 Semantic circularity

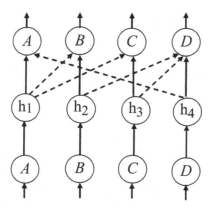

Fig. 11.7 A neural network encoding semantic circularity

positive activation $h(-W \cdot h(O_D \cdot W))$. As a result, if A successfully defeats B and C, then D prevails, and thus defeats A. In this case, B and C prevail, and defeat D, in a cycle.

Let us look at this cycle in more detail in the neural network. Let us assume, for convenience, that $W = 1$, $h(x) = 1$ if $x \geq 1$, $h(x) = -1$ if $x \leq -1$, and $h(x) = x$ for $-1 < x < 1$.[7] We start with the input vector $[1,1,1,1]$, and obtain an output vector $[0,0,0,-1]$. We then use $[0,0,0,-1]$ as input to obtain an output $[1,0,0,-1]$. Let us use $\mapsto$ to denote the above mapping from input to output vectors, so that we have $[1,1,1,1] \mapsto [0,0,0,-1] \mapsto [1,0,0,-1] \mapsto [1,-1,-1,-1] \mapsto [1,-1,-1,1] \mapsto [0,-1,-1,1] \mapsto [-1,-1,-1,1] \mapsto [-1,0,0,1] \mapsto [-1,1,1,1] \mapsto [-1,1,1,-1] \mapsto [0,1,1,-1] \mapsto [1,1,1,-1] \mapsto [1,0,0,-1] \mapsto \ldots \mapsto [1,0,0,-1] \mapsto \ldots$, which shows that we have reached an infinite loop.

Can we learn anything from the sequence of arguments computed by the network? Initially, there is a situation in which A seems to prevail. Then, A and D together prevail. Then, D alone. Then B, C, and D together, then B and C only, and finally A, B, and C, before we go back to the situation in which A alone seems to prevail. One way to deal with this problem would be to simply assume that the loop itself indicates that no argument should prevail at the end. One may argue, however, that this does not really solve the problem. Alternatively, one could try to use the information obtained during the computation of the arguments to resolve the loop. In the example above, for instance, it seems that either $\{A,D\}$ or $\{B,C\}$ could serve as a basis for a stable set of arguments. More information would be needed, but one might start by searching for information in support of $\{A,D\}$ and in support of $\{B,C\}$, and only then in support of the other combinations. It seems that the only real solution to the problem of semantic loops is to have new information in the form of new evidence about the relative strength of the arguments and to learn from it, as we discuss in the following section.

---

[7] This gives an approximation of the standard sigmoid activation function.

11.3.2 Argument Learning

Consider again the neural network of Fig. 11.7. Suppose that new evidence becomes available in favour of arguments A and C so that we would like both arguments to prevail. We do not know how this should affect arguments B and D, but we know now that, given the input vector $[1,1,1,1]$, we would like the network of Fig. 11.7 to produce an output $[1,?,1,?]$, instead of $[0,0,0,-1]$. Since we do not have any information about B or D, the natural candidates for ? are the original values (so that $[1,?,1,?]$ becomes $[1,0,1,-1]$). This will produce an error of zero for output neurons B and D during learning, which is the best way of reflecting the lack of new information about such concepts. An error of zero will produce no changes in the weights directly associated with B and D, but of course the changes in other weights may affect the overall result of the network. Let us exemplify this in the case of the network of Fig. 11.7 for our training example $[1,1,1,1] \mapsto [1,0,1,-1]$.

We used the standard backpropagation learning algorithm[8] [224]. As before, the use of backpropagation was made possible because the network was recurrent only for the computation of the arguments, not during learning. The recurrent connections were important for the reasoning process, and had weights always fixed at 1. During learning, we were interested in establishing a new mapping from the input to the output, and thus a learning algorithm that applied to feedforward networks such as backpropagation sufficed. We used $W = 4.0$ (solid arrows in Fig. 11.7), and $W' = -4.0$ (dotted arrows).[9] Recall that $\theta = 0$ and that any other connection not shown in Fig. 11.7 is given weight zero initially.

The thresholds of output neurons A (θ_A) and C (θ_C) were changed through learning to -0.8, the weights from h_1 to A (W_{A,h_1}) and from h_3 to C (W_{C,h_3}) were changed to 4.8, and the weights from h_4 to A (W_{A,h_4}) and from h_1 to C (W_{C,h_1}) were changed to -3.2. In addition, some very minor changes occurred in the weights linking the input to the hidden layer of the network and, as expected, no changes occurred in the weights leading to output neurons B or D, namely W_{B,h_i} and W_{D,h_i}, $1 \leq i \leq 4$ (recall that, for the purpose of learning, the network is fully-connected).

The computation of the arguments in the trained network goes as follows. In addition to the transition from $[1,1,1,1]$ to $[1,0,1,-1]$, learned as expected, the network then maps $[1,0,1,-1]$ into $[1,-1,1,-1]$, which is a stable state. The newly learned sequence $[1,1,1,1] \mapsto [1,0,1,-1] \mapsto [1,-1,1,-1] \mapsto [1,-1,1,-1]$ is now loop free; the stable state $[1,-1,1,-1]$ corresponds to the acceptance of $\{A,C\}$ as prevailing arguments.

As another example, let us consider the Nixon diamond problem. In the traditional Nixon diamond problem, Nixon is a *Quaker* (Q) and a *Republican* (R). Quakers are generally *pacifists* (P), whereas Republicans are generally *nonpacifists* ($\neg P$).

---

[8] We used tanh as the activation function, a learning rate of 0.1, and a term of momentum of 0.4. We trained the network on the single training example $([1,1,1,1], [1,0,1,-1])$ until a mean square error of 0.01 was reached.

[9] This was done because $\tanh(4.0) = 0.999$, whereas $\tanh(1.0) = 0.761$. As a result, $W = 4.0$ gives a good approximation to $h(W) = 1$, as in our previous assumption.

This produces an inconsistency in a number of formalisations of the problem [7]. Briefly, if the strength of the support for Nixon's pacifism is the same as the strength of the support for his nonpacifism, the neural network will conclude that both P and $\neg P$ prevail. If, in addition, we assume that P attacks $\neg P$ and, vice versa, $\neg P$ attacks P, both with the same strength, then the stable state of the neural network will contain neither P nor $\neg P$. Finally, if we are faced with a situation in which we need to choose between P and $\neg P$, we can learn to enforce a stable state in the network in which one but not the other argument prevails.

Suppose we need to make a decision about Nixon's pacifism. We need to seek new information. We find out that Nixon is a *football fan* (F), and that football fans are normally nonpacifists. We then use this information to convince ourselves that Nixon is indeed a nonpacifist. We need to add an input, a hidden, and an output neuron to our original network to represent F. Then, to make sure that F attacks and defeats P, we simply train with the example $[1, 1, 1, 1, 1] \mapsto [1, 1, -1, 1, 1]$, given arguments $Q, R, P, \neg P, F$ in that order.

There are also situations in which the number of times that an example occurs should be relevant to the decision about the strength of an argument. In such cases, alternative forms of learning would need to be investigated, since the backpropagation algorithm does not cater for varying relevance. We believe that this is an interesting research area, with many open research issues to be addressed in the near future.

11.3.3 Cumulative (Accrual) Argumentation

We have mentioned that neural networks deal with cumulative argumentation in the sense that a number of arguments, none of which are individually stronger than a given argument, may defeat that argument collectively. There is some controversy about whether arguments accrue. Whereas Pollock denied the existence of cumulative argumentation [210], Verheij defended the assertion that arguments can be combined either by subordination or by coordination, and may accrue in stages [265]. In this section, we give an example of accrual by coordination, which happens to be a natural property of neural networks.

Consider the following scenario. *Suppose you are the head of state of a country who needs to decide whether or not to go to war in order to remove a violent dictator from power. First, you consider the prospect of the loss of lives of fellow countrymen and women in action, and the killing of innocent civilians, which forms a strong argument against going to war. Let us call this argument A_1. In support for going to war, according to documented evidence from your intelligence services, the dictator possesses chemical and biological weapons, having made use of such weapons in the past. We call this argument A_2. You also happen to possess what you believe is credible information about the fact that the dictator has recently acquired uranium from another country, most probably in order to continue with an* *unauthorised nuclear-weapons-capability programme. Let this be called argument* A_3. *In addition, recent information indicates that the dictator has the capability and the will – having done so in the past – to attack neighbouring countries. Let us name this argument* A_4. *Finally, you receive evidence that the dictator has provided safe haven for well-known members of an active international terrorist network. This is argument* A_5. *The task at hand is to decide whether or not it is right to remove the dictator.*

Let B denote the proposition *it is right to remove the dictator*, and consider the situation in which A_1 attacks B while $A_2, \ldots, A_5$ support B. Assume, further, that A_1 is stronger than B, i.e. $v(A_1, B) = 1$. We apply the Neural Argumentation Algorithm and obtain the neural network of Fig. 11.8. Taking $A_{min} = 0.5$, we calculate $W > 2.2$. Taking, for example, $W = 3$, we calculate $W' < -4.5$. Let us take $W' = -5$.

According to the algorithm, $W = 3$ and $W' = -5$ form an acceptable set of weights. Although A_1 is supposed to defeat B if contrasted with any of $A_2, \ldots, A_5$, the cumulative support of $A_2, \ldots, A_5$ for B actually allows it to prevail. This can be seen in the network by inspecting the input potential of neuron B, which is approximately $(4 \cdot W) + W' = 7$, i.e. a relatively large positive value, which activates neuron B. Of course, a different outcome could be obtained by ensuring that W' was large enough (in absolute terms) to counteract the influence of all the other arguments together. A value of $W' = -16$, for example, would produce an input potential of -4, which would be sufficient to deactivate neuron B. Of course, these values should depend on your degree of belief in the arguments for and against the war. These values could have been learned from examples (e.g. previous cases) so that one could make an informed decision.

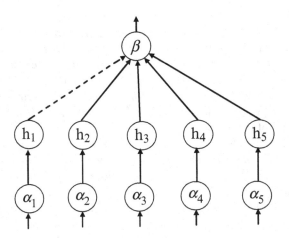

Fig. 11.8 Cumulative-support argumentation

11.4 Fibring Applied to Argumentation

An interesting application of fibring (see Chap. 9) is in the area of legal reasoning and argumentation. In [108], for example, Gabbay and Woods argued for the combined use of labelled deductive systems (LDS) and Bayesian networks [202] to support reasoning about legal evidence under uncertainty. In addition, they argued that neural networks, as learning systems, could play a role in this process by being used to update/revise degrees of belief and the rules of the system whenever new evidence was presented. The three different representations – logical (LDS), Bayesian, and connectionist – all expand the value-based argumentation framework of [22].

Returning to the moral-debate example of Sect. 11.2, notice that some aspects of the argumentation network are probabilistic. For example, the question of whether Carla has abundant insulin (E) depends on the time and is a matter of probability. The question of whether Hal will be able to compensate Carla with replacement insulin (C) is also a matter of probability. If Carla has abundant insulin, the chances that Hal will be able to compensate her are higher. The probability matrices of this Bayesian network ($E \rightarrow C$) influence whether Hal is endangering Carla's life by stealing some of her insulin (D). In the same argumentation network, some other aspects may change as the debate progresses and actions are taken; the strength of one argument in attacking another may change in time. This is a learning process that can be implemented using, as we have seen, the neural network of Fig. 11.2, in which the weights record the strengths of the arguments. The neural network is an autoassociative, single-hidden-layer feedforward network with an input layer (A, B, D), an output layer (A, B, D), and a hidden layer (h_1, h_2, h_3). The hidden neurons are used in the network to provide a greater flexibility as to what can be learned as combinations of the input neurons. Training changes the initial weights (the initial belief in the strength of arguments and counter-arguments, which could be random), according to examples of the relationship between the arguments A, B, and D. Roughly speaking, if the absolute value of the weight from neuron h_1 to output neuron A is greater than the sum of the absolute values of the weights from neurons h_2 and h_3 to A, then one can say that argument A prevails.

Now that we have two concrete models of the arguments involved in the moral-debate example – a probabilistic model and a learning/action model – we can reason about the problem at hand in a more realistic way. We just need to put the two models together consistently. We can use the fibring methodology for networks described in Chap. 9. The (more abstract) argumentation network of Fig. 11.1 can be used to tell us how the networks (Bayesian and neural) are to be fibred. From Fig. 11.1, one can see that both arguments C and E attack argument D directly. As a result, we would like the probabilities in our Bayesian network $E \rightarrow C$ to influence the activation of neuron D in the neural network. Thus, the network $E \rightarrow C$ needs to be embedded into node D. Again from the argumentation network (Fig. 11.1), one can see that argument C also attacks argument B directly. As a result, we would like the probabilities associated with C to influence the activation of neuron B. As before, this can be done by embedding the Bayesian network C into neuron B. This produces the recursive network of Fig. 11.9.

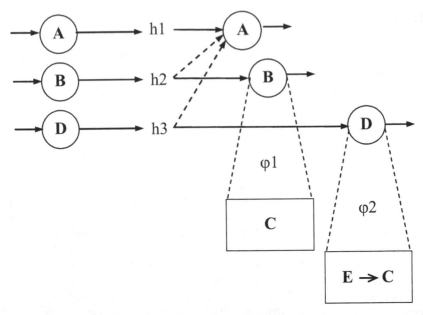

Fig. 11.9 Fibring of Bayesian and neural networks applied to argumentation

Let us consider again the embedding of $E \rightarrow C$ into D. We have seen that the embedding is guided by the arrow in the original argumentation network. An arrow in an argumentation network indicates an *attack*. As a result, the higher the probability $P(C/E)$ is (see Fig. 11.9), the lower the activation value of neuron D should be. Similarly, the higher the probability $P(C)$, the lower the value of B should be. Thus, we take $\varphi 1 : \mathbf{s}^{\mathbf{B}}_{new} = \mathbf{s}^{\mathbf{B}}_{old} - P(\mathbf{C})$ and $\varphi 2 : \mathbf{s}^{\mathbf{D}}_{new} = \mathbf{s}^{\mathbf{D}}_{old} - P(\mathbf{C/E})$, where $P(\mathbf{X}) \in [0, 1]$ and $\mathbf{s} \in (0, 1)$. In the combined system, the new state of output neuron D ($\mathbf{s}^{\mathbf{D}}_{new}$) will be fed into input neuron D and affect the new state of A (through hidden neuron h_3 and the negative weight from h_3 to A), such that the higher the value of D, the lower the value of A. The same will happen through B according to the dynamics of the embedding and embedded networks.

In this argumentation case study, we have seen that the general methodology of fibring can be applied to neural networks and to other systems such as Bayesian networks. In symbolic systems, the fibring of two logics that do not allow, for example, for embedded implication may result in a logic with embedded implication. In the same way, the fibring of (Bayesian and neural) networks may result in embedded networks such as $(A \rightarrow B) \rightarrow C$, which are strictly more expressive than standard networks, i.e. do not have a flattened counterpart network.[10] This is an indication,

---

[10] The idea of fibring Bayesian networks emerged from the observation that causal relations may themselves take part in causal relations. This was simply and effectively exemplified in the very first section of Williamson and Gabbay's 'Recursive causality in Bayesian networks and self-fibring networks' [270]. The example given there states that the fact that smoking causes cancer, for instance, causes the government to restrict tobacco advertising. Such a recursive definition of causal

now from the point of view of neural-symbolic integration, that fibring may be used to produce simple neural-network architectures (an important requirement for effective learning) that can represent powerful logics.

11.5 Discussion

In this chapter, we have presented a model of computation that allows the deduction and learning of argumentative reasoning. The model combines value-based argumentation frameworks and neural-symbolic learning systems by providing a translation from argumentation networks to neural networks. A theorem then shows that such a translation is correct. We have shown that the model works not only for acyclic argumentation networks, but also for circular networks, and it enables cumulative argumentation through learning.

A neural implementation of argumentative reasoning may be advantageous from a purely computational point of view owing to the parallelism of neural networks. A relevant long-term goal is to facilitate learning capabilities in value-based argumentation frameworks, as arguments may evolve over time, with certain arguments being strengthened and others weakened. At the same time, we seek to enable the parallel computation of argumentation frameworks by making use of the parallelism of neural networks.

As future work, one could perform further study on the fibring of neural networks [67] in connection with the framework of Williamson and Gabbay [270]. This framework incorporates the idea of recursive causality, according to which causal relations may take causal relations as input values. The model presented here could also consider probabilistic weights in argumentation frameworks in the style of [119]. This would allow a quantitative approach to argumentation in an integrated model of argumentative reasoning under uncertainty and inductive learning.

Neural-symbolic learning systems may serve as an underlying framework for the study of the fibring of networks and logics, and the self-fibring of networks. In this setting, an appropriate fibring of two networks A and B, for example, would be one in which the logic extracted from the fibred network is the same as the logic obtained from fibring the logics extracted from networks A and B. There are many possible avenues of research on the fibring of networks (neural, Bayesian, etc.), the study of their logical interpretation, and their application in argumentation.

---

relations was then used to define what Williamson and Gabbay call a *recursive Bayesian network*, a Bayesian network in which certain nodes may be Bayesian networks in their own right. This was defined with the help of the concept of *network variables*, which are variables that may take Bayesian networks as values. Thus, a network variable *SC* may be used to represent the fact that *smoking causes cancer*, and then *SC* causes *A*, where *A* stands for *restricting advertising*. This may be written as $SC \rightarrow A$, where $SC = S \rightarrow C$, or simply as $(S \rightarrow C) \rightarrow A$.

Chapter 12
Reasoning about Probabilities in Neural Networks

In this chapter, we show that artificial neural networks can reason about probabilities, thus being able to integrate reasoning about uncertainty with modal, temporal, and epistemic logics, which have found a large number of applications, notably in game theory and in models of knowledge and interaction in multiagent systems [87, 103, 207]; artificial intelligence and computer science have made extensive use of decidable modal logics, including in the analysis and model checking of distributed and multiagent systems, in program verification and specification, and in hardware model checking. Finally, the combination of knowledge, time, and probability in a connectionist system provides support for integrated knowledge representation and learning in a distributed environment, dealing with the various dimensions of reasoning of an idealised agent [94, 202].

12.1 Representing Uncertainty

To represent uncertainty, we add a probabilistic dimension to the framework of connectionist modal logic (CML) presented in Chap. 5. We follow Halpern's work in order to do so [121], and associate probabilities with possible worlds. In this way, the different probabilities that agents envisage are captured not by different probability distributions, but by the set of worlds that the agents consider possible. As a result, we need a (temporal) translation algorithm (see Chap. 6) that caters for an agent that envisages multiple possible worlds at the same time point. Let us first consider the *two-coin problem* as described in [121], as an example of how to represent uncertainty in neural-symbolic systems. In what follows, we say that $p_i(\alpha) = x$ if the probability of formula α, according to agent i, is equal to x, where x is a real number in $[0, 1]$. We then allow neurons to be labelled as $\alpha = x$, indicating that x is the probability of α when the neuron is activated. There are two agents involved in the problem. Agent 1 holds two coins; one of them is fair (coin 1) and the other is biased (coin 2). Agent 1 is able to identify which coin is fair and which coin is

A.S. d'Avila Garcez et al., *Neural-Symbolic Cognitive Reasoning,* Cognitive Technologies,   161
© Springer-Verlag Berlin Heidelberg 2009

biased. Agent 2, however, knows only that one coin is fair and the other is twice as likely to land *heads* as *tails*, and cannot tell them apart. Thus, the probability p_{c_1} of coin 1 landing heads is $p_{c_1}(heads) = 1/2$, and the probability of coin 1 landing tails is $p_{c_1}(tail) = 1/2$. The probability p_{c_2} of coin 2 landing heads is $p_{c_2}(heads) = 2/3$, and the probability of coin 2 landing tails is $p_{c_2}(tails) = 1/3$.

Agent 1 chooses one of the coins to toss. Agent 2 does not know which coin agent 1 has chosen, nor even the probability that the fair coin has been chosen. What is the probability, according to agent 2, that the result of the coin toss will be heads? What is the probability according to agent 1? The difference between agent 1 and agent 2 is captured not by the probability distributions that they use, but by the set of worlds that they consider possible. We argue, as a result, that the CML framework, extended to reason about knowledge and time, is suitable for representing the kinds of problems discussed in [121]. Let us discuss the background knowledge of the agents involved in the problem. Below, we use **f** for *fair*, **b** for *biased*, **h** for *heads*, and **t** for *tails*. Moreover, as one would expect, knowledge persists through time.

Suppose that at time t_0, no coin has been chosen yet. At time t_1, agent 1 has chosen a coin to toss, and at time t_2, agent 1 has tossed the coin. At time t_1, agent 1 must know whether she has selected a biased coin ($t_1 : K_1 \mathbf{b}$) or a fair coin ($t_1 : K_1 \mathbf{f}$). We say that agent 1 is in one of the states B or F depending on the coin that she has selected (biased or fair, respectively). We represent this as a neural-symbolic system by having ω_{1B} as a possible world in which agent 1 has selected the biased coin at time t_1. Similarly, we have ω_{1F} as a possible world in which agent 1 has selected the fair coin at time t_1. Obviously, the associated probabilities $p(\mathbf{h}) = 2/3$ and $p(\mathbf{t}) = 1/3$ must hold in ω_{1B}, whereas $p(\mathbf{h}) = 1/2$ and $p(\mathbf{t}) = 1/2$ must hold in ω_{1F}. In contrast, agent 2 is uncertain about the situation. All agent 2 knows at t_1 is that $p(\mathbf{h}) = 1/2$ or $p(\mathbf{h}) = 2/3$, and that $p(\mathbf{t}) = 1/2$ or $p(\mathbf{t}) = 1/3$. We represent this by using two worlds: ω_{2B} as a possible world in which agent 2 considers that $p(\mathbf{h}) = 2/3$ and $p(\mathbf{t}) = 1/3$, and ω_{2F} as a possible world in which agent 2 considers that $p(\mathbf{h}) = 1/2$ and $p(\mathbf{t}) = 1/2$.

Notice how what is known by the agents is implemented in the various neural networks: at t_1, either $p(\mathbf{h}) = 2/3$ or $p(\mathbf{h}) = 1/2$, but not both, will be activated for agent 1 (according to the inputs to the networks representing ω_{1B} and ω_{1F}); at the same time, both of $p(\mathbf{h}) = 2/3$ and $p(\mathbf{h}) = 1/2$ will be activated for agent 2 in worlds ω_{2B} and ω_{2F}, respectively, indicating the fact that agent 2 is uncertain about the situation.

At time t_2, agent 1 knows the result of the coin toss, and she assigns a probability 1 to it. Agent 2 also knows the result of the toss (we assume that he can see it), but 'never learns what happened' [121]. As a result, at time t_2, there are two possible worlds: ω_H, in which $p(\mathbf{h}) = 1$ and $p(\mathbf{t}) = 0$, and ω_T, in which $p(\mathbf{h}) = 0$ and $p(\mathbf{t}) = 1$.

Figure 12.1 represents the reasoning process at t_1 and t_2, where **ct** indicates that the selected coin has been tossed. As discussed above, in ω_H, input neuron **h** is activated, and if **ct** is also activated, neurons $\mathbf{h} = 1$ and $\mathbf{t} = 0$ will be activated (using the rules $\mathbf{ct} \wedge \mathbf{h} \rightarrow (p(\mathbf{h}) = 1)$ and $\mathbf{ct} \wedge \mathbf{h} \rightarrow (p(\mathbf{t}) = 0)$). Similarly, in ω_T, input

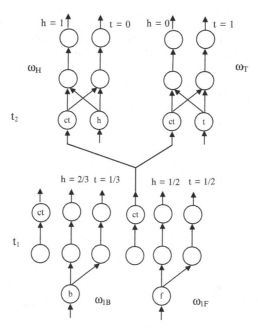

Fig. 12.1 A representation of the two-coin problem

neuron **t** is activated, and if **ct** is also activated, neurons **h** = 0 and **t** = 1 will be activated (using the rules **ct** ∧ **t** → ($p(\mathbf{h}) = 0$) and **ct** ∧ **t** → ($p(\mathbf{t}) = 1$)). In Fig. 12.1, the connection between worlds can be established by the use of the *tomorrow* operator ○, as detailed in what follows.

The above example illustrates the need to consider a pair (ω, t), where ω is one of the worlds envisaged by an agent at time t. This allows us to reason about situations such as the one described in the two-coin problem, where each agent i can reason about different possible worlds ω at a time point t, represented by $t : K_i^\omega \alpha$, where α represents qualitative information about the probability of a literal. More generally, in what follows, we consider *knowledge and probability rules* of the form $t : \bigcirc K_{[\mathcal{A}]}^{[\mathcal{W}]} L_1, \ldots, \bigcirc K_{[\mathcal{A}]}^{[\mathcal{W}]} L_k \to \bigcirc K_{[\mathcal{A}]}^{[\mathcal{W}]} L_{k+1}$, where $[\mathcal{W}]$ denotes an element selected from the set of possible worlds $\mathcal{W}$, for each literal L_j, $1 \leq j \leq k+1$, $1 \leq t \leq n$, and $k, n \in \mathbb{N}$. In addition, L_j can be either a literal or a probabilistic statement of the form $p(\alpha) = x$, as defined above. Note also that ○ is not required to precede every single literal.

Normally, we shall have rules such as $t : K_{[\mathcal{A}]}^\omega L_1, \ldots, K_{[\mathcal{A}]}^\omega L_k \to \bigcirc K_{[\mathcal{A}]}(p(\alpha) = x)$. Although a single rule might refer to different worlds, normally (as in the examples given in this chapter) a single ω is selected from $[\mathcal{W}]$ for each rule. Recall that $t : \bigcirc K_i \alpha$ denotes that α holds in every accessible possible world from the point of view of agent i at time $t + 1$. Finally, note that probabilistic statements are not generally preceded by negation.

Returning to the two-coin problem, the following would be the rules for the
agents involved in the situation where ω_{iB} and ω_{iF} denote the worlds in which
agent i considers that the coin is biased and fair, respectively, $i \in \{1,2\}$:

$t_1 : K_i^{\omega_{iB}} \mathbf{b} \rightarrow K_i^{\omega_{iB}} (p(\mathbf{h}) = 2/3);$
$t_1 : K_i^{\omega_{iB}} \mathbf{b} \rightarrow K_i^{\omega_{iB}} (p(\mathbf{t}) = 1/3);$
$t_1 : K_i^{\omega_{iF}} \mathbf{f} \rightarrow K_i^{\omega_{iF}} (p(\mathbf{h}) = 1/2);$
$t_1 : K_i^{\omega_{iF}} \mathbf{f} \rightarrow K_i^{\omega_{iF}} (p(\mathbf{t}) = 1/2);$
$t_1 : K_1^{\omega_{1B}} \mathbf{ct};$
$t_1 : K_1^{\omega_{1F}} \mathbf{ct}.$

In addition, the following rules model the situations once agent i knows that a
coin has been tossed:

$t_2 : K_i^{\omega_H} \mathbf{ct} \wedge K_i^{\omega_H} \mathbf{h} \rightarrow (p(\mathbf{h}) = 1);$
$t_2 : K_i^{\omega_H} \mathbf{ct} \wedge K_i^{\omega_H} \mathbf{h} \rightarrow (p(\mathbf{t}) = 0);$
$t_2 : K_i^{\omega_T} \mathbf{ct} \wedge K_i^{\omega_T} \mathbf{h} \rightarrow (p(\mathbf{h}) = 0);$
$t_2 : K_i^{\omega_T} \mathbf{ct} \wedge K_i^{\omega_T} \mathbf{h} \rightarrow (p(\mathbf{t}) = 1).$

Finally, to interconnect the networks, we have the following rule, expressing the
fact that when $\mathbf{ct}$ holds in ω_{1F}, then $\mathbf{ct}$ holds in both ω_H and ω_T:

$t_1 : K_i^{\omega_{1F}} \mathbf{ct} \rightarrow \bigcirc K_i \mathbf{ct}, \mathcal{R}(\omega_{1F}, \omega_H), \mathcal{R}(\omega_{1F}, \omega_T).$

12.2 An Algorithm for Reasoning about Uncertainty

We now present an algorithm to translate knowledge and probability rules into
neural-network ensembles. The equations used in this algorithm to calculate the
values of weights and thresholds were obtained from the CILP Translation Algorithm (see Chap. 4). The main difference between the two algorithms is that here
probabilities can be associated with neurons and that probabilities can be combined
with time and knowledge operators, along the lines of [121]. The present algorithm
distinguishes between the case in which the tomorrow operator occurs in the head
of a clause (step 3) and the case in which it does not (step 4).

Notation Let $\mathcal{P}$ contain q knowledge and probability rules. We number each L_j
from 1 to $k+1$ such that, when a neural network $\mathcal{N}$ is created, input and output
neurons are created to represent each L_j. We also number worlds $\omega_t \in \mathcal{W}$ from 1 to
$u, u \in \mathbb{N}$. We use $A_{min} \in (0,1)$ to denote the minimum activation for a neuron to be
considered active (i.e. its associated literal is considered *true*), a bipolar semilinear
activation function $h(x) = 2/(1+e^{-\beta x}) - 1$, and inputs in $\{-1,1\}$. Let k_l denote the
number of literals in the body of rule r_l, μ_l the number of rules in $\mathcal{P}$ with the same
literal as the consequent for each rule r_l, $MAX_{r_l}(k_l, \mu_l)$ the greater of the elements
k_l and μ_l for rule r_l, and $MAX_{\mathcal{P}}(k_1, \ldots, k_q, \mu_1, \ldots, \mu_q)$ the greatest element among
all k_l's and μ_l's for $\mathcal{P}$. We also use $\overrightarrow{k}$ as a shorthand for $(k_1, \ldots, k_q)$, and $\overrightarrow{\mu}$ as a
shorthand for $(\mu_1, \ldots, \mu_q)$.

Knowledge and Probability Translation Algorithm

1. For each world $\omega_l \in \mathcal{W}$, for each time point t, do: Create a CILP neural network $\mathcal{N}_{\omega_l,t}$.

2. Calculate the weight W such that

$$W \geq \frac{2}{\beta} \cdot \frac{\ln(1+A_{min}) - \ln(1-A_{min})}{MAX_{\mathcal{P}}(\overrightarrow{k},\overrightarrow{\mu}) \cdot (A_{min}-1) + A_{min}+1}.$$

3. For each rule r_l in $\mathcal{P}$ of the form

$$t : \bigcirc K_{[\mathcal{A}]}^{\omega_1} L_1, \ldots, \bigcirc K_{[\mathcal{A}]}^{\omega_{u-1}} L_k \to \bigcirc K_{[\mathcal{A}]}^{\omega_u} L_{k+1} :$$

   (a) Add a hidden neuron L° to $\mathcal{N}_{\omega_u,t+1}$ and set $h(x)$ as the activation function of L°.
   (b) Connect each neuron $\bigcirc K_{[\mathcal{A}]}^{\omega_1} L_i$ $(1 \leq i \leq k)$, $(1 \leq \iota \leq u-1)$ in $\mathcal{N}_{\omega_1,t}$ to L°. If L_i is a positive literal, then set the connection weight to W; otherwise, set the connection weight to $-W$. Set the threshold of L° to $((1+A_{min}) \cdot (k_l - 1)/2) \cdot W$.
   (c) Connect L° to $K_{[\mathcal{A}]}^{\omega_u} L_{k+1}$ in $\mathcal{N}_{\omega_u,t+1}$ and set the connection weight to W. Set the threshold of $K_{[\mathcal{A}]}^{\omega_u} L_{k+1}$ to $((1+A_{min}) \cdot (1-\mu_l)/2) \cdot W$.
   (d) Add a hidden neuron $L^{\bullet}$ to $\mathcal{N}_{\omega_1,t}$ and set $h(x)$ as the activation function of $L^{\bullet}$.
   (e) Connect the neuron $K_{[\mathcal{A}]}^{\omega_u} L_{k+1}$ in $\mathcal{N}_{\omega_u,t+1}$ to $L^{\bullet}$ and set the connection weight to W. Set the threshold of $L^{\bullet}$ to zero.
   (f) Connect $L^{\bullet}$ to $\bigcirc K_{[\mathcal{A}]}^{\omega_1} L_i$ in $\mathcal{N}_{\omega_1,t}$ and set the connection weight to W. Set the threshold of $K_{[\mathcal{A}]}^{\omega_1} L_i$ to $((1+A_{min}) \cdot (1-\mu_l)/2) \cdot W$.

4. For each rule in $\mathcal{P}$ of the form

$$t: \bigcirc K_{[\mathcal{A}]}^{\omega_1} L_1, \ldots, \bigcirc K_{[\mathcal{A}]}^{\omega_{u-1}} L_k \to K_{[\mathcal{A}]}^{\omega_u} L_{k+1} :$$

   (a) Add a hidden neuron L° to $\mathcal{N}_{\omega_u,t}$ and set $h(x)$ as the activation function of L°.
   (b) Connect each neuron $\bigcirc K_{[\mathcal{A}]}^{\omega_1} L_i$ $(1 \leq i \leq k)$, $(1 \leq \iota \leq u-1)$ in $\mathcal{N}_{\omega_1,t}$ to L°. If L_i is a positive literal, then set the connection weight to W; otherwise, set the connection weight to $-W$. Set the threshold of L° to $((1+A_{min}) \cdot (k_l - 1)/2) \cdot W$.
   (c) Connect L° to $K_{[\mathcal{A}]}^{\omega_u} L_{k+1}$ in $\mathcal{N}_{\omega_u,t}$ and set the connection weight to W. Set the threshold of $K_{[\mathcal{A}]}^{\omega_u} L_{k+1}$ to $((1+A_{min}) \cdot (1-\mu_l)/2) \cdot W$.

Theorem 27 (Correctness of Knowledge and Probability Translation Algorithm). *For each set of knowledge and probability rules $\mathcal{P}$, there exists a neural-network ensemble $\mathcal{N}$ such that $\mathcal{N}$ computes $\mathcal{P}$.*

Proof. This follows directly from the proof of the analogous theorem for single CILP networks (Theorem 8, Chap. 4) and the proof that CML computes a fixed-point semantics for modal programs (Theorem 12, Chap. 5) extended to cater for pairs (ω, t), instead of ω only, as done in Chap. 6, Theorem 13. The only difference from Theorem 13 is that here we allow for the renaming of literals L_i as $p_i(\alpha) = x$.   ∎

12.3 The Monty Hall Puzzle

As an example case study, let us consider the Monty Hall puzzle. *Suppose you are in a game show and are given a choice of three doors. Behind one is a car, behind the others are goats. You pick door 1. Before opening door 1, Monty Hall, the host (who knows what is behind each door), opens door 2, which has a goat behind it. He then asks if you still want to take what is behind door 1, or what is behind door 3 instead. Should you switch?* [121].

At time t_0, two goats and a car are placed behind the doors. At time t_1, a door is randomly selected by you, and another door, always having a goat behind it, is opened by Monty Hall. At time t_2, you have the choice of whether or not to change your selected door, and depending on your choice, you will have different probabilities of winning the car, as outlined below (for details, see [121]).

Your chances of picking the right door are 1/3, and your chances of picking the wrong door are 2/3. When Monty Hall opens door 2, it becomes known that the probability of the car being behind door 2 is zero $(t_2 : p(door_2) = 0)$. The probability of the car not being behind door 1 remains 2/3 and, as a result, the probability of the car being behind door 3 is 2/3 $(t_2 : p(door_3) = 2/3)$. Therefore, once you learn that $p(door_2) = 0$, you ought to change from door 1 to door 3. This is summarised below:

$t_k : p(door_1) = 1/3, k \in \{0,1,2\};$
$t_j : p(door_2) = 1/3, j \in \{0,1\};$
$t_j : p(door_3) = 1/3, j \in \{0,1\};$
$t_2 : K(goat_2) \rightarrow p(door_2) = 0;$
$t_2 : K(goat_2) \rightarrow p(door_3) = 2/3.$

We model the puzzle as follows. At t_2, there are two possible worlds, one in which your policy is to change (ω_c), and another one in which your policy is to stick to your original option (ω_s). In ω_c, your chances of getting the car are 2/3, and in ω_s your chances are 1/3. Figure 12.2 shows the implementation of the rules for the puzzle in a neural-symbolic system, where g_2 denotes the fact that there is a goat behind door 2, D_i denotes the probability that the car is behind door i, *win* indicates your chance of winning the car, and c denotes that you have chosen to change from door 1 to door 3. The rules are as follows:

$t_1 : g_2,$
$t_1 : g_2 \rightarrow \bigcirc g_2,$
$t_2 : K_i^{\omega_c} \mathbf{c} \rightarrow K_i^{\omega_c}(win = 2/3),$
$t_2 : K_i^{\omega_s} \neg \mathbf{c} \rightarrow K_i^{\omega_s}(win = 1/3).$

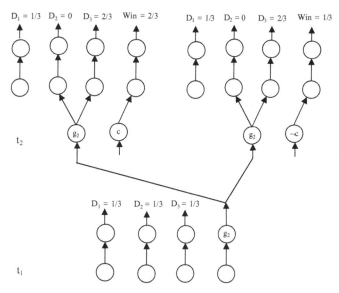

Fig. 12.2 A representation of the Monty Hall puzzle

12.4 Discussion

The knowledge representation formalism presented in this chapter provides neural-symbolic learning systems with the ability to reason about uncertainty in addition to time and knowledge. An important feature of the approach is that a temporal dimension can be combined with an epistemic dimension, at the same time allowing for probabilistic reasoning. We have illustrated this by showing that our formalism is applicable to some well-known problems of reasoning about uncertainty.

Although the approach proposed here allows reasoning with probabilities, it does not cater for the computing of probabilities. A natural next step would be to process qualitative probabilistic statements such as $(i > 0.8) \to x$. Further, the integration of other logical systems which are relevant to artificial intelligence, such as BDI logics [219], would offer interesting foundational and application-oriented developments. The use of neural-symbolic systems also facilitates knowledge evolution and revision through learning. It would be interesting to apply the above formalism to knowledge evolution in the context of distributed systems and model checking.

Chapter 13
Conclusions

This chapter reviews the neural-symbolic approach presented in this book and provides a summary of the overall neural-symbolic cognitive model. The book deals with how to represent, learn, and compute expressive forms of symbolic knowledge using neural networks. We believe this is the way forward towards the provision of an integrated system of expressive reasoning and robust learning. The provision of such a system, integrating the two most fundamental phenomena of intelligent cognitive behaviour, has been identified as a key challenge for computer science [255]. Our goal is to produce computational models with integrated reasoning and learning capability, in which neural networks provide the machinery necessary for cognitive computation and learning, while logic provides practical reasoning and explanation capabilities to the neural models, facilitating the necessary interaction with the outside world.

Three notable hallmarks of intelligent cognition are the ability to draw rational conclusions, the ability to make plausible assumptions, and the ability to generalise from experience. In a logical setting, these abilities correspond to the processes of deduction, abduction, and induction, respectively. Although human cognition often involves the interaction of these three abilities, they are typically studied in isolation (a notable exception is [186]). For example, in artificial intelligence, symbolic (logic-based) approaches have been concerned mainly with deductive reasoning, whereas connectionist (neural-network-based) approaches have focused mainly on inductive learning. It is well known that this connectionist/symbolic dichotomy in artificial intelligence reflects a distinction between brain and mind, but we argue this should not dissuade us from seeking a fruitful synthesis of these paradigms [56, 58, 71].

In our research programme, we are seeking to integrate the processes of reasoning and learning within the neural-computation paradigm. When we think of neural networks, what springs to mind is their ability to learn from examples using efficient algorithms in a massively parallel fashion. In neural computation, induction is typically seen as the process of changing the weights of a network in ways that reflect the statistical properties of a data set (a set of examples), allowing useful generalisations over unseen examples. When we think of symbolic logic, we recognise its

A.S. d'Avila Garcez et al., *Neural-Symbolic Cognitive Reasoning,* Cognitive Technologies, 169
© Springer-Verlag Berlin Heidelberg 2009

rigour, and semantic clarity, and the availability of automated proof methods which can provide explanations of the reasoning process, for example through a proof history. In neural computation, deduction can be seen as a network computation of output values as a response to input values, given a particular set of weights. Standard feedforward and partially recurrent networks have been shown capable of deductive reasoning of various kinds depending on the network architecture, including nonmonotonic [66], modal [79], intuitionistic [77], and abductive [58] reasoning.

Our goal is to offer a unified framework for learning and reasoning that exploits the parallelism and robustness of connectionist architectures. To this end, we have chosen to work with standard neural networks, whose learning capabilities have been already demonstrated in significant practical applications, and to investigate how they can be enhanced with more advanced reasoning capabilities. The main insight of this book is that, in order to enable effective learning from examples and background knowledge, one should keep network structures as simple as possible, and try to find the best symbolic representation for them. We have done so by presenting translation algorithms from nonclassical logics to single-hidden-layer neural networks. It was essential to show equivalence between the symbolic representations and the neural networks, thus ensuring a sound translation of background knowledge into a connectionist representation. Such results have made our nonclassical neural-symbolic systems into cognitive massively parallel models of symbolic computation and learning. We call such systems, combining a connectionist learning component with a logical reasoning component, *neural-symbolic learning systems* [66].

In what follows, we briefly review the work on the integration of nonclassical logics and neural networks presented in the book (see also [33]). We then look at the combination of different neural networks and their associated logics by the use of the fibring method [67]. As seen in Chap. 9, the overall model consists of a set (an ensemble) of simple, single-hidden-layer neural networks – each of which may represent the knowledge of an agent (or a possible world) at a particular time point – and connections between networks representing the relationships between agents/possible worlds. Each ensemble may be seen as being at a different level of abstraction so that networks at one level may be fibred onto networks at another level to form a structure combining metalevel and object-level information. We claim that this structure offers the basis for an expressive yet computationally tractable model of integrated, robust learning and expressive reasoning.

13.1 Neural-Symbolic Learning Systems

For neural-symbolic integration to be effective in complex applications, we need to investigate how to represent, reason with, and learn expressive logics in neural networks. We also need to find effective ways of expressing the knowledge encoded in a trained network in a comprehensible symbolic form. There are at least two lines of action. The first is to take standard neural networks and try to find out which logics they can represent. The other is to take well-established logics and concepts (e.g. recursion) and try to encode these in a neural-network architecture. Both require a principled approach, so that whenever we show that a particular logic can be represented by a particular neural network, we need to show that the network and the logic are in fact equivalent (a way of doing this is to prove that the network computes a formal semantics of the logic). Similarly, if we develop a knowledge extraction algorithm, we need to make sure that it is correct (sound) in the sense that it produces rules that are encoded in the network, and that it is *quasi*-complete in the sense that the extracted rules increasingly approximate the exact behaviour of the network.

During the last twenty years, a number of models for neural-symbolic integration have been proposed (mainly in response to John McCarthy's note 'Epistemological challenges for connectionism'[1] [176], itself a response to Paul Smolensky's paper 'On the proper treatment of connectionism' [237]). Broadly speaking, researchers have made contributions in three main areas, providing either (i) a logical character-isation of a connectionist system, (ii) a connectionist implementation of a logic, or (iii) a hybrid system bringing together features from connectionist systems and sym-bolic artificial intelligence [132]. Early relevant contributions include [135,229,242] on knowledge representation, [80, 250] on learning with background knowledge, and [30, 65, 144, 227, 244] on knowledge extraction. The reader is referred to [66] for a detailed presentation of neural-symbolic learning systems and applications.

Neural-symbolic learning systems contain six main phases: (1) *background knowledge insertion,* (2) *inductive learning from examples,* (3) *massively parallel deduction,* (4) *fine-tuning of the theory,* (5) *symbolic knowledge extraction,* and (6) *feedback* (see Fig. 13.1). In phase (1), symbolic knowledge is translated into the initial architecture of a neural network with the use of a *translation algorithm.* In phase (2), the neural network is trained with examples by a neural learning algo-rithm, which revises the theory given in phase (1) as *background knowledge.* In phase (3), the network can be used as a massively parallel system to compute the logical consequences of the theory encoded in it. In phase (4), information obtained from the computation carried out in phase (3) may be used to help fine-tune the

---

[1] In [176], McCarthy identified four knowledge representation problems for neural networks: the problem of *elaboration tolerance* (the ability of a representation to be elaborated to take additional phenomena into account), the *propositional fixation* of neural networks (based on the assumption that neural networks cannot represent relational knowledge), the problem of how to make use of any available *background knowledge* as part of learning, and the problem of how to obtain domain *descriptions* from trained networks, as opposed to mere discriminations. Neural-symbolic integra-tion can address each of the above challenges. In a nutshell, the problem of elaboration tolerance can be resolved by having networks that are fibred so as to form a modular hierarchy, similarly to the idea of using self-organising maps [112, 125] for language processing, where the lower levels of abstraction are used for the formation of concepts that are then used at the higher levels of the hierarchy. Connectionist modal logic [79] deals with the so-called propositional fixation of neural networks by allowing them to encode relational knowledge in the form of accessibility relations; a number of other formalisms have also tackled this issue as early as 1990 [11, 13, 134, 230], the key question being that of how to have simple representations that promote effective learning. Learning with background knowledge can be achieved by the usual translation of symbolic rules into neural networks. Problem descriptions can be obtained by rule extraction; a number of such translation and extraction algorithms have been proposed, for example [30, 65, 80, 132, 144, 165, 192, 227, 242].

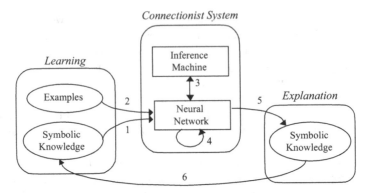

Fig. 13.1 Neural-symbolic learning systems

network in order to better represent the problem domain. This mechanism can be used, for example, to resolve inconsistencies between the background knowledge and the training examples. In phase (5), the result of training is explained by the extraction of revised symbolic knowledge. As with the insertion of rules, the *extraction algorithm* must be provably correct, so that each rule extracted is guaranteed to be a rule of the network. Finally, in phase (6), the knowledge extracted may be analysed by an expert to decide if it should feed the system again, closing the learning and reasoning cycle.

Our neural-network models consist of feedforward and partially recurrent networks, as opposed to the symmetric networks investigated, for example, in [240]. It uses a localist rather than a distributed representation,[2] and it works with backpropagation, the neural learning algorithm most successfully used in industrial-strength applications [224].

13.2 Connectionist Nonclassical Reasoning

We now turn to the question of expressiveness. We believe that for neural computation to achieve its promise, connectionist models must be able to cater for nonclassical reasoning. We believe that the neural-symbolic community cannot ignore the achievements and impact that nonclassical logics have had in computer science [71]. Whereas nonmonotonic reasoning dominated research in artificial intelligence in the 1980s and 1990s, temporal logic has had a large impact in both academia and industry, and modal logic has become a lingua franca for the specification and analysis

---

[2] We depart from distributed representations for two main reasons: localist representations can be associated with highly effective learning algorithms such as backpropagation, and in our view, localist networks are at an appropriate level of abstraction for symbolic knowledge representation. As advocated in [200], we believe one should be able to achieve the goals of distributed representations by properly changing the levels of abstraction of localist networks, whereas some of the desirable properties of localist models cannot be exhibited by fully-distributed ones.

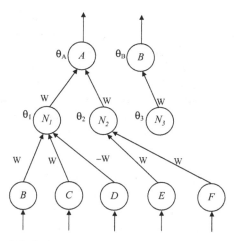

Fig. 13.2 Neural-network for logic programming

of knowledge and communication in multiagent and distributed systems [87]. In this section, we consider modal and temporal reasoning as key representatives of nonclassical reasoning.

The basic idea behind more expressive, connectionist nonclassical reasoning is simple, as seen in previous chapters of this book. Instead of having a single network, if we now consider a set of networks such as the one in Fig. 13.2, and we label them, say, as ω_1, ω_2, etc., then we can talk about a concept L holding in ω_1 and the same concept L holding in ω_2 separately. In this way, we can see ω_1 as one possible world and ω_2 as another, and this allows us to represent modalities such as necessity and possibility, and time, and also argumentation [69], epistemic states [74], and intuitionistic reasoning [77]. It is important to note that this avenue of research is of interest in connection with McCarthy's conjecture about the propositional fixation of neural networks [176] because there is a well-established translation between propositional modal logic and the two-variable fragment of first-order logic, as we have seen in Chap. 5 (see e.g. [264]), indicating that relatively simple neural-symbolic systems may go beyond propositional logic.

13.2.1 Connectionist Modal Reasoning

Recall that modal logic deals with the analysis of concepts such as *necessity* (represented by $\Box L$, read as 'box L', and meaning that L is *necessarily true*), and *possibility* (represented by $\Diamond L$, read as 'diamond L', and meaning that L is *possibly true*). A key aspect of modal logic is the use of *possible worlds* and a binary (accessibility) relation $\mathcal{R}(\omega_i, \omega_j)$ between worlds ω_i and ω_j. In possible-world semantics, a proposition is necessary in a world if it is true in all worlds which are possible in relation to that world, whereas it is possible in a world if it is true in at least one world which is possible in relation to that same world.

Connectionist modal logic (CML), presented in Chap. 5, uses ensembles of neural networks (instead of single networks) to represent the language of modal logic programming [197]. The theories are now sets of modal clauses, each of the form $\omega_i : ML_1, \ldots, ML_n \rightarrow MA$, where ω_i is a label representing a world in which the associated clause holds, and $M \in \{\Box, \Diamond\}$, together with a finite set of relations $\mathcal{R}(\omega_i, \omega_j)$ between worlds ω_i and ω_j. Such theories are implemented in a network ensemble, each network representing a possible world, with the use of ensembles and labels allowing the representation of accessibility relations.

In CML, each network in the ensemble is a simple, single-hidden-layer network like the network of Fig. 13.2, to which standard neural learning algorithms can be applied. Learning, in this setting, can be seen as learning the concepts that hold in each possible world independently, with the accessibility relation providing information on how the networks should interact. For example, take three networks all related to each other. If a neuron $\Diamond a$ is activated in one of these networks, then a neuron a must be activated in at least one of the networks. If a neuron $\Box a$ is activated in one network, then neuron a must be activated in all the networks. This implements in a connectionist setting the possible-world semantics mentioned above. It is achieved by defining the connections and the weights of the network ensemble, following a translation algorithm. Details of the translation algorithm, along with a soundness proof, have been given in Chap. 5.

As an example, consider Fig. 13.3. This shows an ensemble of three neural networks labelled N_1, N_2, N_3, which might *communicate* in different ways. We look at N_1, N_2, and N_3 as *possible worlds*. Input and output neurons may now represent $\Box L$, $\Diamond L$, or L, where L is a literal. $\Box A$ will be *true* in a world ω_i if A is *true* in all worlds ω_j to which ω_i is related. Similarly, $\Diamond A$ will be *true* in a world ω_i if A is

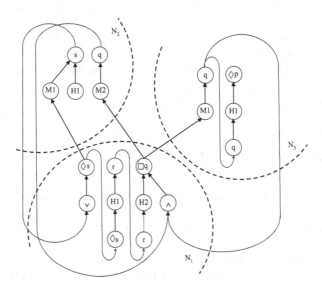

Fig. 13.3 Neural-network ensemble for modal reasoning

true in some world ω_j to which ω_i is related. As a result, if neuron $\Box A$ is activated in network N_1, denoted by $\omega_1 : \Box A$, and world ω_1 is related to worlds ω_2 and ω_3, then neuron A must be activated in networks N_2 and N_3. Similarly, if neuron $\Diamond A$ is activated in N_1, then a neuron A must be activated in an arbitrary network that is related to N_1.

It is also possible to make use of CML to compute that $\Box A$ holds in a possible world, say ω_i, whenever A holds in *all* possible worlds related to ω_i, by connecting the output neurons of the related networks to a hidden neuron in ω_i which connects to an output neuron labelled $\Box A$. Dually for $\Diamond A$, whenever A holds in *some* possible world related to ω_i, we connect the output neuron representing A to a hidden neuron in ω_i which connects to an output neuron labelled $\Diamond A$. Owing to the simplicity of each network in the ensemble, when it comes to learning, we can still use backpropagation on each network to learn the local knowledge in each possible world.

13.2.2 Connectionist Temporal Reasoning

The Connectionist Temporal Logic of Knowledge (CTLK), presented in Chap. 6, is an extension of CML which considers temporal and epistemic knowledge [72]. Generally speaking, the idea is to allow, instead of a single ensemble, a number n of ensembles, each representing the knowledge held by a number of agents at a given time point t. Figure 13.4 illustrates how this dynamic feature can be combined with the symbolic features of the knowledge represented in each network, allowing not only the analysis of the current state (the current possible world or time point), but also the analysis of how knowledge changes over time.

Of course, there are important issues to do with (1) the optimisation of the model of Fig. 13.4 in practice, (2) the fact that the number of networks may be bounded, and (3) the trade-off between space and time computational complexity. The fact, however, that this model is sufficient to deal with such a variety of reasoning tasks is encouraging.

The definition of the number of ensembles s that are necessary to solve a given problem clearly depends on the problem domain, and on the number of time points that are relevant to reasoning about the problem. For example, in the case of the archetypal distributed-knowledge-representation problem of the muddy children puzzle [87], we know that it suffices to have s equal to the number of children that are muddy. The definition of s for a different domain might not be as straightforward, possibly requiring a fine-tuning process similar to that performed during learning, but with a varying network architecture. These and other considerations, including more extensive evaluations of the model with respect to learning, are still required. Recently, this model has been applied effectively to multiprocess synchronisation and learning in concurrent programming [157] and in a neural-symbolic model for analogical reasoning [34].

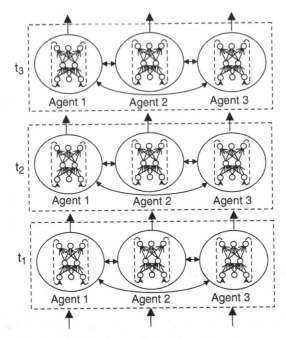

Fig. 13.4 Neural-network ensemble for temporal reasoning

13.3 Fibring Neural Networks

In CML, one may need to create copies of certain concepts. As a result, CML does not deal directly with infinite domains, since this would require infinitely many copies. An alternative is to map the instances of a variable onto the real numbers, and then use the real numbers as inputs to a neural network as a way of representing the instances. This has been done in [136]. However, the question of how to construct such a network to compute and learn a program remained unanswered, since no translation algorithm was given in [136]. A follow-up paper providing such an algorithm for first-order covered programs has appeared recently [13]. In [11], the idea of representing variables as real numbers was also followed, and a translation algorithm from first-order acyclic programs to neural-network ensembles was proposed. This algorithm makes use of *fibring* of neural networks [67]. Briefly, the idea is to use a neural network to iterate a global counter n. For each clause C_i in the logic program, this counter is combined (fibred) with another neural network, which determines whether C_i outputs an atom of level n for a given interpretation I. This allows us to translate programs with an infinite number of ground instances into a finite neural-network structure (e.g. $\neg even(x) \rightarrow even(s(x))$ for $x \in \mathbb{N}, s(x) = x+1$), and to prove that the network indeed approximates the fixed-point semantics of the program. The translation is made possible because fibring allows one to implement a key feature of symbolic computation in neural networks, namely *recursion*, as we describe below.

The idea of fibring neural networks is simple. Fibred networks may be composed not only of interconnected neurons but also of other networks, forming a recursive architecture. A fibring function then defines how this architecture behaves, by defining how the networks in the ensemble relate to each other. Typically, the fibring function will allow the activation of neurons in one network (*A*) to influence the change of weights in another network (*B*). Intuitively, this may be seen as training network *B* at the same time that network *A* runs. Interestingly, even though they are a combination of simple, standard neural networks, fibred networks can approximate any polynomial function in an unbounded domain, thus being more expressive than standard feedforward networks.

Figure 13.5, reproduced from Chap. 9, exemplifies how a network (*B*) can be fibred into another network (*A*). Of course, the idea of fibring is not only to organise networks as a number of subnetworks; in Fig. 13.5, the output neuron of *A* is expected to be a neural network (*B*) in its own right. The input, weights, and output of *B* may depend on the activation state of *A*'s output neuron, according to the fibring function φ. Fibred networks can be trained by examples in the same way that standard networks are. For instance, networks *A* and *B* could have been trained separately before they were fibred. Networks can be fibred in a number of different ways as far as their architectures are concerned; network *B* could have been fibred into a hidden neuron of network *A*.

As an example, network *A* could have been trained with a robot's visual system, while network *B* could have been trained with its planning system, and fibring would serve to perform the composition of the two systems [101]. Fibring can be very powerful. It offers the extra expressiveness required by complex applications at low computational cost (that of computing the fibring function φ). Of course, we would like to keep φ as simple as possible so that it can be implemented itself by

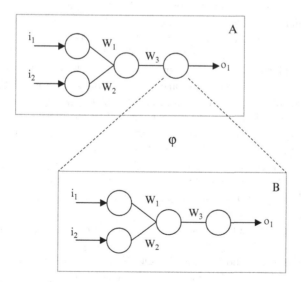

Fig. 13.5 Fibring neural networks

simple neurons in a fully-connectionist model. Interesting work remains to be done in this area, particularly in regard to the question of how one should go about fibring networks in real applications.

13.4 Concluding Remarks

Connectionist modal logic and its variations offer an illustration of how the area of neural networks may contribute to the area of logic, while fibring is an example of how logic can bring insight into neural computation. CML offers parallel models of computation to modal logic that, at the same time, can be integrated with an efficient learning algorithm. Fibring is a clear example of how concepts from symbolic computation may help in the development of neural models. This does not necessarily conflict with the ambition of biological plausibility; for example, fibring functions can be understood as a model of *presynaptic weights*, which play an important role in biological neural networks.

Connectionist nonclassical reasoning and network fibring bring us to our overall cognitive model, which we may call *fibred network ensembles*. In this model, a network ensemble A (representing, for example, a temporal theory) may be combined with another network ensemble B (representing, for example, an intuitionistic theory). Along the same lines, metalevel concepts (in A) may be combined and brought into the object level (B), without necessarily blurring the distinction between the two levels. One may reason in the metalevel and use that information in the object level, a typical example being (metalevel) reasoning about actions in (object-level) databases containing inconsistencies [96]. Relations between networks/concepts in the object level may be represented and learned in the metalevel as described in Chap. 10. If two networks denote, for example, $P(X,Y)$ and $Q(Z)$, a metanetwork can learn to map a representation of the concepts P and Q (for instance using the hidden neurons of networks P and Q) onto a third network, denoting, say, $R(X,Y,Z)$, such that, for example, $P(X,Y) \wedge Q(Z) \rightarrow R(X,Y,Z)$.

Figure 13.6 illustrates fibred network ensembles. The overall model takes the most general knowledge representation ensemble of the kind shown in Fig. 13.4, and allows a number of such ensembles to be combined at different levels of abstraction through fibring. Relations between concepts at a level n may be generalised at level $n+1$ with the use of metalevel networks. Abstract concepts at level n may be specialised (or instantiated) at level $n-1$ with the use of a fibring function. Evolution of knowlege with time occurs at each level. Alternative outcomes, possible worlds, and the nonmonotonic reasoning process of multiple interacting agents can be modelled at each level. Learning can take place inside each modular, simple network or across networks in the ensemble.

Both the symbolic and the connectionist paradigms have virtues and deficiencies. Research into the integration of the two has important implications that are beneficial to computing and to cognitive science. Concomitantly, the limits of effective integration should also be pursued, in the sense that integration might become

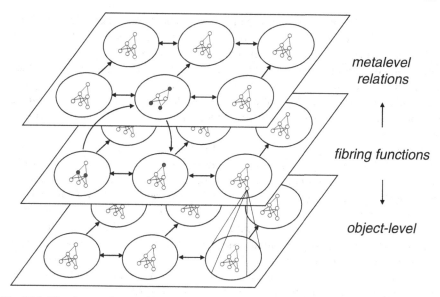

Fig. 13.6 Fibred network ensembles

disadvantageous in comparison with purely symbolic or purely connectionist systems. We believe that this book has contributed to the synergetic integration of connectionism and symbolism.

Of course, the question of how we humans integrate reasoning and learning is only starting to be answered [109, 241]. We argue that the prospects are better if we investigate the connectionist processes of the brain together with the logical processes of symbolic computation, rather than as two isolated paradigms. Of course, we shall need to be precise as we develop the framework further and test our model of fibred network ensembles in real cognitive tasks.

The challenges for neural-symbolic integration today emerge from the goal of effective integration of expressive reasoning and robust learning. One cannot afford to lose on learning performance when adding reasoning capability to neural models. This means that one cannot depart from the key concept that neural networks are composed of simple processing units organised in a massively parallel fashion (i.e. one cannot allow some clever neuron to perform complex symbol processing). Ideally, the models should be amenable to advances in computational neuroscience and brain imaging, which can offer data and also insight into new forms of representation. Finally, there are computational challenges associated with the more practical aspects of the application of neural-symbolic systems in areas such as engineering, robotics, and the Semantic Web. These challenges include the effective, massively parallel computation of logical models, the efficient extraction of comprehensible rules, and, ultimately, the striking of the right balance between computational tractability and expressiveness. References [57, 59–61] contain a number of recent papers dealing with some of today's challenges.

In summary, by paying attention to the developments on either side of the division between the symbolic and the subsymbolic paradigms, we are getting closer to a unifying theory, or at least promoting a faster, principled development of the cognitive and computing sciences and artificial intelligence. This book has described a family of connectionist nonclassical reasoning systems and hinted at how they may be combined at different levels of abstraction by fibring. We hope that it serves as a stepping stone towards such a theory to reconcile the symbolic and connectionist approaches.

Human beings are quite extraordinary at performing practical reasoning as they go about their daily business. *There are cases where the human computer, slow as it is, is faster than artificial intelligence systems. Why are we faster? Is it the way we perceive knowledge, as opposed to the way we represent it? Do we know immediately which rules to select and apply? We must look for the correct representation, in the sense that it mirrors the way we perceive and apply the rules* [100]. Ultimately, neural-symbolic integration is about asking and trying to answer these questions, and about the associated provision of neural-symbolic systems with integrated capabilities for expressive reasoning and robust learning. We believe that this book has offered a principled computational model towards this goal.

References

[1] S. Abramsky. Computational interpretations of linear logic. *Theoretical Computer Science*, 111(1–2):3–57, 1993.

[2] V. Ajjanagadde. Reasoning with function symbols in a connectionist system. In *Proceedings of the Eleventh Annual Conference of the Cognitive Science Society*, pages 388–395, 1989.

[3] V. Ajjanagadde. *Rule-Based Reasoning in Connectionist Networks*. PhD thesis, University of Minnesota, 1997.

[4] C.E. Alchourrón, P. Gärdenfors, and D.C. Makinson. On the logic of theory change: Partial meet contraction and revision functions. *Journal of Symbolic Logic*, 50:510–530, 1985.

[5] N. Alechina, M. Mendler, V. de Paiva, and E. Ritter. Categorical and Kripke semantics for constructive S4 modal logic. In L. Fribourg, editor, *Computer Science Logic, CSL'01*, volume 2142 of Lecture Notes in Computer Science, pages 292–307. Springer, 2001.

[6] N. Angelopoulos and S.H. Muggleton. Machine learning metabolic pathway descriptions using a probabilistic relational representation. *Electronic Transactions in Artificial Intelligence*, 7, 2002.

[7] G. Antoniou. *Nonmonotonic Reasoning*. MIT Press, Cambridge, MA, 1997.

[8] G. Antoniou, D. Billington, and M.J. Maher. Sceptical logic programming based default reasoning: Defeasible logic rehabilitated. In R. Miller and M. Shanahan, editors, *COMMONSENSE 98, The Fourth Symposium on Logical Formalizations of Commonsense Reasoning*, pages 1–20, London, 1998.

[9] K.R. Apt and R.N. Bol. Logic programming and negation: A survey. *Journal of Logic Programming*, 19–20:9–71, 1994.

[10] S.N. Artëmov. Explicit provability and constructive semantics. *Bulletin of Symbolic Logic*, 7(1):1–36, 2001.

[11] S. Bader, A.S. d'Avila Garcez, and P. Hitzler. Computing first-order logic programs by fibring artificial neural networks. In *Proceedings of the AAAI International FLAIRS Conference*, pages 314–319, 2005.

[12] S. Bader and P. Hitzler. Dimensions of neural-symbolic integration – a structured survey. In S.N. Artëmov, H. Barringer, A.S. d'Avila Garcez, L.C. Lamb, and J. Woods, editors, *We Will Show Them! Essays in Honour of Dov Gabbay*, pages 167–194. College Publications, International Federation for Computational Logic, 2005.

[13] S. Bader, P. Hitzler, S. Holldobler, and A. Witzel. A fully connectionist model generator for covered first-order logic programs. In *Proceedings of the International Joint Conference on Artificial Intelligence, IJCAI-07*, pages 666–671, Hyderabad, India, 2007. AAAI Press, 2007.

[14] P. Baldi and S. Brunak. *Bioinformatics: The Machine Learning Approach*. MIT Press, 2001.

[15] M. Baldoni, L. Giordano, and A. Martelli. A modal extension of logic programming: Modularity, beliefs and hypothetical reasoning. *Journal of Logic and Computation*, 8(5):597–635, 1998.

[16] C. Balkenius and P. Gärdenfors. Nonmonotonic inference in neural networks. In *Principles of Knowledge Representation and Reasoning, Proceedings of the Second International Conference, KR91*, pages 32–39, 1991.

[17] D.H. Ballard. Parallel logical inference and energy minimization. In *Proceedings of the National Conference on Artificial Intelligence, AAAI-86*, pages 203–208, 1986.

[18] H. Barringer, D.M. Gabbay, and J. Woods. Temporal dynamics of support and attack networks: From argumentation to zoology. In D. Hutter and W. Stephan, editors, *Mechanizing Mathematical Reasoning, Essays in Honor of Jörg H. Siekmann on the Occasion of His 60th Birthday*, volume 2605 of Lecture Notes in Computer Science, pages 59–98. Springer, 2005.

[19] R. Basilio, G. Zaverucha, and V.C. Barbosa. Learning logic programs with neural networks. In *11th International Conference on Inductive Logic Programming, ILP01*, volume 2157 of Lecture Notes in Computer Science, pages 15–26. Springer, 2001.

[20] R. Basilio, G. Zaverucha, and A.S. d'Avila Garcez. Inducing relational concepts with neural networks via the LINUS system. In *Proceedings of the Fifth International Conference on Neural Information Processing, ICONIP'98*, pages 1507–1510, 1998.

[21] M. Baudinet. Temporal logic programming is complete and expressive. In *Proceedings of ACM Symposium on Principles of Programming Languages*, pages 267–280, Austin, Texas, 1989.

[22] T.J.M. Bench-Capon. Persuasion in practical argument using value-based argumentation frameworks. *Journal of Logic and Computation*, 13:429–448, 2003.

[23] B. Bennett. Spatial reasoning with propositional logics. In *Proceedings of the Fourth International Conference on Principles of Knowledge Representation and Reasoning, KR-94*, pages 51–62, 1994.

[24] B. Bennett, C. Dixon, M. Fisher, U. Hustadt, E. Franconi, I. Horrocks, and M. de Rijke. Combinations of modal logics. *Artificial Intelligence Review*, 17(1):1–20, 2002.

[25] P. Besnard and A. Hunter. Towards a logic-based theory of argumentation. In *Proceedings of 17th National Conference on Artificial Intelligence, AAAI-00*, pages 411–416. AAAI Press, 2000.

[26] C. Bishop. *Neural Networks for Pattern Recognition*. Oxford University Press, Oxford, 1995.

[27] C. Bishop. *Pattern Recognition and Machine Learning*. Springer, 2006.

[28] P. Blackburn, M. de Rijke, and Y. Venema. *Modal Logic*. Cambridge University Press, 2001.

[29] H. Blair and V.S. Subrahmanian. Paraconsistent logic programming. *Theoretical Computer Science*, 68:135–154, 1989.

[30] G. Bologna. Is it worth generating rules from neural network ensembles? *Journal of Applied Logic*, 2(3):325–348, 2004.

[31] A. Bondarenko, P. Dung, R.A. Kowalski, and F. Toni. An abstract, argumentation theoretic approach to default reasoning. *Artificial Intelligence*, 93:63–101, 1997.

[32] R.V. Borges, L.C. Lamb, and A.S. d'Avila Garcez. Combining architectures for temporal learning in neural-symbolic systems. In *Proceedings of the 6th International Conference on Hybrid Intelligent Systems, HIS 2006*, page 46. IEEE Computer Society, 2006.

[33] R.V. Borges, L.C. Lamb, and A.S. d'Avila Garcez. Reasoning and learning about past temporal knowledge in connectionist models. In *Proceedings of the Twentieth International Joint Conference on Neural Networks, IJCNN 2007*, pages 1488–1493, 2007.

[34] R.V. Borges, A.S. d'Avila Garcez, and L.C. Lamb. A neural-symbolic perspective on analogy. *Behavioral and Brain Sciences*, 31(4):379–380, 2008.

[35] N.K. Bose and P. Liang. *Neural Networks Fundamentals with Graphs, Algorithms, and Applications*. McGraw-Hill, 1996.

[36] B. Boutsinas and M.N. Vrahatis. Artificial nonmonotonic neural networks. *Artificial Intelligence*, 132:1–38, 2001.

[37] G. Brewka. *Nonmonotonic Reasoning: Logical Foundations of Commonsense*, volume 12 of Cambridge Tracts in Theoretical Computer Science. Cambridge University Press, 1990.

[38] G. Brewka. Cumulative default logic: In defense of nonmonotonic inference rules. *Artificial Intelligence*, 50(2):183–205, 1991.

[39] G. Brewka. Dynamic argument systems: A formal model of argumentation processes based on situation calculus. *Journal of Logic and Computation*, 11(2):257–282, 2001.

[40] G. Brewka and T. Eiter. Preferred answer sets for extended logic programs. *Artificial Intelligence*, 109:297–356, 1999.

[41] K. Broda, D.M. Gabbay, L.C. Lamb, and A. Russo. Labelled natural deduction for conditional logics of normality. *Logic Journal of the IGPL*, 10(2):123–163, 2002.

[42] K. Broda, D.M. Gabbay, L.C. Lamb, and A. Russo. *Compiled Labelled Deductive Systems: A Uniform Presentation of Non-Classical Logics*, Studies in Logic and Computation. Research Studies Press/Institute of Physics Publishing, Baldock, UK/Philadelphia, PA, 2004.

[43] A. Browne and R. Sun. Connectionist inference models. *Neural Networks*, 14:1331–1355, 2001.

[44] C. Brzoska. Temporal logic programming and its relation to constraint logic programming. In *Proceedings of the International Symposium on Logic Programming*, pages 661–677. MIT Press, 1991.

[45] M.A. Castilho, L. Farinas del Cerro, O. Gasquet, and A. Herzig. Modal tableaux with propagation rules and structural rules. *Fundamenta Informaticae*, 32(3–4):281–297, 1997.

[46] A. Chagrov and M. Zakharyaschev. *Modal Logic*. Clarendon Press, Oxford, 1997.

[47] Y. Chauvin and D. Rumelhart, editors. *Backpropagation: Theory, Architectures and Applications*. Lawrence Erlbaum, 1995.

[48] C.I. Chesñevar, A.G. Maguitman, and R.P. Loui. Logical models of argument. *ACM Computing Surveys*, 32(4):337–383, December 2000.

[49] K.L. Clark. Negation as failure. In H. Gallaire and J. Minker, editors, *Logic and Databases*, pages 293–322. Plenum Press, New York, 1978.

[50] E.M. Clarke and H. Schlingloff. Model checking. In J.A. Robinson and A. Voronkov, editors, *Handbook of Automated Reasoning*, volume II, chapter 24, pages 1635–1790. Elsevier, 2001.

[51] I. Cloete and J.M. Zurada, editors. *Knowledge-Based Neurocomputing*. MIT Press, Cambridge, MA, 2000.

[52] G. Cybenco. Approximation by superposition of sigmoidal functions. In *Mathematics of Control, Signals and Systems 2*, pages 303–314, 1989.

[53] B. DasGupta and G. Schnitger. Analog versus discrete neural networks. *Neural Computation*, 8:805–818, 1996.

[54] B.A. Davey and H.A. Priestley. *Introduction to Lattices and Order*. Cambridge University Press, 1990.

[55] R. Davies and F. Pfenning. A modal analysis of staged computation. *Journal of the ACM*, 48(3):555–604, 2001.

[56] A.S. d'Avila Garcez. Fewer epistemological challenges for connectionism. In S.B. Cooper, B. Lowe, and L. Torenvliet, editors, *Proceedings of Computability in Europe, CiE 2005*, volume 3526 of Lecture Notes in Computer Science, pages 139–149. Springer, 2005.

[57] A.S. d'Avila Garcez, J. Elman, and P. Hitzler, editors. *Proceedings of IJCAI International Workshop on Neural-Symbolic Learning and Reasoning, NeSy05*, Edinburgh, 2005.

[58] A.S. d'Avila Garcez, D.M. Gabbay, O. Ray, and J. Woods. Abductive reasoning in neural-symbolic systems. *TOPOI: An International Review of Philosophy*, 26:37–49, 2007.

[59] A.S. d'Avila Garcez and P. Hitzler, editors. *Proceedings of ECAI International Workshop on Neural-Symbolic Learning and Reasoning, NeSy08*, Patras, Greece, 2008.

[60] A.S. d'Avila Garcez, P. Hitzler, and G. Tamburrini, editors. *Proceedings of ECAI International Workshop on Neural-Symbolic Learning and Reasoning, NeSy06*, Trento, Italy, 2006.

[61] A.S. d'Avila Garcez, P. Hitzler, and G. Tamburrini, editors. *Proceedings of IJCAI International Workshop on Neural-Symbolic Learning and Reasoning, NeSy07*, Hyderabad, India, 2007.

[62] A.S. d'Avila Garcez. Extended theory refinement in knowledge-based neural networks. In *Proceedings of IEEE International Joint Conference on Neural Networks, IJCNN'02*, Honolulu, Hawaii, 2002.

[63] A.S. d'Avila Garcez. On Gabbay's fibring methodology for Bayesian and neural networks. In D. Gillies, editor, *Laws and Models in Science*. King's College London, 233–245, 2004.

[64] A.S. d'Avila Garcez, K. Broda, and D.M. Gabbay. Metalevel priorities and neural networks. In P. Frasconi, M. Gori, F. Kurfess, and A. Sperduti, editors, *Proceedings of ECAI 2000, Workshop on the Foundations of Connectionist-Symbolic Integration*, Berlin, 2000.

[65] A.S. d'Avila Garcez, K. Broda, and D.M. Gabbay. Symbolic knowledge extraction from trained neural networks: A sound approach. *Artificial Intelligence*, 125:155–207, 2001.

[66] A.S. d'Avila Garcez, K. Broda, and D.M. Gabbay. *Neural-Symbolic Learning Systems: Foundations and Applications*, Perspectives in Neural Computing. Springer, 2002.

[67] A.S. d'Avila Garcez and D.M. Gabbay. Fibring neural networks. In *Proceedings of 19th National Conference on Artificial Intelligence, AAAI-04*, pages 342–347, San Jose, CA, 2004.

[68] A.S. d'Avila Garcez, D.M. Gabbay, and L.C. Lamb. Argumentation neural networks. In *Proceedings of the 11th International Conference on Neural Information Processing, ICONIP'04*, volume 3316 of Lecture Notes in Computer Science, pages 606–612. Springer, 2004.

[69] A.S. d'Avila Garcez, D.M. Gabbay, and L.C. Lamb. Value-based argumentation frameworks as neural-symbolic learning systems. *Journal of Logic and Computation*, 15(6):1041–1058, 2005.

[70] A.S. d'Avila Garcez and L.C. Lamb. Reasoning about time and knowledge in neural-symbolic learning systems. In S.B. Thrun, L. Saul, and B. Schoelkopf, editors, *Advances in Neural Information Processing Systems 16*, Proceedings of NIPS 2003, pages 921–928. MIT Press, 2004.

[71] A.S. d'Avila Garcez and L.C. Lamb. Neural-symbolic systems and the case for non-classical reasoning. In S.N. Artëmov, H. Barringer, A.S. d'Avila Garcez, L.C. Lamb, and J. Woods, editors, *We Will Show Them! Essays in Honour of Dov Gabbay*, pages 469–488. College Publications, International Federation for Computational Logic, 2005.

[72] A.S. d'Avila Garcez and L.C. Lamb. A connectionist computational model for epistemic and temporal reasoning. *Neural Computation*, 18(7):1711–1738, 2006.

[73] A.S. d'Avila Garcez, L.C. Lamb, K. Broda, and D.M. Gabbay. Distributed knowledge representation in neural-symbolic learning systems: A case study. In *Proceedings of AAAI International FLAIRS Conference*, pages 271–275 St. Augustine, FL, 2003. AAAI Press, 2007.

[74] A.S. d'Avila Garcez, L.C. Lamb, K. Broda, and D.M. Gabbay. Applying connectionist modal logics to distributed knowledge representation problems. *International Journal on Artificial Intelligence Tools*, 13(1):115–139, 2004.

[75] A.S. d'Avila Garcez, L.C. Lamb, and D.M. Gabbay. A connectionist inductive learning system for modal logic programming. In *Proceedings of the 9th International Conference on Neural Information Processing, ICONIP'02*, pages 1992–1997, Singapore, 2002. IEEE Press, 2007.

[76] A.S. d'Avila Garcez, L.C. Lamb, and D.M. Gabbay. Neural-symbolic intuitionistic reasoning. In A. Abraham, M. köppen, and K. Franke, editors, *Design and Application of Hybrid Intelligent Systems*, volume 104 of Frontiers in Artificial Intelligence and Applications, pages 399–408. IOS Press, Amsterdam, 2003.

[77] A.S. d'Avila Garcez, L.C. Lamb, and D.M. Gabbay. Connectionist computations of intuitionistic reasoning. *Theoretical Computer Science*, 358(1):34–55, 2006.

[78] A.S. d'Avila Garcez, L.C. Lamb, and D.M. Gabbay. A connectionist model for constructive modal reasoning. In *Advances in Neural Information Processing Systems 18*, Proceedings of NIPS 2005, pages 403–410. MIT Press, 2006.

[79] A.S. d'Avila Garcez, L.C. Lamb, and D.M. Gabbay. Connectionist modal logic: Representing modalities in neural networks. *Theoretical Computer Science*, 371(1–2):34–53, 2007.

[80] A.S. d'Avila Garcez and G. Zaverucha. The connectionist inductive learning and logic programming system. *Applied Intelligence Journal, Special Issue on Neural Networks and Structured Knowledge*, 11(1):59–77, 1999.

[81] M. Davis. The early history of automated deduction. In J.A. Robinson and A. Voronkov, editors, *Handbook of Automated Reasoning*, volume I, chapter 1, pages 3–15. Elsevier Science, 2001.

[82] L.A. Doumas and J.E. Hummel. A symbolic–connectionist model of relation discovery. In *Proceedings of XXVII Annual Conference of the Cognitive Science Society, CogSci2005*, pages 606–611, Stresa, Italy, July 2005.

[83] P.M. Dung. On the acceptability of arguments and its fundamental role in nonmonotonic reasoning, logic programming and *n*-person games. *Artificial Intelligence*, 77:321–357, 1995.

[84] S. Dzeroski and N. Lavrac, editors. *Relational Data Mining*. Springer, September 2001.

[85] J.L. Elman. Finding structure in time. *Cognitive Science*, 14(2):179–211, 1990.

[86] H.B. Enderton. *A Mathematical Introduction to Logic*. Academic Press, 1972.

[87] R. Fagin, J. Halpern, Y. Moses, and M. Vardi. *Reasoning About Knowledge*. MIT Press, 1995.

[88] L. Farinas del Cerro and A. Herzig. Modal deduction with applications in epistemic and temporal logics. In D.M. Gabbay, C.J. Hogger, and J.A. Robinson, editors, *Handbook of Logic in Artificial Intelligence and Logic Programming*, volume 4, pages 499–594. Oxford University Press, 1995.

[89] M. Fischer, D.M. Gabbay, and L. Vila, editors. *Handbook of Temporal Reasoning in Artificial Intelligence*. Elsevier, 2005.

[90] M. Fitting. *Proof Methods for Modal and Intuitionistic Logics*. Reidel, Dordrecht, 1983.

[91] M. Fitting. A Kripke–Kleene semantics for general logic programs. *Journal of Logic Programming*, 2:295–312, 1985.

[92] M. Fitting. Metric methods: Three examples and a theorem. *Journal of Logic Programming*, 21:113–127, 1994.

[93] N. Friedman, L. Getoor, D. Koller, and A. Pfeffer. Learning probabilistic relational models. In *Proceedings of International Joint Conference on Artificial Intelligence, IJCAI'99*, pages 1300–1309, 1999.

[94] N. Friedman and D. Koller. Being Bayesian about network structure: A Bayesian approach to structure discovery in Bayesian networks. *Machine Learning*, 50:95–126, 2003.

[95] L.M. Fu. *Neural Networks in Computer Intelligence*. McGraw-Hill, 1994.

[96] D.M. Gabbay and A. Hunter. Making inconsistency respectable: Part 2 – meta-level handling of inconsistency. In *Symbolic and Quantitative Approaches to Reasoning and Uncertainty, ECSQARU'93*, volume 747 of Lecture Notes in Computer Science, pages 129–136. Springer, 1993.

[97] D.M. Gabbay. Theoretical foundations for non-monotonic reasoning in expert systems. In K.R. Apt, editor, *NATO Advanced Study Institute on Logics and Models of Concurrent Systems*, pages 439–457. Springer, 1985.

[98] D.M. Gabbay. The declarative past and imperative future. In H. Barringer, editor, *Proceedings of the Colloquium on Temporal Logic and Specifications*, volume 398 of Lecture Notes in Computer Science, pages 409–448. Springer, 1989.

[99] D.M. Gabbay. *Labelled Deductive Systems*, volume 1. Oxford University Press, Oxford, 1996.

[100] D.M. Gabbay. *Elementary Logics: A Procedural Perspective*. Prentice Hall, London, 1998.

[101] D.M. Gabbay. *Fibring Logics*, volume 38 of Oxford Logic Guides. Oxford University Press, Oxford, 1999.

[102] D.M. Gabbay and F. Guenthner, editors. *Handbook of Philosophical Logic*, volumes 1–18. Springer, 2000–2008. Volumes 15–18 in press.

[103] D.M. Gabbay, I. Hodkinson, and M. Reynolds. *Temporal logic: Mathematical Foundations and Computational Aspects*, volume 1, volume 28 of Oxford Logic Guides. Oxford University Press, Oxford, 1994.

[104] D.M. Gabbay, C. Hogger, and J.A. Robinson, editors. *Handbook of Logic in Artificial Intelligence and Logic Programming*, volumes 1–5. Oxford University Press, Oxford, 1994–1999.

[105] D.M. Gabbay and A. Hunter. Making inconsistency respectable: A logical framework for inconsistency in reasoning. In P. Jorrand and J. Kelemen, editors, *FAIR*, volume 535 of Lecture Notes in Computer Science, pages 19–32. Springer, 1991.

[106] D.M. Gabbay, A. Kurucz, F. Wolter, and M. Zakharyaschev. *Many-Dimensional Modal Logics: Theory and Applications*, volume 148 of Studies in Logic and the Foundations of Mathematics. Elsevier Science, 2003.

[107] D.M. Gabbay and N. Olivetti. *Goal-Directed Proof Theory*. Kluwer, 2000.

[108] D.M. Gabbay and J. Woods. The law of evidence and labelled deduction: A position paper. *Phi News*, 4, October 2003.

[109] D.M. Gabbay and J. Woods. *A Practical Logic of Cognitive Systems*. Volume 2: *The Reach of Abduction: Insight and Trial*. Elsevier, 2005.

[110] D. Gamberger and N. Lavrac. Conditions for Occam's razor applicability and noise elimination. In M. Someren and G. Widmer, editors, *Proceedings of the European Conference on Machine Learning*, pages 108–123, Prague, 1997.

[111] A.J. García and G.R. Simari. Defeasible logic programming: An argumentative approach. *Theory and Practice of Logic Programming*, 4(1):95–138, 2004.

[112] P. Gärdenfors. *Conceptual Spaces: The Geometry of Thought*. MIT Press, 2000.

[113] M. Garzon. *Models of Massive Parallelism: Analysis of Cellular Automata and Neural Networks*, Texts in Theoretical Computer Science. Springer, 1996.

[114] R.W. Gayler and R. Wales. Connections, binding, unification and analogical promiscuity. In K. Holyoak, D. Gentner, and B. Kokinov, editors, *Advances in Analogy Research: Integration of Theory and Data from the Cognitive, Computational and Neural Sciences*, pages 181–190. Sofia, Bulgaria, 1998.

[115] M. Gelfond and V. Lifschitz. The stable model semantics for logic programming. In *Proceedings of the Fifth Logic Programming Symposium*, pages 1070–1080. MIT Press, 1988.

[116] M. Gelfond and V. Lifschitz. Classical negation in logic programs and disjunctive databases. *New Generation Computing*, 9:365–385, 1991.

[117] J.L. Gersting. *Mathematical Structures for Computer Science*. Computer Science Press, New York, 1993.

[118] C.L. Giles and C.W. Omlin. Extraction, insertion and refinement of production rules in recurrent neural networks. *Connection Science, Special Issue on Architectures for Integrating Symbolic and Neural Processes*, 5(3):307–328, 1993.

[119] R. Haenni, J. Kohlas, and N. Lehmann. Probabilistic argumentation systems. In J. Kohlas and S. Moral, editors, *Handbook of Defeasible Reasoning and Uncertainty Management Systems*, volume 5, pages 221–288. Kluwer, 2000.

[120] N. Hallack, G. Zaverucha, and V. Barbosa. Towards a hybrid model of first-order theory refinement. In S. Wermter and R. Sun, editors, *Hybrid Neural Systems*, volume 1778 of Lecture Notes in Artificial Intelligence, pages 92–106. Springer, 1998.

[121] J.Y. Halpern. *Reasoning About Uncertainty*. MIT Press, 2003.

[122] J.Y. Halpern, R. Harper, N. Immerman, P.G. Kolaitis, M.Y. Vardi, and V. Vianu. On the unusual effectiveness of logic in computer science. *Bulletin of Symbolic Logic*, 7(2):213–236, 2001.

[123] J.Y. Halpern, R. van der Meyden, and M.Y. Vardi. Complete axiomatizations for reasoning about knowledge and time. *SIAM Journal on Computing*, 33(3):674–703, 2004.

[124] D. Harel. Dynamic logic. In D.M. Gabbay and F. Guenthner, editors, *Handbook of Philosophical Logic*, volume 2, pages 497–604. Reidel, Boston, 1984.

[125] S. Haykin. *Neural Networks: A Comprehensive Foundation*. Prentice Hall, 1999.

[126] J. Henderson. Estimating probabilities of unbounded categorization problems. In *Proceedings of European Symposium on Artificial Neural Networks*, pages 383–388, Bruges, Belgium, April 2002.

[127] J. Hertz, A. Krogh, and R.G. Palmer. *Introduction to the Theory of Neural Computation*, Studies in the Science of Complexity. Addison-Wesley, Santa Fe Institute, 1991.

[128] J.W. Hines. A logarithmic neural network architecture for unbounded non-linear function approximation. In *Proceedings of IEEE International Conference on Neural Networks*, volume 2, pages 1245–1250, Washington, DC, June 1996.

[129] J. Hintikka. *Knowledge and Belief.* Cornell University Press, Ithaca, NY, 1962.

[130] G.E. Hinton, editor. *Connectionist Symbol Processing.* MIT Press, 1991.

[131] H. Hirsh and M. Noordewier. Using background knowledge to improve inductive learning: a case study in molecular biology. *IEEE Expert*, 10:3–6, 1994.

[132] P. Hitzler, S. Holldobler, and A.K. Seda. Logic programs and connectionist networks. *Journal of Applied Logic, Special Issue on Neural-Symbolics Systems*, 2(3):245–272, 2004.

[133] S. Hölldobler. A structured connectionist unification algorithm. In *Proceedings of the National Conference on Artificial Intelligence, AAAI-90*, pages 587–593, 1990.

[134] S. Hölldobler. Automated inferencing and connectionist models. Postdoctoral thesis, Intellektik, Informatik, TH Darmstadt, 1993.

[135] S. Hölldobler and Y. Kalinke. Toward a new massively parallel computational model for logic programming. In *Proceedings of the Workshop on Combining Symbolic and Connectionist Processing, ECAI 1994*, pages 68–77, 1994.

[136] S. Hölldobler, Y. Kalinke, and H.P. Storr. Approximating the semantics of logic programs by recurrent neural networks. *Applied Intelligence Journal, Special Issue on Neural Networks and Structured Knowledge*, 11(1):45–58, 1999.

[137] S. Hölldobler and F. Kurfess. CHCL: A connectionist inference system. In B. Fronhofer and G. Wrightson, editors, *Parallelization in Inference Systems*, pages 318–342. Springer, 1992.

[138] V. Honavar and L. Uhr, editors. *Artificial Intelligence and Neural Networks: Steps Toward Principled Integration.* Academic Press, 1994.

[139] J.J. Hopfield. Neural networks and physical systems with emergent collective computational abilities. *Proceedings of the National Academy of Sciences of the U.S.A.*, 79: 2554–2558, 1982.

[140] K. Hornik, M. Stinchcombe, and H. White. Multilayer feedforward networks are universal approximators. *Neural Networks*, 2:359–366, 1989.

[141] G.E. Hughes and M.J. Cresswell. *A New Introduction to Modal Logic.* Routledge, London, 1996.

[142] E.B. Hunt, J. Marin, and P.J. Stone. *Experiments in Induction.* Academic Press, New York, 1966.

[143] M.R.A. Huth and M.D. Ryan. *Logic in Computer Science: Modelling and Reasoning About Systems.* Cambridge University Press, 2000.

[144] H. Jacobsson. Rule extraction from recurrent neural networks: A taxonomy and review. *Neural Computation*, 17(6):1223–1263, 2005.

[145] M.I. Jordan. Attractor dynamics and parallelisms in a connectionist sequential machine. In *Proceedings of the Eighth Annual Conference of the Cognitive Science Society*, pages 531–546, 1986.

[146] A.C. Kakas, P. Mancarella, and P.M. Dung. The acceptability semantics of logic programs. In *Proceedings of the Eleventh International Conference on Logic Programming ICLP-94*, pages 504–519. MIT Press, 1994.

[147] K. Engesser and D.M. Gabbay. Quantum logic, Hilbert space, revision theory. *Artificial Intelligence*, 136(1):61–100, 2002.

[148] R. Khardon and D. Roth. Learning to reason. *Journal of the ACM*, 44(5):697–725, 1997.

[149] B. Kijsirikul, S. Sinthupinyo, and K. Chongkasemwongse. Approximate match of rules using backpropagation neural networks. *Machine Learning*, 43(3):273–299, 2001.

[150] S. Kobayashi. Monad as modality. *Theoretical Computer Science*, 175(1):29–74, 1997.

[151] J.F. Kolen. *Exploring the Computational Capabilities of Recurrent Neural Networks.* PhD thesis, Ohio State University, 1994.

[152] E. Komendantskaya. First-order deduction in neural networks. In *Proceedings of the 1st Conference on Language and Automata Theory and Applications, LATA'07*, pages 307–318, Tarragona, Spain, March 2007.

[153] R.A. Kowalski and F. Toni. Abstract argumentation. *Artificial Intelligence and Law*, 4(3–4): 275–296, 1996.

[154] S. Kraus. *Strategic Negotiation in Multi-Agent Environments.* MIT Press, Cambridge, MA, 2001.

[155] S. Kraus, D. Lehmann, and M. Magidor. Nonmonotonic reasoning, preferential models and cumulative logics. *Artificial Intelligence*, 44:167–208, 1990.

[156] S. Kripke. Semantical analysis of modal logic I: Normal modal propositional calculi. *Zeitschrift für mathematische Logic and Grundlagen der Mathematik*, pages 67–96, 1963.

[157] L.C. Lamb, R.V. Borges, and A.S. d'Avila Garcez. A connectionist cognitive model for temporal synchronisation and learning. In *Proceedings of the Twenty-Second AAAI Conference on Artificial Intelligence, AAAI 2007*, pages 827–832. AAAI Press, 2007.

[158] N. Landwehr, A. Passerini, L. De Raedt, and P.L. Frasconi. kFOIL: Learning simple relational kernels. In *Proceedings of the National Conference on Artificial Intelligence, AAAI 2006*, pages 389–394. AAAI Press, 2006.

[159] N. Lavrac and S. Dzeroski. *Inductive Logic Programming: Techniques and Applications*, Ellis Horwood Series in Artificial Intelligence Ellis Horwood, 1994.

[160] N. Lavrac, S. Dzeroski, and M. Grobelnik. Experiments in learning nonrecursive definitions of relations with LINUS. Technical report, Josef Stefan Institute, Yugoslavia, 1990.

[161] S. Lawrence, C. Lee Giles, and A. Chung Tsoi. Lessons in neural networks training: Overfitting may be harder than expected. In *Proceedings of the National Conference on Artificial Intelligence, AAAI-96*, pages 540–545, 1996.

[162] C. Lewis. *A Survey of Symbolic Logic*. University of California Press, Berkeley, 1918.

[163] J.W. Lloyd. *Foundations of Logic Programming*. Springer, 1987.

[164] J.W. Lloyd. *Logic for Learning: Learning Comprehensible Theories from Structured Data*. Springer, 2003.

[165] A. Lozowski and J.M. Zurada. Extraction of linguistic rules from data via neural networks and fuzzy approximation. In I. Cloete and J.M. Zurada, editors, *Knowledge-Based Neurocomputing*, pages 403–417. MIT Press, 2000.

[166] V. Lukaszewicz. *Nonmonotonic Reasoning: Formalization of Commonsense Reasoning*. Ellis Horwood, 1990.

[167] M. Maidl. The common fragment of CTL and LTL. In *Proceedings of the 41st IEEE Symposium on Foundations of Computer Science*, pages 643–652, 2000.

[168] D.C. Makinson. General patterns in nonmonotonic reasoning. In D.M. Gabbay, C.J. Hogger, and J.A. Robinson, editors, *Handbook of Logic in Artificial Intelligence and Logic Programming*, volume 3, pages 35–110. Oxford University Press, 1994.

[169] O. Mangasarian, J. Shavlik, and E. Wild. Knowledge-based kernel approximation. *Journal of Machine Learning Research*, 5:1127–1141, 2004.

[170] Z. Manna and R. Waldinger. *The Logical Basis for Computer Programming. Volume 1: Deductive Reasoning*. Addison-Wesley, Boston, 1985.

[171] W. Marek and M. Truszczynski. *Nonmonotonic Logic: Context Dependent Reasoning*. Springer, 1993.

[172] P. Martin-Lof. Constructive mathematics and computer programming. In *Logic, Methodology and Philosophy of Science VI*, pages 153–179. North-Holland, 1982.

[173] G. Mayraz and G.E. Hinton. Recognizing handwritten digits using hierarchical products of experts. *IEEE Transactions on Pattern Analysis and Machine Intelligence*, 24:189–197, 2002.

[174] J. McCarthy. Programs with common sense. In *Proceedings of the Teddington Conference on the Mechanization of Thought Processes*, pages 75–91, London, 1959. Her Majesty's Stationery Office.

[175] J. McCarthy. Circumscription: A form of nonmonotonic reasoning. *Artificial Intelligence*, 13:27–39, 1980.

[176] J. McCarthy. Epistemological challenges for connectionism. *Behavioral and Brain Sciences*, 11(1):44, 1988.

[177] W.S. McCulloch and W. Pitts. A logical calculus of the ideas immanent in neural nets. *Bulletin of Mathematical Biophysics*, 5:115–133, 1943.

[178] C. McMillan, M.C. Mozer, and P. Smolensky. Rule induction through integrated symbolic and subsymbolic processing. In J. Moody, S. Hanson, and R. Lippmann, editors, *Advances in Neural Information Processing Systems 4, Proceedings of NIPS 1991*, pages 969–976. Morgan Kaufmann, San Mateo, CA, 1992.

[179] C. McMillan, M.C. Mozer, and P. Smolensky. Dynamic conflict resolution in a connectionist rule-based system. In *Proceedings of the 13th International Joint Conference on Artificial Intelligence, IJCAI-93*, pages 1366–1371, 1993.

[180] M. Mendler. Characterising combinatorial timing analysis in intuitionistic modal logic. *Logic Journal of the IGPL*, 8(6):821–852, 2000.

[181] R.S. Michalski. Pattern recognition as rule-guided inference. *Pattern Analysis and Machine Intelligence*, 2(4):349–361, 1980.

[182] R.S. Michalski. Learning strategies and automated knowledge acquisition: An overview. In L. Bolc, editor, *Computational Models of Learning*, pages 1–19. Springer, 1987.

[183] R.S. Michalski, I. Mozetic, J. Hong, and N. Lavrac. The multi-purpose incremental learning system AQ15 and its testing application to three medical domains. In *Proceedings of the National Conference on Artificial Intelligence, AAAI-86*, volume 2, pages 1041–1045, 1986.

[184] T.M. Mitchell. *Machine Learning*. McGraw-Hill, 1997.

[185] T.M. Mitchell and S.B. Thrun. Explanation-based learning: A comparison of symbolic and neural network approaches. In *Tenth International Conference on Machine Learning*, Amherst, MA, 1993.

[186] R.J. Mooney and D. Ourston. A multistrategy approach to theory refinement. In R.S. Michalski and G. Teccuci, editors, *Machine Learning: A Multistrategy Approach*, volume 4, pages 141–164. Morgan Kaufmann, San Mateo, CA, 1994.

[187] R.J. Mooney and J.M. Zelle. Integrating ILP and EBL. *SIGART Bulletin*, 5:12–21. 1994.

[188] R.C. Moore. Semantic considerations on nonmonotonic logic. *Artificial Intelligence*, 25(1):75–94, 1985.

[189] S.H. Muggleton and L. De Raedt. Inductive logic programming: Theory and methods. *Journal of Logic Programming*, 19:629–679, 1994.

[190] I. Niemelä. Logic programs with stable model semantics as a constraint programming paradigm. *Annals of Mathematics and Artificial Intelligence*, 25:241–273, 1999.

[191] M.O. Noordewier, G.G. Towell, and J.W. Shavlik. Training knowledge-based neural networks to recognize genes in DNA sequences. In *Advances in Neural Information Processing Systems 3, Proceedings of NIPS 1990*, pages 530–536, 1991.

[192] H. Nunez, C. Angulo, and A. Catala. Rule based learning systems for support vector machines. *Neural Processing Letters*, 24(1):1–18, 2006.

[193] D. Nute. Defeasible reasoning. In *Proceedings of the Hawaii International Conference on Systems Science*, pages 470–477. IEEE Press, 1987.

[194] D. Nute. Defeasible logic. In D.M. Gabbay, C.J. Hogger, and J.A. Robinson, editors, *Handbook of Logic in Artificial Intelligence and Logic Programming*, volume 3, pages 353–396. Oxford University Press, 1994.

[195] D.W. Opitz. *An Anytime Approach to Connectionist Theory Refinement: Refining the Topologies of Knowledge-Based Neural Networks*. PhD thesis, University of Wisconsin, Madison, 1995.

[196] D.W. Opitz and J.W. Shavlik. Heuristically expanding knowledge-based neural networks. In *Proceedings of the International Joint Conference on Artificial Intelligence, IJCAI-93*, pages 1360–1365, 1993.

[197] M.A. Orgun and W. Ma. An overview of temporal and modal logic programming. In *Proceedings of the International Conference on Temporal Logic, ICTL'94*, volume 827 of Lecture Notes in Artificial Intelligence, pages 445–479. Springer, 1994.

[198] M.A. Orgun and W.W. Wadge. Towards a unified theory of intensional logic programming. *Journal of Logic Programming*, 13(4):413–440, 1992.

[199] M.A. Orgun and W.W. Wadge. Extending temporal logic programming with choice predicates non-determinism. *Journal of Logic and Computation*, 4(6):877–903, 1994.

[200] M. Page. Connectionist modelling in psychology: A localist manifesto. *Behavioral and Brain Sciences*, 23:443–467, 2000.

[201] M. Pazzani and D. Kibler. The utility of knowledge in inductive learning. *Machine Learning*, 9:57–94, 1992.

[202] J. Pearl. *Causality: Models, Reasoning and Inference*. Cambridge University Press, 2000.

[203] F. Pfenning and H.-C. Wong. On a modal lambda calculus for S4. *Electronic Notes in Theoretical Computer Science*, 1:515–534, 1995.

[204] G. Pinkas. Symmetric neural networks and propositional logic satisfiability. *Neural Computation*, 3(2):282–291, 1991.

[205] G. Pinkas. Reasoning, nonmonotonicity and learning in connectionist networks that capture propositional knowledge. *Artificial Intelligence*, 77:203–247, 1995.

[206] G.D. Plotkin and C.P. Stirling. A framework for intuitionistic modal logic. In *Proceedings of the First Conference on Theoretical Aspects of Reasoning About Knowledge, TARK'86*, pages 399–406. Morgan Kaufmann, 1986.

[207] A. Pnueli. The temporal logic of programs. In *Proceedings of 18th IEEE Annual Symposium on Foundations of Computer Science*, pages 46–57, 1977.

[208] J.B. Pollack. Recursive distributed representations. *Artificial Intelligence*, 46(1):77–105, 1990.

[209] J. Pollock. Defeasible reasoning. *Cognitive Science*, 11:481–518, 1987.

[210] J. Pollock. Self-defeating arguments. *Minds and Machines*, 1(4):367–392, 1991.

[211] H. Prakken and G. Sartor. Argument-based extended logic programming with defeasible priorities. *Journal of Applied Non-Classical Logics*, 7:25–75, 1997.

[212] H. Prakken and G.A.W. Vreeswijk. Logical systems for defeasible argumentation. In D.M. Gabbay and F. Guenthner, editors, *Handbook of Philosophical Logic*, 2nd edition. Kluwer, 2000.

[213] F.P. Preparata and R.T. Yeh. *Introduction to Discrete Structures*. Addison-Wesley, 1973.

[214] G. Priest. *An Introduction to Non-Classical Logic*. Cambridge University Press, Cambridge, 2001.

[215] T.C. Przymusinski. On the declarative semantics of logic programs with negation. In J. Minker, editor, *Foundations of Deductive Databases and Logic Programming*, pages 193–216. Morgan Kaufmann, 1988.

[216] J.R. Quinlan. Induction of decision trees. *Machine Learning*, 1:81–106, 1986.

[217] R. Ramanujam. Semantics of distributed definite clause programs. *Theoretical Computer Science*, 68:203–220, 1989.

[218] D.A. Randell, Z. Cui, and A.G. Cohn. A spatial logic based on regions and connection. In *Proccedings of the Third International Conference on Principles of Knowledge Representation and Reasoning, KR-92*, pages 165–176, 1992.

[219] A.S. Rao and M.P. Georgeff. Decision procedures for BDI logics. *Journal of Logic and Computation*, 8(3):293–343, 1998.

[220] R. Reiter. A logic for default reasoning. *Artificial Intelligence*, 13:81–132, 1980.

[221] O.T. Rodrigues. *A Methodology for Iterated Information Change*. PhD thesis, Department of Computing, Imperial College, London, 1997.

[222] D. Roth. Learning to reason: The non-monotonic case. In *Proceedings of the 14th International Joint Conference on Artificial Intelligence, IJCAI-95*, pages 1178–1184, 1995.

[223] D. Roth and W. Yih. Relational learning via propositional algorithms: An information extraction case study. In *Proceedings of the International Joint Conference on Artificial Intelligence, IJCAI-01*, pages 1257–1263, Seattle, August 2001.

[224] D.E. Rumelhart, G.E. Hinton, and R.J. Williams. Learning internal representations by error propagation. In D.E. Rumelhart and J.L. McClelland, editors, *Parallel Distributed Processing: Explorations in the Microstructure of Cognition*, volume 1, pages 318–362. MIT Press, 1986.

[225] S. Russell. Machine learning. In M.A. Boden, editor, *Handbook of Perception and Cognition*, Artificial Intelligence Series, chapter 4. Academic Press, 1996.

[226] Y. Sakakibara. Programming in modal logic: An extension of PROLOG based on modal logic. In *Logic Programming 86*, volume 264 of Lecture Notes in Computer Science, pages 81–91. Springer, 1986.

[227] R. Setiono. Extracting rules from neural networks by pruning and hidden-unit splitting. *Neural Computation*, 9:205–225, 1997.

[228] L. Shastri. A connectionist approach to knowledge representation and limited inference. *Cognitive Science*, 12(13):331–392, 1988.

[229] L. Shastri. Advances in SHRUTI: A neurally motivated model of relational knowledge representation and rapid inference using temporal synchrony. *Applied Intelligence Journal, Special Issue on Neural Networks and Structured Knowledge*, 11:79–108, 1999.

[230] L. Shastri and V. Ajjanagadde. From simple associations to semantic reasoning: A connectionist representation of rules, variables and dynamic binding. Technical report, University of Pennsylvania, 1990.

[231] J.W. Shavlik. An overview of research at Wisconsin on knowledge-based neural networks. In *Proceedings of the International Conference on Neural Networks, ICNN96*, pages 65–69, Washington, DC, 1996.

[232] J. Shawe-Taylor and N. Cristianini. *Kernel Methods for Pattern Analysis*. Cambridge University Press, 2004.

[233] Y. Shin and J. Ghosh. The pi–sigma network: An efficient higher-order neural network for pattern classification and function approximation. In *Proceedings of the International Joint Conference on Neural Networks, IJCNN91*, volume 1, pages 13–18, Seattle, July 1991.

[234] H.T. Siegelmann. Neural and super-Turing computing. *Minds and Machines*, 13(1):103–114, 2003.

[235] H.T. Siegelmann and E.D. Sontag. On the computational power of neural nets. *Journal of Computer and System Sciences*, 50(1):132–150, 1995.

[236] A. Simpson. *The Proof Theory and Semantics of Intuitionistic Modal Logics*. PhD thesis, Edinburgh University, 1993.

[237] P. Smolensky. On the proper treatment of connectionism. *Behavioral and Brain Sciences*, 44:1–74, 1988.

[238] P. Smolensky. Tensor product variable binding and the representation of symbolic structures in connectionist networks. *Artificial Intelligence*, 46:159–216, 1990.

[239] P. Smolensky. Grammar-based connectionist approaches to language. *Cognitive Science*, 23(4):589–613, 1999.

[240] P. Smolensky and G. Legendre. *The Harmonic Mind: From Neural Computation to Optimality-Theoretic Grammar*. MIT Press, Cambridge, MA, 2006.

[241] K. Stenning and M. van Lambalgen. Human reasoning and cognitive science, MIT Press, Cambridge, MA, 2008.

[242] R. Sun. Robust reasoning: Integrating rule-based and similarity-based reasoning. *Artificial Intelligence*, 75(2):241–296, 1995.

[243] R. Sun and F. Alexandre. *Connectionist Symbolic Integration*. Lawrence Erlbaum Associates, Hillsdale, NJ, 1997.

[244] S.B. Thrun. Extracting provably correct rules from artificial neural networks. Technical report, Institut für Informatik, Universität Bonn, 1994.

[245] S.B. Thrun. *Explanation-Based Neural Network Learning: A Lifelong Learning Approach*. Kluwer Academic, Boston, MA, 1996.

[246] S.B. Thrun, J. Bala, E. Bloedorn, I. Bratko, B. Cestnik, J. Cheng, K. De Jong, S. Dzeroski, S.E. Fahlman, D. Fisher, R. Haumann, K. Kaufman, S. Keller, I. Kononenko, J. Kreuziger, R.S. Michalski, T.M. Mitchell, P. Pachowicz, Y. Reich, H. Vafaie, K. Van de Welde, W. Wenzel, J. Wnek, and J. Zhang. The MONK's problems: A performance comparison of different learning algorithms. Technical Report CMU-CS-91-197, Carnegie Mellon University, 1991.

[247] D. Touretzky and G.E. Hinton. Symbols among neurons. In *Proceedings of the International Joint Conference on Artificial Intelligence, IJCAI-85*, pages 238–243. Morgan Kaufmann, 1985.

[248] D. Touretzky and G.E. Hinton. A distributed connectionist production system. *Cognitive Science*, 12(3):423–466, 1988.

[249] G.G. Towell and J.W. Shavlik. Using symbolic learning to improve knowledge-based neural networks. In *Proceedings of the National Conference on Artificial Intelligence, AAAI-92*, pages 177–182, 1992.

[250] G.G. Towell and J.W. Shavlik. Knowledge-based artificial neural networks. *Artificial Intelligence*, 70(1):119–165, 1994.

[251] A.M. Turing. Computer machinery and intelligence. *Mind*, 59:433–460, 1950.

[252] W. Uwents and H. Blockeel. Classifying relational data with neural networks. In S. Kramer and B. Pfahringer, editors, *Proceedings of 15th International Conference on Inductive Logic Programming*, volume 3625 of Lecture Notes in Computer Science, pages 384–396. Springer, 2005.

[253] L.G. Valiant. A theory of the learnable. *Communications of the ACM*, 27(11):1134–1142, 1984.

[254] L.G. Valiant. Robust logics. *Artificial Intelligence*, 117:231–253, 2000.

[255] L.G. Valiant. Three problems in computer science. *Journal of the ACM*, 50(1):96–99, 2003.

[256] J. van Benthem. *Modal Logic and Classical Logic*. Bibliopolis, Naples, 1983.

[257] J. van Benthem. Correspondence theory. In D.M. Gabbay and F. Guenthner, editors, *Handbook of Philosophical Logic*, chapter II.4, pages 167–247. Reidel, Dordrecht, 1984.

[258] D. van Dalen. Intuitionistic logic. In D.M. Gabbay and F. Guenthner, editors, *Handbook of Philosophical Logic*, 2nd edition, volume 5. Kluwer, 2002.

[259] F. van der Velde and M. de Kamps. Neural blackboard architectures of combinatorial structures in cognition. *Behavioral and Brain Sciences*, 29(1):37–70, 2006.

[260] M.H. van Emden and R.A. Kowalski. The semantics of predicate logic as a programming language. *Journal of the ACM*, 23(4):733–742, 1976.

[261] A. van Gelder, K. Ross, and J. Schlipf. The well-founded semantics for general logic programs. *Journal of the ACM*, 38(3):620–650, 1991.

[262] V. Vapnik. *The Nature of Statistical Learning Theory*. Springer, 1995.

[263] V. Vapnik and A. Chervonenkis. On the uniform convergence of relative frequencies of events to their probabilities. *Theory of Probability and Its Applications*, 16(2), 264–280, SIAM, 1971.

[264] M.Y. Vardi. Why is modal logic so robustly decidable. In N. Immerman and P. Kolaitis, editors, *Descriptive Complexity and Finite Models*, volume 31 of Discrete Mathematics and Theoretical Computer Science, pages 149–184. DIMACS, 1997.

[265] B. Verheij. Accrual of arguments in defeasible argumentation. In *Proceedings of Second Dutch/German Workshop on Nonmonotonic Reasoning*, pages 217–224, Utrecht, 1995.

[266] B. Verheij. *Rules, Reasons, Arguments: Formal Studies of Argumentation and Defeat*. PhD thesis, Maastricht University, The Netherlands, 1996.

[267] G.A.W. Vreeswijk. Abstract argumentation systems. *Artificial Intelligence*, 90(1–2):225–279, 1997.

[268] P.J. Werbos. *Beyond Regression: New Tools for Prediction and Analysis in the Behavioral Sciences*. PhD thesis, Harvard University, Cambridge, MA, 1974.

[269] P.J. Werbos. Backpropagation through time: What does it mean and how to do it. *Proceedings of the IEEE*, 78:1550–1560, 1990.

[270] J. Williamson and D.M. Gabbay. Recursive causality in Bayesian networks and self-fibring networks. In D. Gillies, editor, *Laws and Models in Science*. King's College London, 173–221, 2004.

[271] M.J. Wooldridge. *Introduction to Multi-Agent Systems*. Wiley, New York, 2001.

[272] Y. Xiong, W. Wu, X. Kang, and C. Zhang. Training pi–sigma network by online gradient algorithm with penalty for small weight update. *Neural Computation*, 19(12):3356–3368, 2007.

[273] Z.H. Zhou, Y. Jiang, and S.F. Chen. Extracting symbolic rules from trained neural network ensembles. *AI Communications*, 16(1):3–15, 2003.

Index

abduction, 169
abductive reasoning, 141
Abramsky, S., ix
accrual (cumulative) argumentation, 155
agent
  common knowledge, 69
  individual knowledge, 69
  knowledge about the world, 15
  representation of knowledge, 69
Alchourrón, C.E., 16
alternatives to classical logic, 9
AND/OR neurons, 35
ANNN (artificial nonmonotonic neural
    networks), 53
answer set, 45
  semantics, 46
Apt, K.R., 20
argument computation, 149, 151
argument learning, 149, 154
argumentation and probabilities, 159
argumentation framework, 143
argumentation network, 144, 145
argumentation neural network, 145
arguments
  acceptability, 144
  colouring, 144
  conflicting sets, 151
  indefensible, 144
  prevailing, 144
  relative strength, 144, 145
arity, 12
artificial intelligence, integration
    of symbolic and connectionist
    paradigms, 1
Artëmov, S.N., 108
assignment, 12

background knowledge, 171
backpropagation learning algorithm, 26, 45,
    172
Bader, S., ix
Balkenius, C., 53
Barringer, H., ix, 150
Bayesian networks, 157
belief revision, 16
Bench-Capon, T.J.M., 144
Bennett, B., 3
biologically motivated models, 2
Bol, R.N., 20
brain imaging, 179
Braz, R.S., ix
Brewka, G., 51
Broda, K., ix
Brouwer, L.E.J., 85, 88
Bruck, J., ix

chain, 10
CHCL (Connectionist Horn Clause Logic), 53
CIL (connectionist intuitionistic logic), 101,
    109
CILP
  applications, 52
  classical negation, 45
  theory refinement, 44
  Translation Algorithm, 39
circular argumentation, 150
circularity in argumentation networks, 149
classical logic, 9, 11
classical negation, 45
classical propositional logic, 11
clause
  body, 17
  general, 19
  head, 17

closed-world assumption, 16
CML (connectionist modal logic), 55, 60, 174
   distributed knowledge representation, 69
   learning in CML, 71
cognitive abilities, 15
cognitive models, 1
commonsense reasoning, 14, 16
computational cognitive models, 1
conditional reasoning, 14
conflicting sets of arguments, 151
Connectionist Intuitionistic Algorithm, 93
connectionist intuitionistic implication, 90
connectionist intuitionistic logic, 101, 108
Connectionist Intuitionistic Modal Algorithm, 97
connectionist intuitionistic negation, 91
Connectionist Modal Algorithm, 62
connectionist muddy children puzzle, 68
connectionist nonclassical logic, 4
connectionist nonclassical reasoning, 173
connectionist paradigm, 1
Connectionist Temporal Algorithm, 80
connectionist temporal logic, 78
connectionist temporal reasoning, 175
connectionist wise men puzzle, 104, 109
constant symbols, 12
constructive mathematics, 88
context units, 30
Cook, M., ix
cross-validation, 32
   leaving-one-out, 33
CTLK (Connectionist Temporal Logic of Knowledge), 4, 75, 175
   language, 77
   learning, 83

DasGupta, B., 44
De Raedt, L., ix
deduction, 169
deductive reasoning, 43
defeasible arguments, 143
defeasible logic, 50
definite logic program, 17
distributed knowledge representation in CML, 69
distributed representation, 172
Dung, P., 144

east–west trains example, 135
EBL (explanation-based learning), 53
EBNN (explanation-based neural networks), 53
Eiter, T., 51
Elman, J.L., 29, 31

epistemic entrenchment, 51
epoch, 32
explicit negation, 45
extended logic programs, 45
extraction methods, 140

fibred network ensembles, viii, 4, 178
fibred neural network, 115, 122, 176, 177
fibring
   application to argumentation networks, 157
   applied to argumentation, 157
   conditionals, 117
   fibring modal logic into many-valued logic, 117
fibring function, 5, 116, 122, 177
first-order logic, 12
first-order logic programs, 176
Fitting, M., 59
fixed-point characterisation of the least Herbrand model, 18
formal models of argumentation, 143
Fu, L.M., 54
function symbols, 12

Gärdenfors, P., 16, 53
Gabbay, D.M., 16, 59, 150, 159
Garcez, C., ix
Gelfond, M., 19
Gelfond–Lifschitz reduction, 46
Gelfond–Lifschitz transformation, 20
general logic program, 19
generalised delta rule, 27
Givan, R., ix
goal-directed reasoning, 140
Gori, M., ix
greatest fixed point, 18
greatest lower bound, 10

Hölldobler, S., ix, 36
Halpern, J.Y., ix, 1, 161
Herbrand base, 17
Herbrand model, 17
Herbrand, J., 17
Heyting, A., 88
Hintikka, J., 15, 56
Hinton, G.E., 27
Hitzler, P., ix
Hodges, W., ix
Hodkinson, I.M., ix
Hornik, K., 44
human reasoning, 179
hybrid system, 171

ILP (inductive logic programming), 53, 127
immediate-consequence operator, 18
immediate predecessor, 10
immediate successor, 10
inconsistency, 172
inconsistency handling, 51
induction, 169
inductive learning, 32, 44, 171
inductive logic programming, 53, 127
integration of symbolic and connectionist
    paradigms, 1
intelligent behaviour, 1
interpretation, 12
intuitionistic implication, 89
intuitionistic language, 88
intuitionistic logic, 3, 88
intuitionistic logical systems, 87
intuitionistic modal consequence operator, 96
intuitionistic modal logic, 95
intuitionistic negation, 89

Jordan, M.I., 29

Kalinke, Y., 36
KBANN (Knowledge-Based Artificial Neural
    Networks), 35
KBCNN (Knowledge-Based Conceptual
    Neural Network), 54
Knowledge and Probability Translation
    Algorithm, 165
knowledge evolution, 74, 75, 77
knowledge extraction, 140, 171
knowledge representation, 21
Kolmogorov, A.N., 88
Kowalski, R.A., ix, 89
Kripke models, 57
Kripke, S., 15, 56
Kuehnberger, K.-U., ix

labelled formula, 58
labelled intuitionistic modal program, 95
labelled intuitionistic program, 88
lattice, 10
    complete, 10
    distributive, 10
LDS (labelled deductive systems), 57, 157
learning algorithm, 171
learning and reasoning cycle, 172
learning capability, 28
learning in CML, 71
learning in CTLK, 83
learning with and without background
    knowledge, 72
least fixed point, 18

least upper bound, 10
Lifschitz, V., 19, 45
linear order, 10
localist representation, 172
locally stratified program, 19
logic
    alternatives to classical logic, 9
    classical logic, 9, 11
    classical propositional logic, 11
    first-order logic, 12
    intuitionistic logic, 2, 88
        intuitionistic implication, 89
        intuitionistic negation, 89
    intuitionistic modal logic, 95
    logic as the calculus of computer science, 14
    modal logic, 3, 55, 56
        modalities, 57
        possible-world semantics, 56
        proof procedures for modal logic, 58
    nonclassical logics, viii, 9, 14, 170
    predicate logic, see predicate logic
    propositional logic, expressive power, 11
    role of logic in computer science, vii, 14
    temporal logic, 3, 76
        next-time operator, 76
    two-variable fragment of first-order logic, 6
logic programming, 17
logical consequence, 171
long-term memory, 113
lower bound, 10

Makinson, D.C., ix, 16
McCarthy, J., 2, 16, 45, 127, 171
merging of temporal background knowledge
    and data learning, 84
metalevel, 178
metalevel network, 128
metalevel priority, 49
metanetwork, see Metalevel network
metric space, 11
Michalski, R.S., ix, 32, 135
modal immediate-consequence operator, 59
modal logic, 3, 55, 56
modal logic programming, 55
modal reasoning, 58, 173
model intersection property, 17
Modgil, S., ix
Monty Hall puzzle, 166
Moore, R.C., 16
moral-debate example, 145
    neural network for, 149
muddy children puzzle, 68
    complete solution, 81
    snapshot solution, 81

Muggleton, S.H., ix
multiagent system, 3

natural-deduction-style rules, 58
negation as failure, 16
network ensemble, 31
Neural Argumentation Algorithm, 147
neural computation, 169
Neural network, learning process of, 26
neural-symbolic integration, 170
    objectives, viii
neural-symbolic learning systems, 170
neural-symbolic systems, 179
neuron functionality, 23
    activation function, 24
    activation rule, 23
    activation state, 23
    bipolar function, 25
    feedforward network, 24
    fully connected network, 24
    hidden-layer network, 24
    learning rule, 24
    output rule, 23
    propagation rule, 23
    set of weights, 23
    sigmoid function, 24
    threshold, 24
    universal approximator, 25
Nixon diamond problem, 50, 154
nonclassical logics, viii, 9, 14, 170
nonclassical reasoning, 2
nonmonotonic reasoning, 16
normal logic program, 17
Nute, D., 50

Ockham's (Occam's) razor, 32

Palade, V., ix
Palm, G., ix
paraconsistency, 48
partial order, 10
partially ordered set, 10
penalty logic, 53
Pinkas, G., 53
Pnueli, A., 3
Pollock, J., 155
possible worlds, 173
possible-world semantics, 15, 56
practical reasoning, 16
Prakken, H., 51
predicate logic
    domain, 13
    interpretation, 13
    model, 13

semantics, 14
symbols, 12
syntax, 12
preference handling, 51
preference relation, 50
probabilistic relational model, 129
probabilities and argumentation, 159
probabilities and possible worlds, 161
probability, 157
processing units of neural network, 179
propositional fixation, 2
propositional logic, expressive power, 11

quantifiers, 12
Quinlan, J.R., 32

Rüger, S., ix
Ray, O., ix
recurrent architecture, 29
recurrent backpropagation, 29
recurrent network, 172
recursion in Bayesian networks, 159
recursive causality, 159
recursive neural network, 177
Reiter, R., 16
relational knowledge, 171
relational learning, 128
relationship between argumentation and neural
    networks, 144
robust learning, 179
Rodrigues, O.T., ix
Roth, D., ix
Rumelhart, R.E., 27
Russo, A., ix

Sartor, G., 51
Schnitger, G., 44
semantics for extended modal logic programs,
    58
set of terms, 13
Shastri, L., ix
Shavlik, J.W., ix, 35, 36
short-term memory, 113
Siekmann, J.H., ix
Smolensky, P., 171
stable model, 20
Stinchcombe, M., 44
Sun, R., ix
superiority relation, 50
supervised learning, 26
support vector machine, 129
supported interpretation, 19
symbolic logic, 169
symbolic paradigm, 1

symmetric network, 29
synergies of neural-symbolic
    integration, viii

Tamburrini, G., ix
Taylor, J.G., ix
Temporal Algorithm, 75
temporal immediate-consequence
    operator, 79
temporal knowledge representation, 81
temporal logic, 3, 76
temporal logic programming, 77
temporal model, 78
temporal muddy children puzzle, 81
temporal reasoning, 3, 15, 173, 175
term mapping, 13
test set performance, 32
testing set, 28
timeline, 78
Toni, F., ix
Towell, G.G., 35, 36
training set, 28
training-set performance, 32
translation algorithm, 171
two-coin problem, 161

uncertainty, 157
uncertainty, reasoning about, 161
uncertainty, representation of, 161
upper bound, 10

Valiant, L.G., 1, 84
value-based argumentation framework, 144
van Benthem, J.F.A.K., ix, 56
van Emden, M., 89
Vardi, M.Y., ix, 56
variable assignment, 13
variables, 12, 176
Verheij, B., 155

well-formed formula (wff), 11, 13
well-founded semantics, 20
Werbos, P.J., 27
Wermter, S., ix
White, H., 44
Williams, R.J., 27
Williamson, J., 159
wise men puzzle, 102, 108
Woods, J., ix, 150

Zaverucha, G., ix